A STRANGER IN A STRANGE LAND

A PASTOR'S LETTERS TO HIS PEOPLE

THOMAS SWANSTON

CHRISTIAN FOCUS PUBLICATIONS

Published by
Christian Focus Publications Ltd
Geanies House, Fearn IV20 1TW
Ross-shire, Scotland, UK.

ISBN 1 871 676 835

Cover design
by
Seoris McGillivray

Printed & bound in Great Britain by
Cox & Wyman Ltd, Reading.

CONTENTS

INNER CONFLICT

DOCTRINAL

MISSION

TRAVEL

HIS LAST TWO LETTERS

FAREWELL TO A FRIEND

The West Parish Church, Inverness was filled to capacity on Wednesday, 20th February, 1991, to mourn the passing of Rev. Thomas Swanston, a beloved pastor and friend who had ministered there for twenty years.

The funeral service was conducted by Rev. James Philip, formerly of Gardenstown and now of Holyrood Abbey, Edinburgh. He spoke of the high honour it was to lead such a service of thanksgiving, gathered as they were under such a shadow of grief and sorrow, with a sense of loss too deep for words. He spoke of the man whose presence had warmed and lit up so large a part of so many lives.

He said, 'What a famous statesman of a past day - Earl Grey - once said of his father, could be truly said of Tom Swanston, that "he lit so many fires in cold rooms", and there are homes and families represented here today who would bear glad testimony that this is what they have experienced over more than thirty-six years of fellowship with him and with deep emotion recalled the fellowship shared since as a school teacher in Gardenstown, Mr. Philip's first parish, Tom was found of Christ. He was my son in the faith and with great joy and pride I speak of the worth of his fruitful ministry in Holytown and then in Inverness. They that be wise shall shine as the brightness of the firmament; and they that turn many to righteousness as the stars for ever and ever. There are many, many people in this gathering today who owe their eternal salvation to his faithful ministry and testimony.'

Rev. William Still, Gilcomston South Church, Aberdeen,

whom Rev Swanston acknowledged as his 'beloved mentor' referred to him as 'one in a million' and went on to outline Mr. Swanston's many gifts and qualities: of fisher stock his upbringing had been essentially simple and it was not until he left Portsoy for Aberdeen University that these began to shine. The capacious retentiveness of his mind was taking in stores of knowledge so that in later life there were few subjects of which Tom had not some understanding. Having taken two university degrees he soon found a post in Gardenstown where he fell in with the minister, James Philip and following a car accident on the way home from the Billy Graham Rallies in Glasgow, he gave himself to Christ. Thus it was back to the University to do Divinity, when he became a friend to many and met cross sections of people who deeply influenced his life and pointed the way forward to a ministry of an extensive biblical order in Lanarkshire where he made his mark on a number, including Alistair Malcolm the young minister who read the Scriptures so movingly during the funeral service.

After his time in Holytown, marked by days of trauma and inner turbulence due to his complex personality, he became minister of the West Kirk, Inverness, and it was there that his abundant gifts flourished the most. While maintaining an astonishing variety of friendships at home and abroad, notably in Eastern Europe and USA, there is no doubt that he gave himself and spent himself for the people of the West Kirk.

His literary output through the Letters grew ever more eloquent so that many at home and abroad looked forward with intense anticipation to them. Mr. Still spoke of his musical gifts and his proficiency in culinary arts but went on to say that the overriding passion of his life was the winning of souls for Christ. He took the deepest interest in the effects of his eloquent and comprehensive teaching of the Word of God and the effect it was having on people. We used to say, Tom couldn't be dull if he tried, and the appeal of his letters always aimed at the conscience, joined with his amazing skill with words, including abundant allusions to history, literature and the ordinary things of life; all the gathered strands of an astonishingly fertile mind were geared to one aim: to bring souls to Christ and to see them built up in the faith and in grace, and sent out into the Lord's service. Mr. Still had told of Tom's musical experience in the Salvation Army and as organist in an Episcopal Church in Aberdeen and how this gifted musician had never had a music lesson in his life. Now, in Inverness his musical gifts were overflowing, until he was able to provide whole recitals of his own music, from hymn tunes to choral pieces and works of other genres. His hymn tunes will live and be sung in days to come.

Mr. Swanston's natural spontaneous and unaffected charm made him popular wherever he went; yet, said Mr. Still, his uncompromising stand for his biblical principles was such that it was his heartbroken admission many times that he felt he had failed to make impact; there were those who never responded to his brilliant, impassioned, extensive expositions of Holy Scripture. His last published letter which will undoubtedly become a classic, contains a final cry to such who he felt had not heeded his pleas to give their lives to Christ before it is too late, are left dumbfounded that any soul, however gospel hardened could resist such a classical appeal from a dying pastor, to come to Christ and begin to show signs of the fruits of righteousness in their lives.

He spoke of Mr. Swanston's afflictions progressively ravaging his whole body with incurable pain and immobility. Yet he bore his privations with cheerfulness and pursued his path of devotion to the Lord, and to his people and to his work, with utter dedication.

Mr. Still spoke of the deep holiness of Mr. Swanston, who on his deathbed had deplored his lack of sanctification. He had quoted to him the lines of the hymn, *They who fain would serve Thee best are conscious most of wrong within*. Mr. Still concluded, 'We shall not see his like again and all attempted bitterness in the loss of such a friend and servant of the Lord must be swallowed up in the knowledge that Tom had suffered enough. We must now be glad for him that it is all over forever and he has reached the source of all these wonderful gifts that made his personality scintillate with the radiance of a soul enlivened and beautified by Christ. Tom will love heaven.'

1*

A STRANGER IN A STRANGE LAND

My Dear Friends,
This is the time of year when we raise the voice of public thanksgiving to our Lord for His faithfulness to us in the year that is past, and He has again made gratitude an easy exercise. He is our God, our Providence, our Saviour and our Joy, and I commend to you the Financial Statement prepared so devotedly by our treasurers and auditors. The figures tell at least some of the story of the Lord's goodness. God is blessing us materially and spiritually, the two so often going hand in hand. Beyond these outward and visible tokens of the Lord's favour there have been private and eternal transactions, and it has been cheering to see a constant stream of folk coming to Christ and finding life and salvation. None of this should be taken for granted in these days of unions, readjustments, linkages and closures. As I said at Alasdair McLennan's preaching-in service, 'In such an age of crisis for so many congregations, no church that accords to Christ the centrality that is His right has anything to fear.' And I note that words associated with thanks and thanksgiving occur over 70 times in the New Testament alone, whereas ingratitude is the mark of the godless man, the man without grace, without Christ and without hope.

Apart from the public work that goes on around our fellowship, perhaps the time has come for me to give a private word of testimony. I want you to know how much I am 'at home' among you. I do not profess to be everyone's cup of tea. Neither did Jesus, and so I am in good company. And

*March 1979

some of my critics are not everyone's cup of tea either. A Christian man simply has to be true to his own best, twice-born self and to his spiritual convictions. Nor do I claim that the sermons are the last word in preaching. My failures both as a preacher and as a pastor are painfully plain: I despair at my ineptitudes, my clumsiness, my insensitivity, my infelicities of expression. And yet, whatever my weaknesses may be, you are among the dearest folk on the face of God's earth to me, and though I sometimes chasten you in love, as God does all of us, any man who lifts against you the voice of carping criticism has my personal wrath to reckon with.

But it is not a light or trivial thing for me to say that I am 'at home' in Inverness, for the truth is that it has never been easy for me in life to feel at home, or wanted, anywhere. Anyone who takes the trouble to find out who I am beneath the surface will readily discover that there are vast areas of homelessness and rootlessness in me. Hence the tendency to insularity and independence; and hence also the difficulty in forming deep, permanent, lasting friendships. The 'rootless' bit in me is partly seen in the love of travel. I am a born voyager! In a sense I am running away from things as they are, for too much travel can be a form of escapism from the here-and-now pains of this world. But, more than that, there is a tragic-romantic, perhaps even hopeless, part that strives for the 'ideal' - the ideal relationship, the ideal friendship, the ideal culture, the ideal civilisation. Such a search, of course, is doomed to fail from the start. Perfections such as these are found only in glory.

The roots of any man's rootlessness are, it almost goes without saying, deep; and all the effects on one's inner personality are doubtless beyond cure until Cure-all Day, the day of the general resurrection. We were born, as lads, in Eyemouth, in Berwickshire, but moved to Portsoy when the

Germans started bombing at the start of the war. In Eyemouth, on father's side, we stood spiritually at the tail end of an evangelical tradition nigh unto death. My grandfather, Thomas Swanston was precentor in the Evangelical Union Church, and led the praise until the congregation bought a 'kist o' whistles'. He used to sing for the father of Lord Douglas-Home in the drawing room of the Hirsel. Grandmother, like her husband, was immensely musical and played the piano. I remember church music, rather than Christian teaching, from those years. The revival in which the E.U. church was born, had run to seed. Grandmother died when I was five, the only grandparent I ever knew, and so the world, for a small boy, did not seem like 'home' even then. Then we were whisked to Portsoy.

I hated the first two years there: the boys spoke a dialect that, to me, seemed crude and coarse and (what was worse) unintelligible. Their interests and mine were light-years apart, for their affections appeared to be reserved for 'fitba' But I loved music, and listened in on an old Cossor battery wireless to Dr. Malcolm Sargent and the Huddersfield Choral Society giving their wartime performances of Handel's *Messiah*. The Portsoy lads, and some of my relatives as well, thought I was mad. So the feeling grew that I did not 'belong' here. Did I belong to some other world? Was there another place where I could live and be happy and fulfilled?

I am at one with Malcolm Muggeridge when he says that from his earliest boyhood years he felt an alien, a foreigner, in this world; and he was profoundly stirred when he first heard the phrase 'a stranger in a strange land'. Have you ever felt this way? None of this feeling of lostness in me was helped by the fact that the spiritual life in Portsoy was at a low ebb. The last reawakening of the 1920s was little more than a memory, and only a handful of those who professed Christ at that time were persevering in the Faith. I do recall singing Sankey and Redemption hymns. But that was all that was left of the revival, largely, I fear, because the new converts were never taught the deeper things of Christ. Being fed on saps and milk they did not grow up. So the music of the revival lasted for a while, but its Gospel died. Certainly no-one ever told me that Christ loved me, or that I was a sinner and needed forgiveness and salvation. Remember, I was twenty-seven years of age before I heard the Gospel, here in Scotland, an alleged land of Christian light!

In addition, all the important things in life happened to me away from home: secondary school was not in Portsoy but in Fordyce, at the academy there; further education was at Aberdeen; teaching was at Bracoden School, Gamrie; my first charge was at Holytown, near Glasgow. And always the feeling persisted that this world was not my home, that I did not belong here. I was fated to be a wanderer, a nomad, a loner.

I bless God that much, though not all, of that is ended and gone. After seven years of ministry, I am glad to testify that life for me has never been so rich, so full, so sweet, so rewarding. The loving-kindnesses that are showered upon me by folks who have been compassionate enough to take me into their affections is something that catches the breath and brings a tear to the eye. Such care is better felt than telt! You should see the Manse at Christmas-time when the place explodes into a veritable cornucopia of good things. 'My cup runneth over.'

But what of the future? In the words of Joshua: 'There remains very much land to be possessed'. Inevitably I dream dreams and see visions. A few are concerned solely that the West Kirk should be a 'successful' church or, much worse, a successful religious club. But these are very far down on the list of my order of priorities. It is not required of stewards that they be successful, but that they be found faithful. I should like to see, therefore, less interest in the numbers coming to worship, the monies coming in, and so on, and more interest in true spirituality. I dream of the day when every elder is a man of the Word, a man of prayer, a man with an experimental working knowledge of Christ. I dream of the day when every professor of Christ is also a possessor of Him and of His benefits. I would love to see a thoroughly converted membership, a persuaded people. I long for the day when people will see that it is more important to be a member of Christ than it is to be a member of the church. And is it not high time for some of our young people to hear the call of Christ to full-time worship and enjoy God's presence. One can be mirthful without being frivolous, you know. So I also dream of the day when God the Holy Ghost, in all His livingness, will come to cold little hearts and take away the woodenness, the stolidity, the formality, the deadness.

Perhaps you know that when the early Baptists in the Highlands tried to found churches they met with much opposition from Parish ministers. The Baptist church in Grantown-on-Spey, having owed something to the evangelical work of the Haldane brothers in the north, was just such a place. The local minister said that he was thankful (to God, I wonder?) that he had no 'enthusiasts' in his congregation. In other words, he had no evangelicals in his membership. His folk were all middle-of-the-road folk, 'laird's men' all. That is to say, they were 'for' the Establishment, right or wrong, dead or alive - and preferably dead. My dream is that all who read this letter (as well as those who don't!) will be 'enthusiasts' and as evangelical as the Word of God and their personalities will allow them to be.

Yours sincerely, in that hope,
THOMAS SWANSTON

2*
LIFESTYLES

Dear Friends,

Lifestyles are constantly changing even in the Christian world - sometimes, happily, for the better and sometimes, alas, for the worse. In a sense it is inevitable that change of some sort should be the order of the day for Christians since we are ceaselessly called upon to make Christ our contemporary in every succeeding generation. This is an evangelical art which challenges us to show Him as the Man for every age, without interfering with His authenticity. Whatever else may vary in this inconstant, futile world He Himself is above and beyond mutability. Lifestyles develop and alter, often according to the whims and moods of passing fashions. He remains the same.

And yet it is an observable fact that there are common factors and characteristics in the ways in which Christians have expressed their faith, demonstrated the Gospel and made the Word flesh for men to see. Some years ago, in the course of a sermon, I spoke of the way in which we observed the Lord's Day as lads along the Moray coast during, and shortly after, the Second World War. Quite a number of folk expressed interest in (not to mention astonishment at!) what was said and I feel, therefore, that the time has come for me to set down some of those experiences in print. We can then think of the question of lifestyles.

As growing boys we were brought up 'Church Army'. That, at least, is how the Salvation Army officers used to label us. We were half Auld Kirk, from which we inherited

*July 1983

a sense of worshipfulness, decorum and reverence, and half Salvation Army, in which we rejoiced in the warmth, availability and freeness of the Gospel message. The Lord's Day ran thus:

10.00 am Salvation Army Young People's Directory
11.00 am Morning Worship in the Parish Church
12.00 pm Parish Church Sunday School
2.00 pm Afternoon Sunday School in the Salvation Army
3.00 pm Salvation Army Holiness Meeting
4.00 pm Open-Air meeting. I sported the traditional red 'Sallie-Annie' jersey and cap given to me by Captain John Cross and played the bass drum, the sole-surviving relic of a band formed in the 1920s after a fleeting spiritual awakening.
6.00 pm Evening worship in the Parish Church
7.00 pm Salvation meeting in the Army
8.00 pm Family hymn-singing round the harmonium.

Looking back (in anything but anger) I might hesitate to say whether or not I would expect any child of mine to suffer such a Marathon. It was, by many standards, a Spartan education. Small wonder that the seats of our Sabbath breeks were permanently shiny! And any present-day educational psychologist would indicate that the process was too meeting-centred, too religion-centred, too God-centred, and that its requirements smacked too much of passivity. We were expected to sit still and to listen.

And listen we did, for I recall how my heart was first moved towards the Saviour around the age of ten when I responded to a call to come forward to the Penitent Seat to seek Himself. Not knowing whom or what I sought I knelt there. Whether or not God then did a secret, permanent work of grace I cannot say. Certainly the memory of that day is indelibly fixed. It is unforgettable.

Nor did the performance seem a Marathon to us then. We entertained no suspicions that all of this was something irksome, intolerable, burdensome, onerous, a weariness to healthy, ebullient flesh, alien and imposed from above. It was simply taken for granted that Sunday was the Lord's Day, special for Himself, special for us, and Christians were expected to keep the day in a distinctive way. Not all young lads in Portsoy, of course, ran the Marathon with us for there were pagans, semi-pagans and semi-Christians then as now. But where do many of them stand morally and spiritually today? Such a pattern of living inculcated in us the following:

Firstly, a profound respect for the things of God; a sense of eternity; and awareness of the holiness and privilege of worship; a living conscience towards sin; a longing for Christ and a homesickness for God.

Secondly, an ability to recognise the genuine message of grace so that, even in unsaved and unconverted days, one could detect when preaching had ceased to be biblical and evangelical and had degenerated into the merely moral, the merely exhortatory, the merely ethical, tending towards little more than religiosity and decent churchmanship.

Thirdly, and most important of all, the notion that all saving religion was a costly business, involving deaths and dyings; the conviction that surrender to Christ had to do with sacrifice - of one's personal opinions, own point of view, pleasures, self-esteem, vanity, money, time, talents and pride. Christianity had more to do with slaughter and the charnel house than with the odours of sanctity! To change the metaphor: whatever fair blossoms the Gospel showed to the world (such as the blooms of service for others, caring, love, gentleness, meekness and grace) the roots lay in the stern earth of duty, loyalty, fidelity, allegiance and commitment.

As boyhood years passed into early manhood the old lifestyle was set behind me, though never forgotten, and never entirely despised. The tragedy was that I set such light store by it and the words of Henry Williams Baker have, for me, a pathetic and meaningful ring:

And I, poor sinner, cast it all away;
Lived for the toil or pleasure of each day;
As if no Christ had ever shed His precious blood,
As if I owed no homage to my God.

I was found by the seeking Saviour at the age of twenty-seven under the preaching of my friend and brother James Philip during my teaching years at Gamrie. In those days there was less clear Gospel preaching in the land than there is today and the Evangel was less accessible. A well-defined pattern of living was taken for granted if a man professed a saving experience of Christ, if he stood on the conservative wing theologically, if he viewed Scripture and the Death of Jesus in a particular way and if he claimed to believe in the power of prayer. Here was the lifestyle:

1. Attendance at public worship with one's fellow-Christians twice on the Lord's Day accompanied by a Bible, the latter witnessing to the seriousness of our interest and concern to be educated in holy things.
2. Attendance at some mid-week service for fellowship and Bible Study.
3. Attendance at the main church Prayer Fellowship in the manner of Jesus and His disciples and of the early Christians in the Book of Acts.
4. Attendance (in student years) at the Christian Union Prayer Fellowship on Friday evenings, followed by the main weekly C.U. meeting.

5. Attendance at occasional Missionary Breakfasts on Saturday mornings.
6. An active, personal concern for the Lord's work at home and abroad. My own involvement on the home front was with Inter-Varsity Fellowship (now UCCF) with its evangelical labours among students. On the foreign field my first love was the China Inland Mission, now the Overseas Missionary Fellowship. But there were other concerns also: the Africa Inland Mission, the Southern Morocco Mission, Ludhiana Christian Medical College, the Evangelical Union of South America, Christian Work in Russia and the Communist bloc, numerous social interests etc. We also wrote to missionaries to comfort, uphold and encourage them. It was generally assumed that if a man showed little or no interest in Christian work the probability was he was not interested in Christ.
7. Income was tithed i.e. a tenth was given to the Lord. Most of this went to the local church and the rest was distributed elsewhere. Some believed in tithing before Her Majesty's Inspector of Taxes had deducted his share; others felt that the tithe should come from one's net income. Those zealous for sacrifice and consecration (it was then called 'laying oneself on the altar') gave more than the tithe. They believed, as I do, that the tithe is what we owe. What we give is what we give beyond our duty. The practice of tithing persisted through university years when we were often very hard up indeed. My first annual grant was £92 out of which I had to pay lodgings and buy all books and laboratory equipment. We did our own cooking and laundry since there were no Halls of Residence.
8. The vast majority gave up the tobacco habit after conversion.

9. Total abstinence was the norm in relation to alcohol.
10. We applied ourselves assiduously to the task of personal evangelism, testifying to friends, distributing tracts, busying ourselves with door-to-door visitation. Immediately after coming to Christ I wrote to all my old friends. Some thought that I had gone mad, and they said so. Others felt that I was 'going through a religious phase' and would soon 'get over it'. Others again wrote to say that there was nothing wrong with me that a good party would not cure. A few, more patronisingly, were of the mind that there was nothing fundamentally wrong with 'getting converted' since that sort of thing had happened to Paul, Augustine, St Francis of Assisi, Savonarola and the like, and so was quite respectable if not taken to extremes. Only one friend, to the best of my knowledge, came to Christ. The rest forsook me and fled into the darkness.

The really telling thing is that, give or take a few cultural alterations, the above lifestyle would be acknowledged and recognised by all who stand in the tradition of historic evangelicalism: Finney, Moody, Spurgeon, Booth, the Bonars, McCheyne, the Wesleys, Whitefield, Edwards and the English and Scottish Puritans. And something, in turn, must also follow from all of this (I am sorry if you find this too frank and unhelpful): many today who call themselves 'evangelicals' are not really evangelicals at all in the historic sense. At the risk of sounding offensive, I call them semi-evangelicals.

I am not speaking of conformity or of toeing the party line. Conformity for conformity's sake can be an idol, and is already something of a plague in the churches. Consider the appalling desolations wrought in the Highlands by such a philosophy! The very last thing that any pastor would want to produce is a generation of mere conformists, yes-men and yes-women robbed of their individuality, all saying the same thing and reduced to the level of religious robots. A man may well espouse the name of Christian: but, if so many aspects of the lifestyle are missing, does he have the right to wave the evangelical flag?

It is indisputable that some who read this letter have, for one reason or another, opted for something less than that surrender which one longs to see in all Christ's bairns. Their cool independence, their self-exclusion from the heart of what I seek to do, their enthusiasm for private Christian pursuits coupled with an unwillingness to see the local church as the essential core of Christian testimony... these are great mysteries to me. Surely the time has come for some to cease looking upon our fellowship (and my ministry within it) as a kind of restaurant i.e. a place from which food may be obtained from time to time, but scarcely a place in which one's true life lies?

For all who are prepared to go all the way with Jesus one blesses the Lord without measure. One praises Him for those whose time, talents, monies and pleasures are not their own. One delights increasingly in sweet fellowship with those who take pleasure in bowing the knee to Jesus. Should more not be joining their number? Henry Baker's hymn quoted above (the first line of which is *God made me for Himself*) has a penetrating last verse which I now commend to you.

O Holy Spirit, with Thy fire divine,
    Melt into tears this thankful heart of mine;
Teach me to love what once I seemed to hate,
    And live to God before it be too late.

Yours sincerely
THOMAS SWANSTON

3*
IAN - A BELOVED BROTHER

Dear Friends,
All true love must suffer pain; or, at least, love (by which I mean living love, seeking and saving love, self-giving and sacrificial love) must be prepared, in one way or another, to pay the price of loving. One may, of course, even as a Christian, opt out of love's pains by simply opting out of loving in any practical, caring, personal or evangelical way. The options to the pains of love must surely be legion!

Sing about love, if you may, for singing about it is easy. Write essays on love, on its length and breadth and depth and height, for that too is fairly effortless. Preach (or write Parish letters) about love, and you may have a goodly hear-ing from the Christian public. Talk about love, with fitting illustrations from Christian history, to various interested groups. But if you want to avoid love's pains, seal your heart.

Seal it against the inroads and encroachments of human need. Close your conscience to strident pleas for pity and mercy. Do not allow yourself to be put to any inconvenience by despair other than your own. Do not permit your life to become contaminated. Lock the door fast; bar the windows; seal the shutters; pull up the drawbridge, sterilize the environment. To love at all is to open oneself to hurt, to humiliation, to self-exposure and, all too often, to rejection. All true love suffers pain. This is an immutable law of God's moral universe. In the light of it let me speak about my late brother, Ian.

He was always a difficult, distracted and complex lad even

*January 1985

from earliest fevered years. He was born with what used to be called 'club feet', an ankle deformity, and spent the first year of infant life shuttling, with legs in heavy plaster, between Eyemouth, our native village in Berwickshire, and the Princess Margaret Rose Hospital in Edinburgh. That initial year of peacelessness and pain was almost a prelude, presaging a stormy life filled with torments and frenzies, with strivings and alarms, with ceaseless psychological conflicts. Beneath the affable, well-read, intelligent and likeable fellow to whom people were attracted, this was the real truth about Ian. Throughout his entire life he sensed himself rejected, unloved, unwanted, uncared for and uncherished. He felt that he did not matter to anyone, that he was nobody and nothing. Therefore his motto, unspoken and unwritten, was: JOHANNES CONTRA MUNDUM: Ian against the Universe.

For years, as a brother who loved him, I sought to fathom the root and basis of this sick, needless war. His position in the family hierarchy did not help: he was the middle boy of three. I was the oldest and was idolised by my mother who saw in me the fulfilment of a prophecy which her mother had made on her deathbed, that one day she would bear a son who would preach the Gospel. I was also adored by my paternal grandmother for I bore her late husband's name and was, as it were, auld Tammie come back from the dead.

Further down in the family our brother Bill was worshipped by my father, for he carried father's name. Ian, therefore, fell between two stools. Some explanation of his rootless psyche, his rebel nature, must lie here. Beneath the Ian who was hail-fellow-well-met there were, for those with eyes to see and insight to discern, truly tragic proportions. He himself, and this is hardly surprising, had very little insight into the workings of his own nature; thus did he blunder on through life from crisis to crisis, from disaster to disaster, hounded by guilt, fleeing from the hurts of life into the cheap illusions afforded by the world of strong drink, uncomprehendingly seeking, seeking, seeking...

But what on earth was he looking for? This is the question which exercised me for the greater part of his life of wandering. I see it all now plainly, as if God had spread a map before me: Ian was looking for a home and a fatherland. He was forever changing employers (now the Ben Line; now P & O; now the Blue Funnel Line; now the Black Funnel Line; now BP tankers; now Esso...) and rarely sailed with the same shipping line, or in the same ship, twice. Always it had to be something and someone new! It was quite a bewildering exercise trying to keep up with his employers, for they changed so rapidly.

He knew virtually every nation in the world with a sea coast; and he visited practically every great port in the world of commercial shipping. Once, having returned to his ship from an evening's carousing, he was rescued half-drowned from the vile waters of Bremen harbour. Always he pressed on, looking for the home and the fatherland. Surely the next harbour would be home? Surely the next country would be the fatherland? But it was not to be. Christians know that for the elect child of God our home and fatherland are not to be found here. That we can be at home in this world, finally happy here, finally content and satisfied, is one of life's greatest lies and a bitter and terrible illusion. Therefore God brought Ian to Inverness to bring him home to Himself. He was born to be born again here.

On the evening of his baptism in church, when he confessed his trust in Christ as Saviour and Lord so resolutely, he later described the experience to me privately as a 'moving occasion'. Indeed it was, to many. He was vastly amused to learn that one lady, having learned of the baptism from the magazine, imagined that somehow I had got married quietly and that my wife had produced a child; she therefore congratulated me on the 'happy event at the Manse'! How Ian and I rocked with mirth and merriment!

Later, when he was ordained to the eldership on March 6th 1983, he said that he sensed he had 'come home at last' and that he felt he 'now belonged'. It was the nearest he ever came to expressing emotion, for he rarely betrayed his inner, deepest heart lest the old feelings of lovelessness and rejection overwhelm him yet again. He was marvellous with old people, with children and with animals: but I suspect that these did not constitute a threat to him. Of mature adults he was more cautious since they were a doorway to ancient hurts and risks.

I bless the Lord for the tender-heartedness, care and acceptance shown him by the elders on our Session. His past was never alluded to. He was totally integrated with these loyal men and in that brotherhood of fellowship and grace began to find the home and fatherland for which he longed.

One should not extol or praise men beyond proportion, but I wish to set it on record here that in Ian I have never seen a man so submissive to the will of God and so possessed of such meek resignation of spirit. He never complained, even when in obvious distress and in great discomfort in hospital. He never raised his voice in protest or rebellion against what the Lord had either sent directly or had allowed in his earlier years. He never once lifted himself in aggression against mother, even when she delivered what we dryly called her 'memorial lectures' against his excesses; and in his wildest years of stravaiging the earth he always provided for her needs week by week and showed her filial devotion and care.

So many factors were involved in his recovery from the scourge and curse of alcoholism: the quality of ministry at

Ronachan House, the compassion and understanding of the staff of the Inverness Branch of the Department of Health and Social Security where he was a messenger, but not least do I bless God for all the fellow-feeling shown by many of you who read this. In our sad, groaning creation it is no small thing to turn a sinner from the error of his ways to the wisdom of the just and to show the love of Christ to the lost, confused and helpless sons of men.

On the afternoon before he died, I called to see him. Only a heart of stone could fail to have been moved to pity by that spectacle of emaciation and woe. I say solemnly that, by this appearance at the last, Ian was a poor advertisement for the tobacco industry and the licensed trade. In terms of ruined health, of wrecked bodies and of condemned souls, those two institutions have much to answer for before the Judgement Bar of God.

But the hope of the gospel for those who have fallen asleep in Jesus is sure and springs eternal. He has come home at long last, having sought God in many harbours. He has found his fatherland and attained his Jerusalem. 'So He bringeth them unto their desired haven.' (Ps 107:30).

Therefore we say from the heart, 'Precious in the sight of the Lord is the death of His saints' (Ps 116:15).

Yours in affection and gratitude,
THOMAS SWANSTON

4
PERMANENCE*

Dear Friends,

I want to write to you about the longing that God has placed in our hearts for what endures; and I start with a quotation from Hardy's *The Return of the Native.* Hardy is writing about the 'permanence' of Egdon Heath compared with the 'impermanence' of the sea. 'The great, inviolate place (i.e. Egdon) had an ancient permanence which the sea cannot claim. Who can say of a particular sea that it is old? Distilled by the sun, kneaded by the moon, it is renewed in a year, in a day or in an hour. The sea changed, the fields changed, the rivers, villages and people changed; yet Egdon remained.'

I recall that when I first read these words a strange carillon rang out within me from some hidden, secret belfry. Here was Thomas Hardy, a dour fellow by all accounts, sceptical and irreligious, who appreciated the vital distinction between what lasts and what is changing and ephemeral. For as long as I can remember that appreciation, coupled with a desperate desire for permanence, has been part of my constitution. When, as a boy in the Kirk, I heard the phrases 'strangers and pilgrims on the earth', a 'better country' and 'a city which hath foundations, whose builder and maker is God' (Heb.11:23,16,10), I felt myself sick at heart with a yearning for that 'better country'. I wanted, above all else in this world, to breathe its air, to talk its language, to sing its songs and to trade in its currency. Does this ring a bell with you?

I can trace this yearning - it is almost a lust - largely to the fact that all my boyhood and adolescent years were spent

*January 1990

within sound of the ocean. My ears were ceaselessly assailed by the music of the waves and when, in later student years, I first heard and sang Vaughan Williams' *Sea Symphony*, my being rose at once as if to recognise and greet an old friend. The sea, spectated by me during endless hours of silent, almost worshipful, vigil from the shore became a kind of first-love - a moody, dangerous, fickle mistress for a young man 'chosen in Christ before the foundation', seeking, at the core of his being, to know where one might find a city whose foundations were built, everlasting, by God Himself. I could not escape the impression that the sea never stayed the same for two fractions of a second on end. Always she was on the move, mutating, easing her way into the next storm, swirling and eddying tantalizingly towards change and yet further change. A camera might trap the spectacle for a fleeting moment; but the moment was soon gone and the dark lady had transmuted herself into something other than she was.

Around the sea, of course, was the shore, and it held more lasting objects. Rocks appeared to endure. Generations of departed Moray fishermen could return from the dead and recognise familiar contours and ancient geology. They were, as it seemed fixed. But not for ever! Even rocks decay and turn to dust under pitiless winters, relentless weathers and searing winds. The rocklikeness of the rocks may be set against the temporariness of the seascape but, in the end, mutability and corruption overtake them all. Paul says that the creation has been 'subjected to frustration, not by its own choice, but by the will of the One who subjected it, in hope that the creation itself will be liberated from its bondage to decay' (Rom 8:20-21 NIV). God, in the mystery of providence, has subjected His entire universe to the principles of evanescence and futility with a view to that great and grand and glorious day when, at the Second Coming of Christ, creation itself will be brought into 'the glorious freedom of the children of God' (Rom 8:21).

Surely it is not too hard to apply such sentiments to life itself? Robert Burns described change as 'Nature's mighty law'. The passage of time is undoubtedly marked and measured by it. We certainly change in our appearance as the ravages of the years take their toll and all the potions and lotions of the cosmetic industry do little to disguise the fact that no-one, from crawling baby to tottering geriatric, is getting any younger. Our tastes alter with the passage of time, as well as our attitudes. The dearest friendships, with one exception (Prov 18:24) may wither under the pressures of treachery, unfaithfulness and lack of true love. Marriages, too, may mutate from what they used to be as first-love loses its lustre, as mutual respect vanishes and as affections are taken for granted. Even Christian profession may become tarnished as folk who were once true, earnest and zealous believers grow cold, allow themselves to lapse into secret (and not so secret) backsliding, and gradually depart from what they once were for Jesus and the Gospel. Flux and mutability, what the Book of Common Prayer calls 'the changes and chances of this mortal life', are the order of the day.

But what of the heart's longing for that which endures? C. S. Lewis describes the longing as 'inconsolable'. He writes: 'If I find in myself a desire which no experience in this world can satisfy, the most probable explanation is that I was made for another world.' Made for another world - there's a thought to conjure with! And yet I am not persuaded that all men have this desire. Is it the case that they are unaware of what lies in them at that level?

In the course of nearly thirty years of ministry, I have noticed that many folk, even among regular churchgoers, do not appear to want the far-off country at all. I was reading through some old sermons recently (an infallible sign of gathering decrepitude in any preacher!) and see that, from time to time, I have said something like this: 'A Christian is someone who, by his very constitution, is predestined by God never to be finally at home in this world.' Abraham, Isaac and Jacob were nomads. They lived in tents, in temporary homes, rather than in houses. They were 'strangers and pilgrims', always on the move and ever ready to loosen the tent-pegs and be up and away.

And yet there are folk who seem perfectly happy and at home here. They seek, and long for, no other world. If it could somehow be proved that there was no God, no life after death, no Grand Assize, no judgment, no heaven and no hell it would not disturb them greatly. They are like old Mr. Cumberground in Bunyan, taken up with, and preoccupied by, the here and now, the visible, tangible empires of money, accounts, houses, pleasure, food, holidays, prospects, promotion, advancement and success - pursuits that are not necessarily wrong in themselves, but which, without the saving, sanctifying touch and presence of the Living Christ, lead to lives of appalling boredom and narrow-mindedness. Pity the poor, unconverted unbeliever, whether he comes to church or not; he is the man who, at the end of the day, gets the worst of both worlds!

On the other hand there are the Christians, those who have been born twice. They are foreordained to carry about with them the divine discontentment, the sense of homelessness and home-sickness. And the truly extraordinary thing is this: one might expect that when we come to Christ the longings will somehow go away. In fact they do not: they are merely heightened, sharpened and intensified. To come to Him is to catch a sight of one's true and lasting home, the place where the sickness and the longing can be assuaged and satisfied. Thereafter, nothing can be quite the same again.

> For, ah, the Master is so fair,
> His smile so sweet on banished men,
> That they who meet it unaware
> Can never turn to earth again;
> And they who see Him risen afar,
> At God's right hand to welcome them,
> Forgetful stand of home and land,
> Desiring fair Jerusalem.

Either the Master is 'fair' to you in this way, or He is not. Is He? Either He has smiled savingly and sweetly on your banished estate, or He has not. Has He? Either you see Him risen and standing there to welcome you, or you do not. Do you? Either you have forgotten home and land, or you have not. Have you? Either you desire fair Jerusalem, or you do not. Do you? If you do not, you are still of the earth, earthy: you belong to this world; you are yet a child of time, of dust, of mortality; your home is here. But if the sentiments of the verse apply to you, and have somehow become incarnate in you, then you are a child of heaven; you do not belong to this world; you are a child of eternity; your home is elsewhere.

The last parish letter was about the need to be born again. At the close of the letter I expressed the hope that I might live to see some fruit from what had been written. So far there has been no response at all. Has the time not come for you to make a major decision?

Yours sincerely in that earnest hope,
THOMAS SWANSTON

5
WHAT IS 'EVANGELICAL'?*

Dear Friends,

'There's a fully-committed evangelical, if ever there was one!' Colleague A was speaking of colleague B. My heart failed within me for I happened to know colleague B. True, B is a hard-working man, diligent, approachable and friendly; but his notions of the love of God tend to be rather vague and sentimental; and he has little interest in the great doctrinal issues of the Faith. His private concerns and pursuits are also somewhat odd, and involve him in the holding of views, and engaging in practices, which would never be espoused by any informed, God-honouring evangelical. More sinister is the fact that he is everybody's buddy; he offends no-one, publicly or privately, and has the right, ineffectual word for every occasion. A smooth man! And, most sinister of all, he does have the strangest friends, men and women, who are far from being well-disposed to the Word of the Cross. Does such a man live consistently in the world of truth? Or is his life not truly integrated, being divided into compartments, so that he can switch from one Christian group to another sub-Christian group without any sense of embarrassment or without knowing that he has compromised his profession? And do these facts not suggest a woeful lack of judgment on the part of colleague A? So what is 'evangelical'?

'We wouldn't care to have an evangelical in our pulpit.' The lady was a member of a Vacancy Committee. She seemed very sure of what she wanted (as distinct from what she needed), and her fur coat fairly bristled to emphasize her

*March 1976

opinions. But what did she mean? Her use of the phrase 'our pulpit' was ominous. Did God have no say in the matter? Was she honestly admitting that hers was a church which had no taste for a Biblical ministry? Perhaps her church had 'done' the Gospel? Were they now superior to it, and moving on to higher things? So what is 'evangelical'?

'But he made a decision at a Scripture Union camp; surely he is an evangelical?' The man in question had indeed 'made a decision for Christ'. But his decision, surely, had within it many other decisions, one of which must have been the decision to make a minimum amount of spiritual progress! For he went on to make something of his material life, but little of his spiritual self. He learned a few basic facts about Jesus and the Bible, but failed to add to these character, gentleness, teachability, fruitfulness, and humility. He had got stuck. He never grew up. So what is 'evangelical'?

I wonder whether or not the time has now come for us to think through the meaning of the word. The problem is that it is used by so many in the church, and used so carelessly, that it can mean everything or nothing. It has become a Humpty-Dumpty word, a word that can be twisted to mean what the speaker wants it to mean. On the right wing of the church it is claimed by Reformed Christians who hold the tenets of Calvinism; on the extreme left wing it is the flag waved by very different folk, by Pentecostals or Charismatics, who try to recapture, for the church's blessing and good, spiritual gifts which they claim have been neglected or lost. The 'Tell Scotland' movement was evangelical. Billy Graham is an evangelical preacher. Barthians claim to stand in an 'evangelical' succession. The Salvation Army is 'evangelical'. But these groups are not normally the happiest of bed-fellows, and hold radically differing opinions on points that could be considered fundamental. So what is 'evangelical'?

We need to distinguish between 'evangelical' and 'evangelistic'. The former refers to a message, the latter to methods. 'Evangelical' describes the historic Biblical doctrines which have been handed down by the church as the substance of the apostolic Gospel. 'Evangelistic' describes certain methods of Gospel presentation and practices which were introduced, largely from America, into Christian work and witness during the second half of the nineteenth century - the enquiry room, the penitent form, the 'hot seat' for those anxious about their souls, trained counsellors, decision-making, altar-calls, the filling-in of commitment cards, large-scale Gospel rallies with special music, choirs and appeals. It is possible to be evangelical without being evangelistic, and that is our position here in the West Kirk. We eschew many of the characteristics of 'evangelistic' life since they are foreign to Scottish religion and spiritual culture at their best. There were, in fact, revivals of enduring worth long before such imports and innovations came to Scotland.

As for 'evangelical' we have moved a long way since Sir Thomas More, in the days of Henry VIII, spoke with contempt of the 'evangelickalls'. He meant those who had ceased to talk the language of Rome and who now spoke the language of the Evangel. In much the same way, the evangelicals of south-west Scotland, the 'men of Galloway' came to be called Lollards, because they 'lolled' with their tongues - they too, would not talk the language of the Roman church. Perhaps evangelicals, by their very nature, are protest-ants; they set themselves against error, corruption and worldliness in the church's teaching and life. But the colour of the protest was determined by the century in which you lived.

The Covenanters, doubtless, had mixed emotions. They were political men as well as spiritual. But without exception they championed the Gospel of Christ, and rallied to evangelical truth against the high-handed tyranny of the Stuarts. Thus, in the seventeenth century, to be evangelical was to be for the Covenants. In the eighteenth century to be evangelical was to be for Wesley and Whitefield, and against the Deists. The Deists were men who were almost Unitarian in their views, believing in God and ethics and little more. For the Deists Jesus tended to be the Master, the Great Example, our Elder Brother - almost as if he were a greater-than-Socrates, a super-Guru. Deist sermons were dry, moralistic affairs destitute of either grace or good news for sinners. After all, was it not the function of Presbyterianism to make a man into a gentleman?

Our national poet, Rabbie Burns, appears to have been Deistic rather than Christian. Burns believed in God, of course. But his beliefs fell far short of the full revelation in Jesus. They also failed to have any noticeable effects on his private morals. Burns' God was the Creator, the Architect of the Universe, the Unmoved Mover, the Prime Cause, Providence and the Higher Hand rather than 'the God and Father of our Lord Jesus Christ', a gracious Redeemer and Saviour from sin. 'We have spoken of the almost Deistic strain of teaching that was to be found among men of the Moderate Party. It was in the company and fellowship of men of such a tendency that the gifted Robert Burns moved. He became their spokesman in his caricatures of the Old School Evangelicals of his native Ayrshire.' And again: 'He (i.e. the great Dr. John Love, of Glasgow) came in touch with the circle of serious godliness in Ayrshire which became the butt of the satire of Robert Burns...' (Dr. John MacLeod in *Scottish Theology*).

In the nineteenth century, still reaping harvests from the revivals under Wesley and Whitefield, to be an 'evangelical' was to be against the Moderates - those broad-minded, laissez-faire churchmen, virtual heirs of the Deists and committed to all the worldliness and patronage of the State Church. The Disruption of 1843 marked the inability of the evangelicals, grieved and frustrated, to contain themselves within the system. The flower of the evangelical ministry threw in its lot with the secession and thus was born the Free Church. In that judgment the Church of Scotland lost a third of its ministers and its entire mission field. But the business of the Patronage Act (which had given heritors the right to appoint a minister over a congregation) was only superficially the issue at stake. The real issues were doctrinal and spiritual and had to do with the Evangel and its distinctive teachings: the New Birth, the need for conversion, the authority and inspiration of Scripture, eternal judgment and rewards, the Godhead of the Son, and so on.

Whale, in his book *The Protestant Tradition* speaks of the tension between the once-born Erasmus and the twice-born Luther. That cleavage stands at the heart of the church in every age and is a great gulf fixed. People who believe in the personalness of sin, in the need to be saved personally from it, and in Jesus as the personal answer are 'evangelical'. Those who do not believe are not evangelical, and it may be questioned whether they are Christians at all in any recognisable sense. An evangelical Christian (and, pray, how can one be an unevangelical one?) is someone who has God for his heavenly Father, Jesus for his Saviour and Lord, the Holy Spirit for his Comforter, and the church (the people of God, the Christian community) for his Mother. If you are evangelical you are 'in' on this. If you are not evangelical, where do you stand?

The real divisions in the church today are not the familiar ones that are the preoccupation of the Ecumenical Movement - Presbyterianism against Episcopacy against Roman Catholicism against Methodism against Brethrenism or what have you. The real division is between those who are evangelical and those who are not. It is the old division between the churchy and the Christian; between those who are merely religious and those who are alive for Jesus.

But it cannot be doubted that the auld kirkers are dying out. In some twenty years or so few will remain. Their doom is writ visibly in our time. Only the blind do not see it. The holocaust that is coming on the visible church will remove all such, for nominal Christians have no resources with which to combat persecution. Requiescant in pace: let them rest (if it be possible) in peace. They did enough damage in their day.

Indications are that our world and society are about to be overtaken by grey, middle-aged, faceless, left-wing bores with a taste for power. In the coming judgment the deid auld kirkers, the once-born, the Great Unwashed will simply disappear. Only the evangelicals (give the word as narrow or as broad a connotation as you Biblically may) will survive.

Yours, hopeful that you see the point,

THOMAS SWANSTON

6
CHRISTIAN FELLOWSHIP*

Dear Friends,
There has been some private discussion among the saints recently as to the nature of Christian fellowship in general, and the quality of fellowship found in our own midst in particular, and the theme calls for some honest thought and, at least, a decent airing. The phrase 'arm's-length fellowship' has been used meaning, of course, fellowship at a distance - proper, demure, acknowledged and undoubtedly real in Christ, yet curiously less than the hearty, personal, life-to-life communion of kindred souls that is hinted at in Scripture.

The word translated as 'fellowship' comes from the Greek *koinonia* and that, in turn, is derived from the root *koinos* which means 'common'. This being the case it is possible to have Christian fellowship only with someone with whom, sharing a common sinnerhood, one shares a common-ness of Jesus Christ and His salvation. Fellowship between a Christian and a non-Christian must therefore be fellowship based on other foundations and grounded on other premises such as a common love of sport, or of music, or of cooking, or of friendship or whatever. Paul puts this truth starkly when he says that, in the end of the day, light can have no fellowship with darkness, nor Christ with Belial (2 Cor. 6:14-15).

Take the English word 'fellowship'. It is made of three small words which come from ancient languages (Old English, Middle English and Old Norse): fe (cattle, property and, thence, price); lag (a laying together, a law or principle); and scipe (a state of being, a state of affairs as in worth-ship,

*March 1986

as in worth-ship, workmanship, craftsmanship). In all authentic fellowship there is a price to be paid (unconditional surrender to Christ), a law to bind (unqualified obedience to Christ) and a state of affairs (being in Christ). A Christian cannot have fellowship with anyone who has not paid the price or who is not bound by the law or who is not in Christ.

Yet, pressing inwards, even within the fold of Christ there are different sorts, degrees and levels of friendship. It cannot be questioned that some are saved, yet barely so. They are in the kingdom and that is not in dispute; they are marked by the great Redeemer's blood, sealed by His Spirit and assured by grace of everlasting life. They are 'saved' in the sense that they are not 'lost'. And yet many appear to evidence little progress into the deeper reaches of that Faith once delivered to the saints (Jude 3). They paddle about everlastingly in a world of spiritual shallows and occupy (not to say preoccupy) themselves endlessly with the elementary things and first principles of the Gospel - the need for men to repent towards God and exercise faith in the Lord Jesus Christ, the absolute necessity of the New Birth and of conversion.

These wonders, however, are merely the beginnings of the Gospel, and one despairs of folk who never seem to grow up or make any advance much beyond the basic elements of evangelisticism. With how many Christians can one have fellowship at the level of Matt 10:37-39, or of Romans 6, or of Col 3:1-3?

It is cold comfort to consider that unprogressive Christians have always existed in the churches from the very start (Heb 5:11-6:3), but I am bound to say here that many believers over the years have been a great source of disappointment and amazement to me in this very matter, so poor has been their track record, so irregular and unstable has been their spiritual performance. Others may be, and have been, taken in by glib professions, but not I. Maturity seeks the mature, crucifixion seeks the crucified, surrender seeks the surrendered and deep calls to deep. And, on the other hand, superficiality seeks the superficial, shallowness the shallow and carnality the carnal. It was ever thus. But it need not be so. The process is not inevitable. The entire business of growth has nothing whatsoever to do with intelligence or education or psychology. It is wholly a matter of the acceptance, or refusal, of the Crown Rights of the Redeemer.

To return, more gently, to the theme of fellowship: church buildings, constructed by our forefathers (often in the spirit of triumphalism when Theology was Queen of the Sciences) and handed down to us, were never designed for fellowship in any close, personal sense. The pews, uncomfortable as they are (by intention, one wonders?), were arranged facing the pulpit and the folk who sat in them were expected to attend to the preaching of the Word. Churches, thus, are hearing-places rather than sharing-places. In warmer, summer days a fairish number linger, whether in pews or at the door, to catch up with news and to share the Lord. But the longing for fellowship must require more than this passing encounter. It is difficult to satisfy such a longing in the context of the large numbers we have at morning worship. The mid-week service for Bible study and prayer opens up a few more possibilities: yet even there we sit in stern, regimented rows, and the majority of Christians prefer to listen, even when opportunity is given to share the Word in parallel Scriptures or associated ideas.

We need also to face the fact that many splendid Christians neither need nor want close, personal fellowship. They are perfectly happy with arrangements as they stand and are content to come to regular, traditional services of worship, greet a few fellow-saints in passing and thereafter make for home. This apparent independence may, perhaps, be attributable to special personality factors. At best such Christians can be the most dependable, faithful and loyal members of the Body of Christ, and their very reliability makes them the very salt of the earth. At worst they can be the sort of folk whose wintry isolation would freeze the very marrow in your bones if not the Holy Ghost out of worship. The speed with which some of them make for the doors at the close of worship has to be seen to be believed!

Part of the answer must surely lie in the offering of hospitality for the Lord's sake, and I want to say here that some homes are sadly lacking in this signal grace. Our homes are a stewardship from the Lord, entrusted to us to be used for the Gospel's sake, and it is required of stewards that they be faithful in the things committed to their charge. I have always tried, not always successfully, to set an example in this and was shocked recently, when entertaining a Christian family, to discover that this was their first invitation since they associated with our own fellowship some years ago. This ought not to be.

My predecessor in Holytown, Rev Dr. James Richmond, once preached a startling and provocative sermon on Christ's words: 'What do ye more than others?' (Matt 5:47 AV). In the course of it he told the story of the lackadaisical student who, on the threshold of his final exams, went to the professor and asked: 'How much do I need to know to pass the exam?' To which the professor replied: 'What you really mean is: How little do I need to know?' The student wanted to put up the minimum performance, enough to get through. But how many Christians get by on the Religion of Minimum Performance? There is nothing particularly spiritual in being kind to one's own, or in entertaining the folk whom we happen to like, or in offering hospitality to those with whom we have something in common. The Saviour's question still stands: 'What do ye more than others?'

Finally, I am convinced that rich, satisfying fellowship, such as is desired by a minority among us, is something that must be systematically worked at. Fellowship of such a quality does not come lightly or casually. It does not lie on the surface of things. It is less like manna, which fell on the ground and was there for the gathering, and more like gold, which must be mined. Manna and gold are both gifts from the Lord, but one is more accessible than the other. If you want the fuller, more lasting communion with others in Jesus you must probe, chisel and dig. You will not find fellowship like that in any other way.

Yours very cordially,
THOMAS SWANSTON

7
FOOD, FUN AND FELLOWSHIP*

My Dear Friends,
Food, fellowship and fun: these appear to be the commodities on offer today throughout the evangelical world. Perhaps it has always been so. With passing years the emphases may change a little: sometimes, especially in a time of spiritual dearth when the Word of God is precious and there is no open vision (1 Sam 3: 1), the stress is on the need for good spiritual food. At other times, when Christians begin to feel themselves a little insular and isolated, the demand is for fellowship, for more of the togetherness so warmly commended to us in the Gospel. And at other times, when we have grown too solemn, too sanctimonious and too serious for our own good, the need is for healthy, God-given fun and laughter. Yet the three stand together: food, fellowship and fun. And two things may be said of them:

In the first place, there is obviously some kind of relationship between the three. The quality of Christian fun which we enjoy in each other's company is, or certainly ought to be, determined by the quality of fellowship we have together in Christ; and the quality of fellowship is determined by the quality of food we are offered in worship. It is true to say, on the whole, that indifferent food breeds poorish fellowship; and poorish fellowship breeds irresponsible and irreverent fun. Food, fellowship and fun are inter-related.

In the second place, there is surely an order of priorities among them. It is, after all, more important that we should be receiving wholesome, nourishing food than that we should be

*October 1986

revelling in Christian togetherness; and it is also more important that we should be in spiritual fellowship than that we should make fun and merriment the be-all and end-all of our Christian existence. Food has primacy over fellowship; fellowship has primacy over fun.

But what is meant by 'fun'? I am not thinking here of frivolity or of shallow, time-wasting vanity. The Preacher has a sharp comment to make on the life-style of the inane: 'Like the crackling of thorns under the pot, so is the laughter of fools' (Eccles 7:6 NIV). I can think back to another scenario in Scotland when the church was somehow thought of as a social club, a centre of harmless recreational activities sanctified by religion and good company. That idea has tended to die the hard way but is, even today, found in a few areas. The minister is judged by his ability to organise, and preside over, social activities. As one dry wag put it, he is expected to be 'a Master of Ceremonies rather than a Bachelor of Divinity'.

Last century, when social activities were introduced into the church's life - the church hall, incidentally, is a very recent phenomenon in church history - the primary aim was that these should have an evangelistic purpose. They were originally intended to attract people to church to hear the message of the Gospel. In practice, however, this 'spiritual' end was soon forgotten or set aside, and the social activities tended to become ends in themselves. In many cases they actually developed into substitutes for the church. One could be treated to the spectacle of folk coming to church for entertainment and the like, but who were not prepared to give any allegiance to the Christian message or to worship. What happened was that the games evenings, concerts and sports clubs which centred their activities on church property acquired only a thin veneer of religion, with the accent on 'thin' and the emphasis on 'religion' rather than on Jesus and the Gospel.

Yet evangelical history witnesses to the wonderful and precious reality of true Christian fun. I think of wholesome amusement and hearty entertainment, of laughter, mirth and human joy under the gaze of God and in the sight of the Lord Christ. This kind of fun is a thousand light years away from the foul, bawdy and improper fare served to an insatiable contemporary public on television. Christian humour, shared by kindred consecrated souls, can be among the most refreshing graces on earth. Fun is not, of course, the end of life. Man's chief end is not to have a good time, but to glorify God and enjoy Him for ever.

Yet man, as the chief of God's handiworks, is a laughing creature, and there is no good reason why his laughter should not be sanctified by the Spirit and entered into by Him. I have long held the theory that the only folk in this world who can afford to make merry are the saints of God, the redeemed of the Lord. All others are heading for a lost eternity. The unsaved may indulge themselves in strident jollifications, but their antics are akin to fiddling on the brink of hell. 'Let us eat, drink and be merry, for tomorrow we die' is the sourest of all songs.

But quality fun is determined by quality fellowship. And 'fellowship' in the New Testament is more than the consumption of buns and steaming cups of coffee; it is more than drinking Coca Cola and singing to guitars; it is more than being crowded together in a room with like, or unlike, minds. (In my own wild days, before I was converted to Christ, I used to think the cocktail party the most unsocial and uncivilised of all forms of behaviour: so many people talking so loudly, and so few listening!) Fellowship, according to Scripture is (1) fellowship in the Word, (2) fellowship in the Lord's

Supper and (3) fellowship in prayer. It is all beautifully summed up in one verse: 'They devoted themselves to the apostle's teaching and to the fellowship, to the breaking of bread and to prayer' (Acts 2:42 NIV). Of course, there are other forms of fellowship: we have fellowship in diaconal service, in ministering to the needs of others, in working together as a believing community, in teaching the young, in giving to the Lord's work and servants, in evangelism and outreach. But all these must stand under the basic three: fellowship in the Word, in the church's sacramental life and in prayer.

It cannot be denied that there has been a great longing, in recent years, for closer and more intimate forms of fellowship. This has been accompanied, in some parts, by something of a spirit of anti-clericalism and anti-denominationalism. There is nothing necessarily wrong in anti-clericalism or anti-denominationalism as such. Christians have a duty to support the truth and to attack error. It is right to be against clerics and ministers who manipulate the church of God, and the people of God, for their own ends, or who twist the truth, or who withhold the Gospel from lost, benighted humanity. It is also right to set oneself against denominations which have become anti-Christ or anti-Gospel, or which have lost themselves in a maze of carnality and worldliness. The difficulties arise, however, when Christians set up independent groups claiming to be non-clerical-centred or non-denominational. The evidence is that new groups are very soon led by men who are ministers and clerics in all but name only, and 'non-denominational fellowships' have an uncanny way of developing into denominations!

Small can be beautiful: it can also be desirable, and the house-fellowship and house-church movements (they are not the same), together with the 'shepherding' movement and the 'restoration church' movement, are expressions of this desire for closer fellowship in our generation. But we all need to guard against our need-to-be-needed and our need-to-share as sound motives for seeking more intimate fellowship. We all need to be needed: that is part of our psychological make-up, our constitution under God. We all need to share: we are made that way as Christians. But the need-to-be-needed and the need-to-share are not, in themselves, the surest foundations for fellowship. They may simply represent our psychological motivation and tell us nothing, one way or the other, about our true spirituality. Love of smallness is not, in itself, particularly spiritual; and neither is love of the large! Spiritual worth, quality and character are measured in other ways and by other canons of judgment.

I am bound to say, in all honesty, that the present preoccupation with fellowship is not accompanied, in many circles, with a like desire for food. And, if the quality of the food offered and consumed determines the quality of the fellowship, that is quite a serious matter. So much is on offer today to the Christian public that we need to learn again that nothing less than the whole counsels of God, preached by anointed and crucified men and watered by the costly prayers of the saints, can possibly be considered substantial fare. 'Man shall not live by bread alone,' said Jesus, 'but by every word that proceeds from the mouth of God.' *Every* word? Yes, indeed. *Every* word.

'What is your programme?' asked some kindly saints abroad on one of my preaching trips when I tried to explain the Scottish scene. 'I tell the people what the Bible says,' I replied. 'Of course,' came the rejoinder, 'but what is your programme?' 'That *is* my programme,' I answered. 'Is that *all*?' came the astonished query. I scented blood and pursued the issue: 'All? Surely the Word of God is a substantial *All*!'

It is indeed, and it takes a preacher every atom of grey matter in his head, and every sound commentary he can lay his hands on, together with a thousand deaths daily, to open up livingly, and to apply savingly, what God has spoken.

But perhaps the problem today is that we have bred, or rather misbred, a generation that cannot recognise good food. It is so easy, and so tempting, to be content with the shallow, the superficial, the trivial and the slick. Jesus without tears! To change the metaphor, cream cakes can be fun to eat occasionally; but one would not, should not and could not live on them for any length of time. Wholewheat bread is not nearly so attractive, nor so immediately tasteful; but, in the end of the day, the bread is far better for you than cream cakes. We all need spiritual nourishment. We often read in the daily press of people 'dying through lack of food'. But this is hardly accurate. People do not die from lack of food: they die from the things which lack of food brings on, the things that happen when food is withheld. People without food become hungry: hunger breeds weakness. The body decays and shrinks from the want of good nutrition. The undernourished body cannot cope with the stresses, strains and diseases which can ravage a weakened frame. And so the person dies. This is as true in the spiritual realm as it is in the natural.

Let me close by mentioning the business of acquiring a taste for the Word of God. I know of Christians who speak about a 'limited Gospel'. By this they mean that the Gospel by its very nature appeals only to certain folk. Only the sick need a physician; only sinners need a Saviour; only the thirsty long for water; only the hungry desire food; only the weary long for rest. The Bible assures us that our God can 'satisfy the longing soul and fill the hungry with good things'. To those who are not hungry He has nothing to offer. The words of Mary in the Magnificat have a solemn ring. She says that the rich are sent empty away by God. The invitation there is to come to Him with our emptiness, our poverty and our hunger. Hunger is, at the last, a creation of God. Under His sovereignty He forms it within us. And under that same sovereignty He fills the hungry and satiates them with His infinite resources in the Word. Quality food procures quality fellowship; quality fellowship produces quality fun. The three, may God help us and give us all grace to see this, stand together.

Yours sincerely,
THOMAS SWANSTON

8
UNSTARCHING OF TRUTH*

Dear Friends,
Much has been spoken and written lately about the 'unstarching of the church'. The particular reference is to current trends in, and attitudes to, worship; its modes, content, structures and appeal. It is of this 'unstarching of the church' that I want to write.

It is imperative, you understand, that Christians should do their utmost to rescue and preserve the very best of our spiritual, and by no means insignificant, heritage. I am thinking of the need to retain good Christian verse and worthy music, and of our obligation to use, adapt, convert and apply them to our present-day needs. I would be the first to champion any such rescue attempts, and had to do so publicly when I was Convener of the Presbytery of Hamilton's Praise Committee; this in relation to the rejection of so many fine old evangelical hymns from the New Church Hymnary.

It needs to be said also, however, that there is something consummately unnatural about so many of the forms of our communal worship. On how many other occasions do we sit together in such stiff, martial fashion? And on pews so calculated to be uncomfortable! We sing religious verse written for other days and other situations, to music composed largely when Victoria was on the throne. It is all so dreadfully uncontemporary, so leaden, so staid, so formal, so middle-class, so bourgeois, so uncreative, so unimaginative, and so unconscionably dull. I suppose that one lesson we may learn from this is that the human spirit is capable of bearing

*March 1972

almost any conceivable amount of tedium. The history of the Russian popular press since the Revolution suggests also that men can go on reading the same slick phrases and tenth-rate cliches that once were original and sent blazing sparks into men's souls - but now have died the death. Malcolm Muggeridge maintains that it is a miracle that Russia has not been submerged beneath mountains of turgid prose.

The frightening thing, however, is that Christians have to reckon, as the communists in their reading of *Pravda* do not, with the Living God. The truth is that it is shockingly possible to bore the Holy Ghost out of our worship. He becomes tired of our solemn, pompous antics, and simply absents Himself and goes elsewhere, 'where He listeth'. The Bible has a word for such a removal: Ichabod: the Glory has departed. This is why the Holy Ghost is not found in some churches. He is not there because there is really no room for Him. The churches are too full of religion. He has been frozen out, even where men profess to believe in Him.

There is, then, perhaps some truth in the allegation that the twentieth-century pagan man dismisses worship not because he does not feel the need for it, nor yet because he does not accept traditional dogmas in a half-hearted, remote sort of way; but because he regards worship as he regards the Death of Christ - as irrelevant to his life and needs. It does not reach him loud and clear. It offers him the answers to questions he has not asked. It does not 'speak' to him. To him worship is a sort of hobby that 'religious' people go in for, like golf, music, or marquetry.

It is easy, of course, for Christians, bolstered and protected and upheld by centuries of rich heritage, to say: 'We are God's people, and we have the Gospel. We cannot change our set-up to accommodate outsiders. We cannot alter the course of Christian history, or change the tradition of the fathers to please anyone. If the worldlings wish to be saved, let them come to God and to us on our terms.' Well, traditions of the fathers apart, such an attitude belongs more to the Old Testament than to the New. It was the Jews who treated the outsiders as beggars, and called them 'Gentile dogs'. And the style of let-the-people-come-to-us is rather that of John the Baptist, the last of the Old, than of Jesus, the first of the New. John stood in the wilderness, craggy giant that he was, and men came to him. Jesus went to men and accepted them where they were, and scandalized religious humbugs by doing so.

How, then, do we take the starch out of the church? Not, surely, by further gadgetries and daring experiments, for the church is weary with wasted, ill-begotten and fruitless gimmicks. Reviewing their debris over the past fifty years, I must confess that I have seen old coffee dregs look more interesting, and prove almost as useful. And yet again, there is more to spiritual dynamism than the importation of a few guitars into worship, and the calling of God 'You' instead of 'Thou'. And badly written modern hymns, sung to tunes that sound like foxtrots from the 1920s, are not going to help either. Not by such roads of themselves, nor by any other roads like them, lies the way to spiritual renewal.

I have always been a little suspicious of the neo-pentecostal movement, and especially of its excesses. They are so divisive of fellowships. They are so less than fully spiritual-rational. They almost assume a new Gospel - the Gospel of the Spirit, over against the Gospel of the Word. Yet the phrase I want to use now, much as I do not care for it, comes from the neo-pentecostal airt - 'the Lordship of the Spirit'. One thinks usually in terms of the Lordship of Christ, the Crown rights of the Redeemer, the Sovereignty of Grace. Yet the Spirit is the Lord and Giver of Life, apart from whom there can be no life at all. 'The Lord is that Spirit', and where He is there is liberty: not liberty to be lawless, or run against the Scriptures, but the liberty to be our very best, redeemed, most natural selves in Christ. Perhaps what I am pleading and praying for is a new release of Him into our worship, a new fullness, a new dimension and experience of the living Christ.

Where this is allowed to happen, where God the Holy Ghost is given the lead, and possesses the worship, and fills the house with Christ's glory, certain other things will happen. More Bibles will be in evidence. I do not mean Bibles that are paraded to church as museum-pieces, but Bibles that are used and earnestly searched 'to see whether these things be so' (Acts 17:11). There will also be a new vitality in the singing. There will be a greater volume of praise, as men's worshipping hearts are drawn in warmth to God. And there will be that sheer quality and intensity of music that is found only where surrendered Christians give themselves utterly in an ecstasy and abandon of worth-ship. There will also be, not least, a new ease and power in preaching. The minister will find himself increasingly more able and free to give the people the 'trackless riches of Christ' for the place will know a new spirit of enquiry.

Of course, fellowships and whole churches may opt out of the onward march of God. On the whole the churches of 'western Christendom' have not moved with God this century. Also, the revivals of this century, scattered as they have been, have not occurred in Christendom! Think of Ruanda, of the Congo awakening, of Kenya, and Brazil, and Ruthenia and the Polish Ukraine. God has no interests in western Christendom, or in the British way of life, or in the Scottish way of life or, for that matter, in the Highland way of life. Our God is marching on, and those who do not march with Him are left behind, wherever they happen to live. And the real spiritual movements of any age bypass the churches and fellowships that do not move with God, and they soon become backwaters, stagnant pools. Quiet, peaceful spots, undisturbed save for an occasional ripple. But dreadfully dead.

The alternative to change, you see, is death. But is that not too high a price to pay for maintaining the ecclesiastical status quo?

Yours affectionately, in tremendous hope,
THOMAS SWANSTON

9
ORTHODOXY AND EVANGELICAL VITALITY*

My Dear Friends,
I have long been intrigued by the connection between orthodoxy and evangelical vitality, and I want to write about that now. Do you know the sort of thing I mean? I am thinking of the linkage that there should undoubtedly be between sound doctrine and spiritual zeal, between believing the right things and Gospel-bearing urgency.

The problem sprang again to mind lately when a good lady approached me despairingly, lamenting the fact that her minister treated the saints to 'little other than Spiritless lecturettes' and that the man had 'bored the Holy Ghost out of the church'. I can sympathize with the lady in her distress, but her complaint raises many questions, not the least being how long believers can be expected to sit-it-out through deadish ministerial regimes, in the hope that something better is bound to turn up eventually. Once you have reached rock-bottom, the only way left to you is up! That attitude, however, makes one's adherence to a particular fellowship an endurance test in faith, and I must say here that I question the wisdom of such misguided loyalty. When an under-shepherd has first secured the salvation of his soul, it is his primary calling to create hunger in the sheep of Christ. Given that, it is then his privilege to feed the sheep. Hungry sheep need to be fed, and under-shepherds have an obligation to provide sound and healthy nourishment. But the sheep, too, have at least as great a responsibility to go where the food is. And is nourishment likely to be found under the sound of 'Spiritless

*July 1973

lecturettes' or in fellowships where the pastors have 'bored the Holy Ghost out of the church'?

Even sadder is this that, knowing the man in question, and being at one with him in most of what he stands for, on paper at least, I could imagine that he would regard himself as a minor bastion of apostolic faith in a day of evangelical decline. I am equally as sure that the dear, needy soul is quite unaware of what a dry, wizened, dead little thing his ministry is. 'By their fruits shall ye know them.'

There was a day when I would have put this state of affairs down to personality factors. We are, after all, built differently. Some men have more vivacity, more panache than others; there is more drive about them, a greater dynamic, a higher expectation, a more vital imagination. But even when you have made allowances for such factors as human psychology and indifferent health, the 'wershness' of a man's ministry is not, and can not, in the long run, be entirely due to defective personality. Is the God who made us, and who calls and enables men, not greater than all our poor psychologies? Surely it is of the essence of the Gospel's glory that Christ can work wonders with limited, 'ordinary' material. 'He giveth more grace.' No, it is not a question of personality, but of deliberate refusal of Christ's emancipating and liberating power. When any Christian's ministry dries up, and becomes fruitless and unprofitable for God, it is usually a sign that there is something in Jesus that has been refused. The Holy Ghost is called, in the Nicene Creed, the 'Lord and Giver of Life'. How, therefore, could any man find dull, or make dull, Him whom age cannot wither nor custom stale His infinite variety? Or is it that even the righteous have come to regard Him merely has an Article of the Creed, rather than as an experimental reality?

You do see the problem, don't you? Put it this way:

imagine two worlds, the one dogmatic, the other dynamic. Into the first world put the whole 'propositional' side of the Gospel, the 'facts' of the historic faith, the 'deposit' once for all committed to the saints, handed down to us from the apostolic age, and which we must guard till death if need be (1 Tim 6:20; 2 Tim 1:13; 2:2). Into the second world, put the more energetic, outgoing aspects of the Gospel, the passion for souls, travailing until Christ be formed in men, the missionary outreach and witness of the church before the eyes of a watching world. But how does the dogmatic become dynamic? One thing is clear in the theological ferment and turmoil of our time: sound teaching, of itself, is not enough. It does not necessarily guarantee evangelical life. You can be dead right as well as dead wrong. What, when all is said and done, is the difference between an orthodox/conservative corpse, and a heterodox/liberal corpse? The only certain difference is that one is narrow-minded, guarded and strict, while the other is broad-minded, do-as-you-please and open. But one is as dead as the other.

In the broader, evangelical wing of the church, there are fellowships whose outlook and scope is as barren, as formalistic, and as desolatingly arid as anything you would ever encounter among the unblessed, avant-garde 'progressives'. There are entire churches simply dying of decrepitude and decay: they have fossilized, turned to stone, become museum-pieces: and their Jesus, though unblemished and precise, is amazingly moribund, archaic, uncontemporary, a very un-1973 Man. Can God seriously be expected to find unanointed orthodoxy less of an abomination than unanointed liberalism?

God is the God of truth, and it is truth that He honours, preached and out-lived in consecrated lives. But truth, of itself, does not save. You do not change men simply by promulgating decrees, or by firing distant salvos at unbelief and ungodliness. It is truth anointed by the Spirit, preached by crucified men, watered by the tears of saints, and thrust into men's hearts to do its death-dealing, life-giving work - this is what God blesses, and this is what saves.

There is scarcely a Christian church in our time that is not dying, if not of one or other subtle form of heresy, then certainly of the tradition of the fathers. So much of what we boast - by Grace alone, by Scripture alone, by Faith alone - is just pious, religious cant. We are all saddled and hide-bound by the tradition of the fathers, and it is a deadly thing.

Do you see when the dogmatic becomes the dynamic? When the Holy Ghost comes down and is given free, sovereign reign in the church. It is not our business to set the denominations right, for in the onward march of God today such sectarian issues are of minimal importance. Nor do we criticise or try to be superior to any. How could we when our own beloved denomination is such a Babel of confused voices? It is our duty, however, having given diligence to make our own calling and election sure, to see to it that the anointing of the Spirit is on our own ministries, whatever they may be.

> Our sufficiency is from God, who has also made us able ministers of the New Testament; not of the letter, but of the Spirit; for the letter kills, but the Spirit gives life... and where the Spirit of the Lord is, there is liberty (2 Cor 3:5, 6, 17).

Liberty? Aye, just that. Sweet, smiling, Christian liberty. A suggestion of that, in some new dimension or other, would not be out of place in all our callings. See ye to it.

Yours most affectionately,
THOMAS SWANSTON

10
CONGREGATIONAL PRAISE*

Dear Friends,
The time has come for us to think about the standards of our congregational praise, and two aspects concern us: quality and quantity. We do not err on the side of the former, for Highland voices are sweet and have a lilt all of their own. But as to the latter we are sadly deficient. It is the sheer volume of praise that is missing.

Perhaps in the North we are saddled with the disadvantages of that worthy Celtic institution, the Pentatonic Scale. That is the 5-tone (penta-tonic) scale which forms the basis of so much true Scottish music, especially old Gaelic airs. The Pentatonic Scale, however, does not lend itself easily to manly, vigorous, hearty song. The nearest, but imperfect, examples in the Church Hymnary are *Child in the manger*, *Christ is the world's Redeemer, Come, Holy Ghost, our souls inspire* and *Come, Holy Ghost, our hearts inspire.* It could be argued that it is not the Pentatonic Scale that makes these hymns so fine, but the excellence of the poetry wedded, as it is, to such fine harmonies. Be that as it may, I am concerned that our own singing should be so uncertain and unreliable. On some Sundays it is dreadfully indifferent and weak, while on others it can be a rousing experience. It is the inconsistency that I notice most.

We are hampered in many ways. The organ does not really 'carry' under the deep galleries and in fact, needs to be played full in order to have the sound carry to downstairs' recesses. Would a microphone among, or near, the pipes help? But one

*March 1974

cannot always have the organ sounding full, the problem being that the tracker action is so slow and heavy that it is not an unmixed blessing in worship, and can be a distraction at times from the intensity and zeal of the praise. There are a few folk who scarcely sing at all, leaving the 'auld kist o' whistles' to do the work for them. It needs to be said here that the Free Church could teach us a thing or two about Psalm-singing: not, of course, the slow singing of the Gaelic Psalms (an art and fashion apart) but the normal English Psalms sung with verve and conviction.

What is the *sine qua non*, the one needful constituent element, of praise? Surely not the musicality or the talentedness of the congregation! The singing in some gifted professional fellowships, with paid singers to lead the worship, is woefully dull and lifeless. It is almost sub-Christian in its cold lack of interest. Real praise has its roots elsewhere, not in talent or in musicality or in professionalism, but in the salvation that is in Christ Jesus. Can unbelievers be expected to sing about a Gospel to which they themselves are strangers? Therefore, allowing for factors such as age and health, when folk do not sing with heart, mind, soul, and will, the questions one asks are: 'Do these people really know the Lord? Are they foreigners to His joy? Have they nothing to sing about?'

All living power must out. Watch a Highland burn straining to be off in spate after a heavy rain. Here's another example: do you not think it a sin to take a wild creature, and whip it and tame it and put it in a cage? Such cruelty! Such frustrated unexpressed beauty; such thwarted prowess; such a damming-up of energy! Is it any less a sin to take the heart-thrilling, heart-melting, heart-subduing praises of God and make them sound so tame, so dull, so unenter-prising, so reserved?

Listen to the enthusiastic singing at football matches.

Make no mistake about this, it is hymns they are singing. Sport is one of the leading gods of this age, and one of the major expressions of idolatry. But the gods of sport cannot see, or hear, or save. Our God can. Is He, then, the God of gods, not worthy of our best when we magnify Him in the assembly of His saints? I am not speaking of 'loud' singing, noisy, raucous, coarse, insensitive, but of that perfect fusion of quantity and quality, of volume and intensity, which delights the Father's ear and heart in heaven. This means more to Him than all worlds, than all the songs of the angels, for ransomed sinners know music that unfallen spirits can never fully appreciate.

My ultimate concern is that God should inhabit our songs, and make His home in our words and music (Ps 22:3). My second concern is that some impact should be made on interested strangers who casually drop in to see what religion is all about. That was partly in Paul's mind in 1 Corinthians 14:24-25: 'But, if an unbeliever or outsider enters, he is convicted by all, he is called to account by all, the secrets of his heart are disclosed; and so, falling on his face, he will worship God and declare that God is really among you.' Do you see the point? The quality of the worship is to be such that a stranger to God will be drawn to find Christ. Is this how our worship affects curious outsiders?

Can we, therefore, rise to the challenge of a new dimension of Spirit-filled praise? It is a spiritual matter, an affair of the heart and of right relationships with Christ; a question of release, of emancipation, of an un-selfconscious, spontaneous going-out to Him. That's what God wants to see among us.

With every affectionate hope and greeting,
THOMAS SWANSTON

11
CHRISTIAN ERA*

My Dear People,
Would you say that we have entered the post-Christian era? On the surface, at least, that seems to be the case. It cannot be denied that the majority of people today do not order their lives with much reference to God or to traditional Christian morality. The morality of the average 20th century man is 'ad hoc' morality - he simply makes it up as he goes along, without paying heed to absolute standards such as the Ten Commandments or the Sermon on the Mount. In our western society much of what was once derived from distinctive Gospel principles has been jettisoned - the Biblical rules about marriage, chastity, self-control, divorce, the sanctity of life, observance of the Lord's Day and so on.

Humanists are not slow to tell us that 20th century man is 'man come of age'. He has outgrown the need for God, for faith and for a super-natural explanation of things as they are. The only world that there is, we are told, is this world. The Ages of Faith, when theology was regarded as Queen of the Sciences, are now history. If paradise is to be restored to man it will be restored by hard work and by man's own efforts, not by conversion to Christ and certainly not by a Second Advent. There can be no going back now to a primitive, superstitious and other-worldly understanding of the world. God is dead, man is on his own, and we must build a new future on these assumptions.

Have we, therefore, entered the post-Christian era? It used to be the fashion not so long ago to say so. I recall starting a

*January 1980

parish letter in Holytown with some such words as, 'We have now entered the post-Christian era...' But have we? It is possible for us to have entered a post-Christian era only if, in fact, we have just passed through a Christian era. But have we? Have we lived through a 'Christian era' since Pentecost? Or since Constantine was converted? Or since the Reformation?

The vexing question arises as to whether we can have Christian eras and Christian societies at all. On the face of it neither of these is a truly Biblical concept. The nearest we come to it is in the Old Testament where Israel, the covenant people, was destined to be a theocracy - a nation governed by God. Had the scheme worked, church and nation would have been one. As it is, however, Israel had ideas of her own, and they ruined her. But the idea of a state, or society, or era being 'Christian' is very remote from the New Testament. When John saw the redeemed in heaven he saw a 'great multitude which no man could number from every nation, from all tribes and peoples, standing before the throne and before the Lamb' (Rev 7:9).

Some nations, of course, have had their laws and morality more obviously based on Christian ethical principles than others. And, from time to time in days of revival, whole societies can be transformed by the preaching of the Word so that they become Christianised, rather than Christian, societies. In this connection one thinks of the visible effects of the preaching of men such as Whitefield, Wesley and William Burns. But the only Christian society that Scripture knows is the church, the elect of God, those ransomed by the blood of Christ.

Men have tried to bring in Christian societies other than the church, and it seems as if the judgment of God has rested on all such efforts. The Crusaders failed when they dreamed of a Kingdom of Christ in Jerusalem. Calvin failed in Geneva with his dream of a Christian city-state - virtually with the Kirk Session as the Town Council! The Covenanters failed to bring a like dream to pass in Scotland, as did Cromwell and the Puritans further south.

The idea of a Christian era really derives from the alleged 'conversion' of the emperor Constantine. It is hardly possible for us to determine whether he was truly converted or not; what we do know is that whereas, up to that point in history, the church had been a despised minority, now all was changed. The emperor has been 'saved'. Worldly Roman lords and ladies flocked to the baptistries for immersion in the Triune Name. The unspeakable had happened - Jesus the Crucified had become fashionable. And Jesus, in what developed into Western Christendom, has remained 'fashionable' in that sense, ever since. Christianity became the official religion of the Empire. One could now be a Christian without offending anyone.

Following hard on the heels of this came the idea of 'national churches' - with church and state inexorably linked, sometimes engaged to be married, sometimes flirting with each other, and sometimes well and truly joined in wedlock. The Church of Scotland, the Church of England and the Lutheran churches are all 'national churches'. Did you know that the Prayer Book can be changed only by an Act of Parliament? And all of this is seen at its worst in pre-revolutionary Russia where the Russian Orthodox Church was simply an extension of the monarchy. Czars and aristocrats loaded the cannons, and metropolitans and priests fired them. Small wonder it is that when Lenin came along he decided that throne and church must be destroyed together.

I have noted happily that my old Moral Philosophy professor, Donald MacKinnon, in the introduction to his booklet, *The Stripping of the Altars,* makes the point that the churches 'are in this present emerging from the age of Constantine, emerging from the tunnel of the experience which began with that emperor's adherence to the Christian faith'. He summons the churches to rise to the challenge of this 'post-Constantinian situation' i.e. a situation in which Jesus is no longer approved by the state, patronized, necessarily welcomed or fashionable. We are, it seems, not coming out of a Christian era but out of a Constantinian era - an era in which church and world were so merged that it was difficult to tell the difference between the churchlings and the worldlings. If such an era is coming to an end, I will be the first to shout, 'Hallelujah!'

I have always believed that the Book of Acts is, in some way, 'normative' for the church - a standard to go by, an example to fall back on and from which Christians of all ages should learn. In Acts we see the church small, but marvellously alive. In Jeremiah, the people of God are described as God's 'speckled bird of prey'. Small birds with rare plumage do not last long when turned out of their cages and let loose in the world. In the same way Christians are the odd-men-out in society, the odd-bods who don't quite fit in with the world and with the world's standards and goals. Therefore Christians, with their bright and unmistakable plumage, are attacked.

In Scotland the number of churches is falling fast, as is the number of full-time ministers. Apparently we are to have yet another manpower crisis around the year 1985. The numbers on Communicant Rolls are falling, and fast at that. More and more weddings take place in Registry Offices, and that is as it should be. Christian weddings are for Christians; the Marriage Service is utterly unintelligible to those who are not in touch with Christian realities. But all of this affects only the visible church - the church that we see. There is a real church, however, inside that - an 'ecclesiola in ecclesia' - a little church inside a greater. My impression is that the little church (made up of truly regenerate, converted people who belong to Christ) is growing. But who can tell what, in the providence of God, will be the end of that growth? Will it lead to the Great Tribulation and to persecution? Or to the last reawakening before Christ comes? Or to both?

When Christians live in a world of privilege and patronage they no longer live in a real world. 'In the world ye shall have tribulation.' Christians are more alive in Russia today, and in the whole of Eastern Europe, than they have ever been in their entire history. There is no need at all for them to purge Communion Rolls and rid themselves of dead, useless, unconverted 'members' - the rise of Communism did that! When all is said and done, what nominal Christian (a believer in name only) will allow himself to be victimized, pressurized and persecuted for the sake of a religion that means very little to him? The coming to power of anti-God and anti-Christ regimes simply serves to purify the churches of Christ. It is we, in the freedom and decadence of the west, with our low standards of faith and discipline, who need to be purged and cleansed.

One thing is very plain: the present situation (post-Constantinian, when all men are vaguely considered Christian) is farcical. Well over 70% of my time is now taken up attending to people who have absolutely no connection whatever with the work of Christ, and no interest in it. While one tries to be as understanding and as compassionate as possible when men's hearts are sore, this is becoming something of a problem in times of bereavement. There was a day when nearly all ministers would cancel engagements to help out ('oblige' is the word often used) at the funerals of unbelievers. Such is no longer the case today, and it is now becoming difficult for non-Christian families to find ministerial help in time of mourning. But why should the on-going work of Christ suffer to suit the convenience of the ungodly? 'Let the dead bury their dead. Go thou and preach the kingdom,' said Jesus. Even in Eastern Europe, under avowedly atheistic governments, the clergy are summoned to conduct the funerals of the most unlikely people - Party members included! But the truth is that it is not at all necessary for funerals to be conducted according to Christian custom. Anyone can conduct a funeral - the undertaker (as is common in the large towns and cities), a friend of the family, the manager of the local bingo hall, or ditto of the local bar, or ditto of the local golf club, or ditto of the local football team. There is nothing whatever 'wrong' in a religionless funeral - it is simply a logical conclusion to a life lived without God. A non-Christian is not posthumously canonized simply because a cleric reads the Bible and says prayers over his head. 'Life is the season God has given to fly from hell and rise to heaven.'

Are we entering a post-Christian era? No - because we have never been in a Christian era. The church has come, since the conversion of Constantine, through an age in which worldlings were often pronounced Christians simply because they had been given a veneer of religious varnish. MacKinnon says that this was the age when 'from Caesar the church of Christ learnt to speak with the accents of Caiaphas'. And why not? For Caesar and Caiaphas and the church were in agreement.

It may well be not that we are entering a post-Christian era but that, on the contrary, we are on the verge of a truly exciting Christian era - not one in which the church is triumphant over the world, but one in which the church comes livingly into her own, when truth is seen for what it is, when the world is the world and the church is the church; when saved is saved and lost is lost; when Jesus is Jesus and Caesar is Caesar. And between the two is a great gulf fixed.

Of one thing I am certain - if I am alive when the present semi-Christian era dies, I, for one, will dance on its grave. Care to join me?

Yours sincerely,
THOMAS SWANSTON

12
SIMPLICITY IN CHURCH*

Dear Friends,
Here is a curious thing: movement away from the one to the many, from unity to diversity, tends to destruction and chaos. Israel moved from the one (Ex 20:3) to the many (Jer 44:1-8) and ended her career in a sordid squalor of idolatry. Monogamy, the lifelong commitment of one man to one woman within the bonds of conjugal love, was God's original rule and plan (Gen 2:24) but men soon found a way to multiply wives (Gen 4:19). David at his best rode on a solitary mule, the royal animal (1Kings 1:8). It was left to the ambitious, worldly Solomon to build stables for many horses at Megiddo (1 Kings 10:26). And Solomon, of course, in addition to multiplying horses, multiplied both wives and gods (1 Kings 11:1-13) to his personal ruin and that of his people. In the early church also there were tensions that fractured the Body, spoiled fellowship and marred the communion of the saints. 'Widows' became virtually a class apart and demanded personal attention (Acts 6:1) and 'the poor' too were almost a special group (Gal 2:10; Jas 2:2-6). And out in the wider Gentile world fractious Corinthians campaigned variously for Paul, for Apollos, for Peter and for Christ (1 Cor 1:10-13).

We today, inheriting much of what we have from our Victorian forefathers, run complex churches in which people are divided and sub-divided according to age and sex. There are groups for young men, for middle-aged men, for young women, for older women, for the married and for the un-

*July 1981

married, for junior and senior children, for teenagers, for the elderly, for the uniformed and for the un-uniformed. And in some larger city church units people are separated according to specialized needs: there are groups for the divorced, for unmarried mothers, for the artistically minded, for alcoholics, for Christians with social consciences, for those interested in Third World affairs, for the politically involved and (amazingly!) for Christians keen on studying the Word. The names, as you see, are legion and, in reviewing them, one longs for a breath of Biblical simplicity. It is not, of course, that the Bible discourages original, independent thought, or stifles self-expression. May the Lord ever save us from becoming, as some have become, dull, pedantic evangelicals whose utterances and comments are little more than dreary collections of Victorian evangelistic cliches! And may that selfsame Lord ever teach us and give us grace to think, to think carefully, to think accurately, to think hard and thoroughly, to think creatively and lovingly *inside revealed truth,* the truth about the truths we should believe, the truth about how God wants His church and work to be run. But you will surely concede that there comes a time when 'original thought', diversification and the multiplying of groups no longer minister to the soundness and health of the local Body of Christ?

One hears much these days about 'para-church' groups. The name comes from the Greek prefix *para* which means 'alongside'. (Compare para-trooper, para-military, parachute and others.) Originally para-church groups were formed to be handmaids of the Gospel and helps to local fellowships. They gave mutual encouragement and channelled both seeking and saved souls into mainstream Gospel work at parish level. It is a matter both of history and of observation, however, that many para-church groups become substitutes for the local fellowship. I was appalled on one occasion to hear a Christian elder say that he had no desire to become involved 'any further' in the activities of his own congregation on the grounds that his 'real interests' lay elsewhere. If ever there was an unbiblical remark that is it! For the New Testament has a high opinion of the local assembly, the local congregation, the local *ecclesia* (the Greek for 'church', meaning 'called-out') of committed folk. According to the Scriptures such a gathering is the focus for worship, edification, evangelism and spiritual nourishment.

In a sense the Scriptures have the advantage of us here and speak from a position of strength, while we speak from a position of weakness. We are heirs to a plethora of organisations and para-church groups, some more helpful than others, some less so, and some of no help at all. I refer to the myriad Christian (and sub-Christian, and post-Christian, and almost Christian, and not quite so Christian?) associations that pepper the spiritual landscape, unions and societies for this, that and the other interest. But what is to be done when para-church groups cease to minister to the local Body? Is not something very far wrong when some such come to rival the historic work of Christ and seduce Christians from their primary allegiance?

I ask you this: Are you finding a fullness of life in some other group or association, however well-intentioned or sound, that you are not finding in your local church? That this is so may, in a few cases, be due to the deadness, dullness and formality of the church. But may it not also be due to the fact that you have failed to make the contribution to the local Body that the New Testament expects of you? I heard recently of a young Christian housewife who, in a spirit of enterprise and piety, organised prayer fellowships in her home for the Lord's work abroad. Yet she herself never came to pray with fellow saints in her own congregation but left that particular area of the conflict and warfare to others. How convenient for the enterprising to 'do their own thing' while the praying remnant soldiers bravely on! No-one can question that such an attitude is against both the letter and the spirit of the New Testament.

If I may restate here an old philosophy of mine: every individual Christian witness stands on a tripod. One leg is rooted in allegiance to the local fellowship. Loyalty, faithfulness, obedience and surrender there! The second leg is rooted in some work of Christ at home, here in our poor, benighted godless land. The third is rooted in some work of Christ abroad. 'The field is the world.' But the Scriptures are not in doubt as to where our primary allegiance should lie.

In the book of Acts we see the early church. Christians met together in simple circumstances to study and hear the Word, and to pray together. There was nothing else. That church turned the world upside down. Could we not learn from its simplicities?

Yours sincerely,
THOMAS SWANSTON

13
URGENT CALL TO THE KIRK*

Dear Friends,
In the course of its labours last May, the General Assembly studied what it called a 'timely and positive document *Urgent Call to the Kirk*,' and commended it to the prayerful consideration of Presbyteries and Kirk Sessions. The Assembly rejoiced that 'in congregations, fellowships and assemblies in our country' people were 'coming to a personal knowledge of Christ as Saviour and Lord'. I reproduce here the text of this *Urgent Call to the Kirk*. It was signed by four distinguished churchmen and approved of by the fathers and brethren. I add a few personal comments at the end.

'We believe that the Church of Scotland is in deep spiritual crisis:

There are certainly encouraging signs of renewal in many parishes and presbyteries, where there is an increasing concern for the spiritual needs of people within the Kirk and for the mission of the Gospel to those outside its institutions, for which we rejoice. But taken as a whole and on a national level the situation in the Church of Scotland is very discouraging. Erosion of fundamental belief has sapped its inner confidence, discarding of great Christian convictions has bereft it of vision and curtailed its mission, detachment of preaching from the control of biblical Revelation has undermined its authority as the Church of Christ, neglect in teaching the truth of the Gospel has allowed the general membership to become seriously ignorant of the Christian Faith. With this loss of evangelical substance the Kirk fails to be taken seriously, while increasing stress upon formal and socio-legal structure has the effect of making the institutional Church get in the way between Christ and the people of the land.

This calls for our repentance. The hungry sheep look up and are not

*October 1983

fed; the flock of Christ is scattered and the membership of the Kirk steadily diminishes; a damaging cut-back in churches and worshipping communities takes place; there are fewer and fewer pastors to care for the flock and to seek and save the lost. There is a drastic slump in the position of the Kirk as a 'National Church', for, while eighty per cent of the people believe in God, only one-third are on the roll of any Church, and less than twenty per cent are on the roll of the Church of Scotland.

We call upon the Kirk to commit itself afresh to Jesus Christ and His Gospel and to carry out an evangelical rebuilding of its faith, life and mission:

Jesus Christ and His Gospel must be brought back into the centre of the Church and all its life, thought and activity, for He is the sole source of God's incarnate self-revelation, the unique way to God the Father, the only ground of salvation and the one foundation and norm of the Church. The Spirit of Jesus Christ alone can quicken and renew the Church and make it one body with Christ.

The Truth of Jesus Christ and His Gospel as mediated through the Holy Scriptures must be given its rightful place in the preaching and teaching of the Church, and be allowed to exercise its divine power and authority in cleansing and unifying the mind of the Church and its ministry at all levels.

Mission and evangelism must be given priority and a controlling place in all the worship, life and activity of the Kirk. The re-evangelisation of Scotland is absolutely imperative. It is above all in the regular ongoing evangelism of the parish and pastoral ministry that the crucified and risen Jesus Christ is mediated to the people. This will require many more ministers or pastors of the flock steadily at work throughout Scotland, the opening of centres for worship and mission, but it will also mean the emergence and spiritual mission of the church, and an engagement of every congregation in the urgent task in winning back the three million people of Scotland to Christ and His Church.

The Church's evangelistic message must recover the New Testament stress upon personal faith and commitment to Jesus Christ as Lord and Saviour, upon the universal claims of the Gospel of Christ crucified, risen and coming again upon human society and the whole world of humanity, and indeed upon the physical creation as it is disclosed through our science. Every encouragement must be given to renew the prayer life of the Church in which all members engage in regular intercession for the salvation of mankind. This will require regular Bible Study throughout the Kirk and the steady rehabilitation of evangelical belief, matching renewed proclamation of the Gospel and the teaching of the Truth as it is in Jesus. We respectfully invite the Moderator at the General Assembly, and throughout the year, to lead the Kirk in prayer and intercession for a renewal of the Church and the conversion of Scotland.

This call for a repentant return of the Church of Scotland to Christ clothed with His Gospel is unashamedly evangelical and theological, for the grave crisis facing the Church is essentially spiritual. Only through spiritual and evangelical renewal will the Church of Scotland meet the compelling claims of Christ upon it to carry the Gospel to the millions in our own land who have not been gathered into the fold of Christ but who are desperately hungry for the bread of life.'

Thus far the text of the *Urgent Call*. But what are we to make of it? On the one hand it is immensely heartening to hear such sentiments being expressed in a General Assembly. For many a long and weary day the message of grace has been lightly esteemed in many high ecclesiastical places, and there was a time when to talk of Bible Study and Prayer as being central to Christian work was to put oneself on the fringes of the Church of Scotland's concerns. Such pur-suits were all very well for a few hotheads and enthusiasts, but they were scarcely thought of as the inner and essential core of the church's life. Perhaps things are beginning to change?

On the other hand one's heart has misgivings. The four signatories to the document have all been parish ministers and therefore have known the heat and stresses of the work at that level, and one would hope that the fathers and brethren were sincere and earnest when they endorsed the Urgent Call. But, in fact, the conservative, evangelical wing of the church has been saying these things for many years, and there is little evidence that that voice has been generally heeded.

I also wish to testify that in my entire ministry I have pleaded with both office-bearers and members alike in these very essential matters: and I cannot honestly say that much interest has been shown or much attention paid. Office-bearers and members alike are conspicuous by their absence from Bible Study and Prayer. It is not that they are not friendly, co-operative, helpful, generous and faithful to a degree, for they obviously are: but there is a monumental non-interest in the entire spiritual and 'other-worldly' side of the Gospel. Will you forgive me for being so frank?

There is one last consideration: there is a history of General Assemblies sending down documents and papers for consideration by the churches. And that history does rather suggest that very little comes of these in the end of the day. Not much appears to be accomplished and often the warnings, admonitions, etc., pass unheeded. I suspect that something of that sort will happen to the *Urgent Call to the Kirk*. But, for the sake and future of the Lord's work in Scotland, I hope not.

Yours sincerely,
THOMAS SWANSTON

14
SIGNS OF THE TIMES*

My Dear Friends,
It is always a great sin when Christians fail to discern the moving of God's Spirit. Jesus encourages us, therefore, and in rather strong language, to be always on our toes, instant to note the 'signs of the times'. He said: 'When you see the cloud banking up in the west, you say at once, "It is going to rain," and rain it does. And when the wind is from the south, you say, "There will be a heat wave" and there is. What hypocrites you are! You know how to interpret the appearance of earth and sky; how is it you cannot interpret this fateful hour?' (Luke 12:54-56 NEB).

The imminence of our Annual Congregational Meeting encourages me to think, at this time, of money in relation to the Lord's work 'in this fateful hour' and, in the light of His command to us to 'discern the signs of the times' we stop to review the progress and standing of our congregation. This meeting ought to be one of the most important events of the year, for we gather then to give thanks to the God and Giver of all grace and glory, who has crowned our years, beyond measure and merit, with loving kindness and tender mercies. It is not 'spiritual' to be disinterested in the material welfare of God's house and kingdom, for the most 'spiritual' people ought always to be the most down-to-earth and practical.

In this magazine you will also find the Financial Statement for 1972, and you are asked to study it carefully. We give God the sole glory for all the grace and bounty He has lavished on us. We have done our best, and having done that we confess

*March 1973

that we are 'all unprofitable servants' (Luke 17:10). The large increases in the offerings speak for themselves. There is an unmistakable hunger in men's hearts for the deep things of God, and where that hunger is met, however imperfectly, then people are not slow to lavish good upon Christ's work. 'Giving is a Grace' was the title of a recent pamphlet on stewardship, and never were truer words written. One cannot expect dead souls to give money to the Lord: grace comes first here as it comes before every other blessing: before faith, before repentance, before the New Birth of the Spirit, before life eternal, before Christian character, before fruit-bearing: grace stands first and last. Where, therefore, like a Highland burn in full spate, grace is allowed to course freely and sovereignly through men's parched hearts and beings, laving the barren desert-lands and slaking the thirst, the fruits of grace appear, rich and rare and manifold. *That* is the true meaning of the astonishing growth in the liberality among us.

But is it any part of a minister's calling to speak about money? Most certainly it is, and I do so without shame for Jesus Himself often spoke of it, and with considerably less embarrassment than many of His servants. Think of how many stories He told involving 'filthy lucre': the Rich Fool; the Lost Coin; the Treasure hid in a Field; the parable of the Talents (talentia - weights of silver); the Pearl of Great Price which the merchant bought for a fortune. Besides all this, did not Christ make all wealth? 'The earth is the Lord's and the fullness thereof...Every beast of the forest is Mine, and the cattle upon a thousand hills. I know all the fowls of the mountains: and the wild beasts of the field are Mine. If I were hungry, I would not tell thee: for the world is Mine, and the fullness thereof...The heavens are Thine, the earth also is Thine: as for the world and the fullness thereof, Thou hast founded them' (Pss 24:1; 50:10-12; 89:11).

I know that it is dangerous to equate godliness with prosperity. In the Bible godly living is more often associated with persecution than with affluence! 'In the world,' says Jesus, 'ye shall have tribulation.' But I cannot too loudly proclaim that spiritual soundness and material prosperity generally go hand in hand. When a congregation is right with God, seeking His blessed face and will, and honouring the Son as they honour the Father, there will never be any lack of resources for Gospel work. If you think that our monies have risen chiefly because of large numbers, then you are wrong. The increases are a matter of the quality of generosity. It is the faithful preaching of the Word, with its eager reception by the people, that is the ground of all liberality. The whole stress is on character, on Christian integrity, on worth, on holiness, on cross-bearing, on sacrifice, on discipleship, on obedience, on grace. Given these, money is no problem. Read Psalm 112 where the 'righteous' man is described in terms of a warm heart and open hands.

It is a fact of evangelical history that when men and women respond to the claims of Christ they have a different attitude to earthly possessions. Money becomes God's money for which, as stewards and custodians, we must give account at the Great Assize on the Day of Christ. Daily work becomes God's work, which must be done cheerfully and ungrudgingly as unto the Lord and not to men (Eph 6:5-8). Home becomes God's home, a sanctuary in which Christ is cherished, where His Name and salvation are loved, and to which needy, lost souls can come and find a refuge from the storms of life. The car becomes God's car, a servant of Christ for the blessing and comfort of others.

All this, of course, is part of a much wider canvas, that of the glorious materialism of the Gospel. 'The Word was made flesh, and dwelt among us'. Christ became a man, not an angel. Cups of cold water, given in faith here on earth, are converted into glory hereafter in heaven. On the Last Day there shall be the resurrection of men's bodies. Heaven will be a most tangible, and withal a most merry, place, for Paul speaks about the 'weight of glory' (2 Cor 4:17). This means that, in the long run, although the Gospel has much to say about eternal issues such as judgment, heavenly gain and loss, Christianity is the least 'spiritual' of all religions. If you really want to be 'spiritual' you become a Buddhist and long for Nirvana; or a Hindu and dream of a better reincarnation. But to be a Christian is to believe that this world, from its most noble to its most degraded, is shot through and through with eternity's values. We are all busy manufacturing what we shall be when we die.

One of the heartening things in the past year has been the appearance of so many interested strangers at worship among us. A few gentle (and some not so gentle) critics would say that these are coming 'for the man'. But that is certainly not the whole truth. Naturally enough you would expect a particular sort of message to be associated with a particular sort of man: I preach the way I do because I am the man I am. You say the things you say because you are you. And who will complain about that?

It is not 'for the man' that they come, but for the message, and that is wise policy, for religion that is built on man (and a preacher is simply a holy sinner who has been set apart by God) cannot last. It will die with the man, whoever he is and however friendly and approachable and engaging he may be, and it will deserve to die for the carnal affair that it is. Our Evening Service has, on many occasions, been made up by almost half of outsiders who are neither formal members nor adherents. May God bless the faithful and the true, but I often wonder where my own dear West Kirk folk are when half the worshippers on some evenings are hungry foreigners.

Nor should we underestimate the watering of God's work with many tears and the prayers of the saints, public and private. It is to be regretted that the Prayer Meeting is looked upon as a 'static' gathering, a quaint, old-fashioned meeting for the pious. Believe me, there is nothing old-fashioned about the West Kirk Prayer Meeting! Nor is there anything staid or dull or fusty or pedantic about the prayers that go up every Saturday for all our work at home and for many works of Christ far afield. There ought to be flux and movement about all such intimate fellowships, growth, change, maturation, as with any other healthy organism. It was when the church in the Book of Acts was a vital praying body of men and women that there were 'added to the church such as should be saved' (Acts 2:47).

But you do see where Christian money comes from? It comes from death. There is no fruit without death. That is both a basic fact of nature and a fundamental tenet of the world of grace. Let your mind ponder the elemental simplicities of sowing and reaping: we reap what we sow; but we also reap only the fruit of that which has died to its own life. To be fruitbearers for Christ we must surrender our rights, our will, our own point of view, our notions and ideas, our selves. As Paul puts it? 'Death works in us, but life in you.' Death works. It certainly does! In fact, nothing else works quite like it. Thanks be to God, who always causes us to triumph in Christ.

Yours affectionately and joyously,

THOMAS SWANSTON

15
BACKSLIDING*

Dear Friends,
Back in February, at an evening service, I promised that this month's letter would be about backsliding in general, and about secret backsliders in particular. That promise came out of a conversation that I had with my friend and brother James Philip, of Holyrood Abbey, in which we both remarked on how appalled we were by the number of un-wholehearted Christians in various fellowships throughout Scotland. We too have our share. My words, therefore, are addressed to only one comparatively small group. If you are not in the group, please bear with me.

You should know me well enough by this time to appreciate that there is a large part in me that, even now, would fain draw back from that promise made in public. I do not enjoy labouring the theme of God's judgment on His own. Such exercises, generally speaking, are dreadfully negative. They can also be unhelpful and unconstructive, in the sense that those believers who are being brought to the judgment-bar tend to withdraw even further into their sad, little worlds of sub-evangelical greys.

I did cherish vague hopes, in February, that the people whom I had in mind would give some evidence of a real and deep repentance. Strangely, and against both my prayers and hopes, not one drifting Christian has been restored, and I wonder what this can mean?

But first we need to define terms. By 'backslider' is not meant a formal church member who has stopped coming to

*July 1979

worship, or who no longer takes an active part in church life, or who fails to attend Communion. It is my experience that the vast majority of such are not backsliders at all - they are simply unbelievers. They cannot be backsliders since they never were forward-sliders. They give little evidence of repentance from sin, of being born again of the Spirit, or of any living interest in, or knowledge of, the Saviour. Their names ought not to have been on the roll of the church in the first place. Most are friendly, helpful, nice, obliging folk without a vestige of saving faith.

True backsliders, however, are real Christians. They are in the kingdom, and their salvation is not in doubt. When they die they will go to heaven, and not to hell. But the glory to which they travel will be qualificd by their disobedience on earth; and the rewards that they receive will be diminished and modified by their infidelity here and now. The quality of the Christian life we live now determines the quality of the eternity that we shall inherit hereafter. Some believers will scarcely get into heaven - 'saved so as by fire' is how the New Testament puts it; while others will have an abundant, royal and joyous welcome into the presence of the King. All believers will be saved; but differences in consecration, so painfully obvious down here, will be perpetuated for all eternity up there. Backsliders are therefore not unsaved, unconverted or unregenerate; their hallmark is that they have drawn back from the work, from the travails of Christ, from the fellowship of His sufferings, from the challenge of costly discipleship, and from the very Cross itself - not the historic piece of wood on which the Redeemer died, but the Cross as the principle of death and resurrection in a believer's life.

Nothing to my mind is more solemn or arresting than this - that the word 'backsliding' as such, does not occur in the New Testament. The experience of backsliding, of course, was known in the early church. Demas professed to love and follow Christ, but forsook Paul and 'loved this present world' (2 Tim 4:10). Paul speaks of Christians making 'shipwreck of their faith' (1 Tim 1:19). Others were idle and careless (2 Thess 3:6-13). And one of the Warning Passages in Hebrews speaks of people who are guilty of 'drawing back' (Heb 10:38,39). But the word 'backsliding' as such, is not used. Backsliding, in other words, is thought of as an Old Testament experience. Since the day of Pentecost it is assumed by the New Testament that Christians, once converted, make progress in Christ. They grow up. They mature. To stand still is to go back, for God is always on the move, and those who do not move with Him, instant to heed His voice and instant to obey, are soon left behind.

Some who read this are already years out of touch with my ministry, and no longer stand for what I stand for. Some switched off seven years ago! That is why the messages on the Lord's Day become more and more unintelligible, and less and less applicable to their lives. God does not change, but He does move, and we must move with Him. Backsliders, therefore, are people who are living on the wrong side of the Cross, on the wrong side of the Easter victory, on the wrong side of the Resurrection, on the wrong side of Pentecost. That is why their lives are so dull, so tame, so stale, so flat, and so unprofitable; why their witness bears no fruit among unbelievers; why they are not renowned for soul-winning; why their lives are so prayerless and powerless.

If you are such - and some are young, some middle-aged, some office-bearers, some ordinary members, some single, some married couples - may I put some searching questions to you? Why is it that, when I think of the heart of the ministry here, your name does not immediately spring to mind? You 'do your own thing' in the Christian world; you have your hobby horses, your own Christian interests and pursuits, and you crusade for these and expect other Christians to support you. But, when it comes to what I am trying to do, you are very much on the fringe, away out on the periphery of things. Christians in the area sometimes say to me, 'Oh, you must find Mr. X a great blessing', or 'What a help Mr. and Mrs. Y must be to the work!' But, in all honesty, my answers must invariably be the same - 'Mr. X and Mr. and Mrs. Y? Surely there is some mistake? I place no deep confidence in them at all, largely because they are not 100% behind the work. They call themselves 'evangelical' but I scarcely know where they stand since they rarely say.'

Surely you must be aware that, in the Book of Acts, the local church, the local fellowship, the local assembly, was the strategic centre for Christian activities? Evangelism, outreach, upbuilding, teaching, edification - all had their origins in the local fellowship of saints, and believers owed an allegiance to each other as members of the Body. Their lives were integrated with one another. But you are independent; you go your own way; you choose whatever you want to do; and as for the activities you don't care for - well, you studiously set them aside. It is your *duty* to give yourself in Christ to the fellowship of kindred minds. This is not a question of emotion or of consecration or even of 'laying yourself on the altar' - it is a matter of *duty*. You *ought* to be more a part of what Christ is doing among us.

The church is a place of spiritual nourishment: it is the place where the sheep of Christ are fed, and this is how I conceive of the West Kirk. God brought me here to seek out the lambs and sheep of Christ and to feed them. I am not here to entertain goats! I notice, however, that some are highly selective about the food. Some of it you do not care for, although it is all in the Word. And when did I ever hear a word of blessing, appreciation or encouragement from you? Many backsliders among us are no better, in this respect, than the 'unbelievers' in the churches upon whom they sit so self-righteously in judgment.

Coolish, detached, stand-offish, uninvolved - what am I to do with you? It is good that believers should drink in the Word, and receive it with gladness. But from you backsliders, when am I ever going to receive anything in return? You come, listen, approve (probably) and comment (usually in private) - but what assurance have I that anything has gone in if little or nothing comes out? Do you not think that there is something dishonest and unworthy about being on the receiving end all the time, and about your unwillingness to give your heart's allegiance to the work? How convenient that the church should be a place of nourishment for pilgrims and passers-by!

And why do you (I address myself now to able-bodied believers, sound in mind, wind and limb) persist in calling yourself an 'evangelical', and yet remain so painfully absent from the place of prayer, that powerhouse of every living work of God? The work, unprayed for, cannot survive. Jesus believed in communal prayer, as did the early Apostles, the first Christians and the Reformers. Are we now grown superior to them in our advanced spirituality?

I am bound to say that I am weary to the marrowbone hearing reasons, excuses and rationalizations for Christian absence here. If Saturday is not the most convenient night of the week, why is it that some have been known to attend other local Christian occasions on that evening? And if Saturday is the night when you like to 'be with the family', why is it that some are known to put the children to bed in good time so that they can have friends in for entertainment, or so that they can view their favourite TV programme? This is scarcely the sort of candour on which spiritual revivals are founded. 'Awake, thou that sleepest, and arise from the dead, and Christ shall give thee light!' Nor are low standards of consecration, exhibited in such lifestyles, likely to make the modern pagans sit up and take notice. This is neither the stuff that turned the Roman Empire upside down, nor the stuff of which martyrs are made.

May I ask you, please, to weary and grieve me no longer with these specious excuses and hypocrisies? Others with families come to pray, and so can you. You could come, but you do not, and this is moral, spiritual and volitional refusal of a very high order. It is of small importance that you should be a supporter of me - that stands very far down on my order of priorities. But where do you stand with Jesus? What do you say to Him when you gaze into His kindly but searching eyes? And what excuses and rationalizations will you offer to Him on the Great Day when you have to answer for the stewardship committed to your charge? Let me rehearse again the lifestyle that was taken for granted when I was converted some twenty years ago: twice at public worship every Sunday, accompanied by a Bible; the mid-week meeting for Bible study on Wednesdays; the Christian Union meeting for prayer every Friday, followed by the main meeting; and prayer fellowship every Saturday evening. All of that was considered basic. There were 'extras' such as Missionary Breakfasts on Saturday mornings, and special meetings for visiting Christian workers on other nights; and we were all engaged in outreach and various other forms of Gospel service.

Perhaps I misjudge the situation now, but I do not form the impression that many 'evangelicals' live like this. Times have changed, but have they changed for the better? Christian standards have changed also. For the better? I have heard it said that we must now make a distinction between the 'old evangelicals' and the 'new evangelicals'. To which camp do you belong? Perhaps what I miss most of all in backslidden folk is the ancient quality of fidelity - of dogged, slogging, unquestioned loyalty to the work.

What is the cure for such drifting? A change of lifestyle, of itself, is not enough. A change of heart is needed - almost a second conversion, a second experience of grace, a fresh baptism of the Holy Spirit (if you will pardon the phrase). But be warned - it is far harder to find the Saviour in the first place. A broken love affair is not easily mended and, even when it is mended, sometimes terrible hurt and damage remain. The repentance that is called for will be deep and sore and radical, but it is all that God now holds out to you. And, until that happens, I am sorry to have to tell you that I entertain no hopes whatever of building a lasting work of Christ upon you.

Only crucified men and women are of any use to me in what I am trying to do - crucified men and women who have died the death, death to self, death to their own ambitions, death to their own opinions and points of view, death to how they think a church should be run, death to pride and vanity, death to worldly honour and esteem, death to mere empty, carnal churchmanship, death to the way they spend their spare time, death to their own desires and dispositions. Unless, dear backslidden brother and sister, you are prepared to be identified with Christ in this way, you will have to content yourself with two things: (1) with being an also-ran in the race, and (2) with God's loving judgment on you - on your health, on your marriage, on your family, on your daily work, on your financial affairs. God punishes disobedience. But will you turn again? Will you come home? Will you be what you used to be? Will you embrace His highest and best once more?

'I will restore the years that the locusts have eaten', and 'If any man draws back, my soul shall have no pleasure in him; but we are not of those who draw back to everlasting loss.'

Yours sincerely, in that hope of better days for us all,
THOMAS SWANSTON

16
NEGATIVITY*

Dear Friends,

You probably know that Dr. Billy Graham commands a hearing from the great ones in America. It is surely a testimony to the divine unction that is on his life, and the grace that is in his heart, that he is a known and accepted associate of famous names, having been on intimate terms with the Kennedys, the Eisenhowers and the Nixons. Recently he was asked why he did not exercise more of a ministry of judgment, rebuking the sins of leaders. His answer was: 'I am called to be a New Testament evangelist, not an Old Testament prophet'. Some may feel that this gives too much away to the critics, driving, as it appears to do, a sharp wedge between the Testaments. Yet, however much you dislike the idea of wedges between the Testaments, or even between the offices of prophet and evangelist, it is a fascinating and stimulating reply, don't you think? Have you grasped what he intends? In his preaching he does not want to be - to use an overworked word - 'judgmental'; he wants to avoid the polemical and the provocative, lest they distract men from the main issues of the Gospel; he does not want to pontificate on private sins, or pass verdicts on controversial moral and social issues. He will stick to the 'basics' of heralding Christ, preaching glad tidings, and proclaiming the acceptable year of the Lord. His is a point well made, for I am weary to death of the sour, critical spirit abroad among so many Christians.

Wilfred Owen, the Welsh poet so tragically killed in the First World War, has an evocative phrase: 'voices of sad des-

*October 1974

pondency'. The church is full of them, and it is high time they were shamed into silence. Starting from the issue raised by Dr. Graham, it is instructive how rarely the voices of the early Christians were lifted, in an Old Testament prophetic manner, against the moral and social evils of the Roman Empire. The major, and most obvious, issue of the abolition of slavery is never mentioned. There were wars in plenty throughout the Empire: yet war, that 'greatest moral issue of our generation' (as it has been wrongly called in our day) is not touched on. If, indeed, you want a case for pacifism, you have to strain hard at a few Scriptures. Certainly the early Christians knew of no such doctrine: they were too preoccupied with essentials. The disparity between the rich and the poor, the ignorance of the Gentiles in their 'outer darkness' - these are scarcely hinted at in New Testament writings.

And as for mentioning precise names, and situations ripe for judgment, how many can you think of? Jesus called Herod, 'That fox', and dismissed the church leaders as 'hypocrites'; Paul called the High Priest a 'white-washed sepulchre'; in Revelation there are a few veiled allusions to persons, and some churches are censured; a few private cases are dealt with, but there is little more than this. It is strange how unpolemic the early saints were! Instead, they were positive, constructive, out-going, concentrating on preaching answers rather than working over problems. It is this that I find missing today: positive, loving outreach; and extending of the solutions afforded by grace. The place of these has been taken by judgmental attitudes, by carping criticisms, by a whole negativity of outlook that is foreign to the New Testament.

All this must surely give point to the Chinese proverb: 'It is better to light a candle than to curse the darkness'. There is too much cursing of the darkness, and too little lighting of the candles of Christ. Can Christians, with any honesty, believe that the life-giving, emancipating Gospel of Grace is similar to Ezekiel's scroll written on the back and front with 'words of lamentation and mourning and woe'? (Ezek. 2:10).

Of course, there is plenty to be sad about, and much that could make one lose heart. Increasingly so. The latest fears, predictably, are of the collapse of democracy as we know it in this country, coupled with the dread of a military takeover, or the emergence of a new kind of fascism. The problem of inflation is ever with us, spiralling upwards at the rate of 20% per year. The world population explosion continues to be just that, in spite of all that the experts do. Meanwhile the general mass of folk gradually subside into what Muggeridge, in a wonderfully illuminating phrase, calls 'people's hedonism' - love of pleasure, indulgence in alcohol, mindless amusements, eroticism, over-eating, gambling, and the worship of money. It is all hideously true. And the list could be extended.

But who is dismayed by these things? Not the Lord of glory! He sits in unchallengeable might, in sovereign charge of all evil. None of the above exists without His permission. Is it not time for Christians to learn, share, and preach His detachment, His triumph? David said: 'The Lord sits upon the floods'. His faith contrasts sadly with that of whole areas of the church. Christian witness, more blameworthily evangelical and reformed witness, has returned so sour. It is so full of vinegar; it is so critical. But there is truth also in another proverb: 'More flies are caught with a teaspoonful of honey than with a gallon of vinegar'.

Consider John the Baptist, self-denying, strict, abstemious, ascetic. There was much that could be called 'negative' in his ministry. He was the second Elijah and, like the first before him, set about bringing in God's kingdom in the wrong way. John was no 'grand mixer'; he did not go to the people. Instead, the people came to him, in the wilderness, and many must have walked long distances to hear him. But give John his due, he did not 'criticise'. He did preach moral Law, another matter; and out of the Law came divine judgment and conviction of sin. Had he 'criticised', the people would not have come, for criticism alienates and estranges men.

Perhaps much of the negativity, the lack of constructive witness, in Christians is really something of a stance, a pose that hides serious failings. It cannot be disputed that people suffering from feelings of inferiority, or from inadequacies of personality, often take refuge behind the 'authoritarianism' of sitting in judgment on others. Perhaps the critics have no real Gospel to preach? The word Evangel means Good News: glad tidings of great joy to all people. Remember?

If it is protested that Law-work needs to come before Grace-work, then two things must be said. In the first place, criticising people is not necessarily Law-work. The Law is a schoolmaster to drive men to Christ. Do judgmental attitudes do that? In the second place, it is not necessary to present the Bad News before the Good News, as a study of the Gospels will show. Read the story of little Zacchaeus, and you will see (Luke 19:1-10). He was a horrid, loveless, unlovely, unlovable creature, a quisling and a scoundrel. But Jesus looked into his eyes, and he was undone. No prayers, sermons, tracts, or moral comments. The same holds true for the encounter with the woman of Samaria. Of course, they were convicted of sin and brought to repentance: but Jesus did it all so tactfully, so gently, so delicately. What fundamental respect for human personality He had! Can't we learn from Him?

The truth is that there is more hope today on the Christian scene than there has been for many years, as is witnessed to by the large numbers of young people turning to Christ in many walks of life and from every stratum of intelligence. Such a harvest of souls, so hungry for the authentic Word, so intent on God's Will for their lives, so ready to concentrate on character-building, cannot but bode well for the future, whatever evil may be in store for the church. Naturally there are disappointments, and there will always be people who simply are not behind the living work of Christ: so far the middle-aged, the elderly, and the churchy, generally speaking, have yet to prove themselves. But, among so much barrenness and formality, is it not a heart-warming experience to see the growth of the evangelical party in the national church, with more and more pulpits committed to the preaching of the historic Gospel?

Any navvy can knock down a building. It is so easy to destroy! You do not need to be particularly advanced in spirituality to do that: indeed, a critical spirit is never a mark of spiritual maturity. But to build takes love, imagination, insight, courage, skill. Sinners who are outside Christ cannot be expected to live Christian lives. That many are truthful, chaste, honest, and sober is to the glory of common grace. The miracle is that men are as good as they are. How much worse might they become if God lifted His restraining hand? Once-born men can be expected only to have once-born morals!

Shakespeare writes of people who are 'of such vinegar aspect, that they'll not show their teeth in the way of a smile'. In the onward march of Christ in our time, there is really no room for such mirthless, dry, grey little souls. If only they guessed what dishonour they bring to Him who, sitting in the heavens, can see the worst happen to His cause and Kingdom and yet laugh (Ps 2:4).

Yours ever, rejoicing in God's goodness to us,
THOMAS SWANSTON

17
REVIEW OF CONGREGATION*

My Dear Friends,
It gives me deep and satisfying pleasure to commend to you the Financial Statement which forms part of the magazine at this time of year. There is little need for me to comment on the figures, for they tell their own story of sacrifice and of stewardship gladly rendered. Once the principle is established that spiritual health and material soundness often go hand in hand in the Lord's service, the basic issues are not in doubt. The work is His, not ours, and we are merely the ministers of His bounties. But there are solemn features. We have, at present, 102 persons in the Covenant Scheme. Last year their givings, along with the Income Tax recovered, came to £16,507. That represents 55% of our direct givings income! Does it not seem astonishing to you that 102 people bring in 55% of what we basically need to keep going?

But we are careful, as we must be, to give to our God and Father the glory and the praise for His faithfulness. He is a God of largesse and we have lacked no good thing. Therefore our testimony must ever be Jehovah-Jireh, 'the Lord will provide' (Gen 22:8), and Ebenezer, for 'hitherto hath the Lord helped us' (1 Sam 7:12).

Here we raise our Ebenezer:
Hither by Thy help we've come;
And we hope, by Thy good pleasure,
Safely to arrive at home.

*March 1983

We are greatly indebted to our esteemed and invaluable treasurer, Ian Brough, and to the auditors for all their painstaking labours in the Lord's treasury. Due tribute will be paid at the Annual Congregational Meeting on Wednesday 16th March, when my colleague and brother Rev A. I. MacDonald of the East Church will bring a word from the Lord.

And yet we have our problems, beyond those of the costly maintenance of fabric. I am concerned that our Communicant Roll has fallen so low. In a sense we have brought this upon our own heads by our faithfulness to church law. Kirk Sessions are required annually to attest the Roll of Members and to attend to matters of discipline (a) where there has been failure to come to the Lord's Supper, or (b) where little or no interest has been shown in the worship and work of Christ.

Many sessions, I fear, pay little or no heed to this aspect of law and duty and, as a result, their 'showing' of members on paper gives no real indication of the state of their congregations. I heard recently of a young minister whose Communicant Roll stood in excess of 1600; yet the weekly offerings scarcely rose above £300. The miracle is that such places even survive. One could not expect them to grow. But the statistics are shameful.

There was a day when we in the West Kirk could boast of a membership well into the 600s. The roll today stands at just over 470. A pattern appears to have asserted itself, as it is being asserted all over Scotland where the full counsels of God are recovered in the pulpit: the official, formal membership tends to go down; the worship is well attended; the offerings rise. These are the fruits of an insistence on the truth that quality and character must always come before quantity and 'success' in Christian service. This was the Saviour's emphasis, and should be ours.

As for the careless folk whose names came before the session, most were sent their Transference Certificates in order to allow them to join some other church; with some, the names were put on the Supplementary Roll, signifying that they may still come to the Lord's Supper, but that they are under discipline because of their lack of interest in the Gospel; and with others the names were removed from the roll completely. It has been felt by some that sessions are inclined to be a little severe in such disciplinary measures. My own feeling is that, on the contrary, we are inclined to be over-generous and gentle. The question certainly arises as to whether these 'members' should ever have had their names on the roll of the Christian church in the first place since their lives and affairs are ordered largely according to pagan principle and with no reference to God and eternity.

However, if the Communicant Roll continues to go down and the offerings continue to rise, presumably there is a point at which they pass each other? My interest in this really springs from the fact that, in the eyes of many union and re-adjustment committees, there is the notion that 1,000 is a good, working, average size for a parish church today. That is why, when two vacancies occur in close proximity, if each roll stands at around 500, the question of linkage or union is raised. Here in Inverness we are over-churched, and one looks at the extraordinary growth of the town towards the west, up the Leachkin hill. Sooner or later a new church will have to be built to minister to the needs of the population there. The 'high heid yins' who have to do with church extension would never create another charge (and another salary!) without attending to the readjustment of the churches in town.

I am not at all interested in the addition to our Communion Roll of worldly, unconverted, unsaved people. Any minister or session can increase the roll of the church by resorting to gimmicks, by lowering the standards or by admitting all and sundry. Yet the time has come to be seeking souls. The most natural person to seek the soul of a child or teenager is the parent. Christian parents are under an obligation to lead their children to the Saviour's feet in trust and surrender. Failing the help of Christian parents, it is the duty and calling of the leaders of Bible Classes and youth groups to bring the young to a saving knowledge of Jesus Christ. That is why Sunday Schools, Bible Classes and youth groups exist. They exist for no other purpose. All else is subsidiary, secondary and peripheral - sport and football, games and activities, awards and honours and all. All the groups that meet on church property do so solely for the conversion of sinners to Christ and their upbuilding and edification in the Faith. The groups exist not primarily for entertainment or amusement, either for young or old, but for salvation and redemption. I assume, of course, the presence of converted leaders.

I wonder also if the time has not come for some of our long-standing adherents to take a public stand for Christ and come to the Supper? It is undoubtedly the case that some of you are truly born again of the Spirit. You do know and honour the Lord in your heart. You love His worship and delight to serve. Yet you hold back from the Table. I appreciate that it does take courage to set aside a whole lifetime of wrong thinking about Communion, the needless fears, superstition and guilt associated with it in Highland minds. But giving courage is the Lord's speciality! Set fear aside and come, dear friend, to the feast!

Cordially yours,
THOMAS SWANSTON

18
RELIGION OF MINIMUM PERFORMANCE*

Dear Friends,

This letter is not a complaint, still less a girn, but I wonder if some kind soul would help me with a problem? How does one get folk who name the Lord's Name, and who profess to be His people, to take a living interest in the Lord's work? By 'Lord's work' I am thinking rather of what is popularly known in the churches today as 'mission' i.e. outreach and wider horizons. My difficulty is that I now find it increasingly harder and harder to persuade Christians to commit themselves to much more than the basics of religious profession. Most opt for what has, somewhat dryly, been called *The Religion of the Minimum Performance*.

Many years ago I came to the conclusion, somewhat unwillingly, that the work of Christ throughout the centuries has always been run by consecrated minorities. The unwillingness springs from one's image of the church as 'fair as the moon, bright as the sun, terrible as an army with banners' (Song of Songs 6:10). And one also thinks of Christ as the King of kings and Lord of lords, shepherding the nations with a rod of iron (Rev 17:14; 2:27; 12:5; 19:15). Surely men will flock eagerly and in their multitudes to the service of such a Redeemer! Yet that is not the case, and there are few exceptions to the 'consecrated minority' rule, e.g. in times of spiritual awakening when 'days of the Son of Man' are seen in the churches. Apart from such rare episodes, however, the 'consecrated minority' rule holds.

To that minority, in every generation, have fallen the bur-

* June 1982

den of prayer, the work of personal evangelism and soul-winning, and radical commitment to missionary interest. Hallelujah, indeed, for the consecrated minorities!

Part of the difficulty, of course, is the appalling parochialism which has ever been the curse of the church in every age. Little-minded people, with their closed understandings and their narrow, visionless horizons, have always been a menace to the cause of Christ. The kail-yard (cabbage-patch) mentality is alien to the spirit of the Gospel, and one spends a great deal of time and energy crusading against it. This, if anything, needs to die in the church!

You will recall the old story of the lady who said to her visiting bishop, 'Oh, I don't believe in missionaries.' 'My dear,' said the bishop, 'you have no right to believe in missionaries. Your problem is that you do not believe in Jesus.' To be a 'Jesus person' in today's world is to be committed automatically to the realm of caring, to witness and testifying, to evangelism and to the saving of the lost. Not to be thus surrendered is to place oneself in the category of those in the church at Sardis who had a name that they lived, and behold they were dead (Rev 3:1). He who lives, loves!

On Saturday 7th November of last year, the Africa Inland Mission held a half-day conference in our halls. The event was amply advertised and intimations were sent to most local churches. Attention was drawn to it from our own pulpit for three consecutive Sundays. There were excellent speakers from Kenya, Sudan and Zaire, three strategic areas for Christian concern, especially when one thinks of militant Marxism and resurgent Islam. Fewer than thirty came to the afternoon session, and only eight came from our own fellowship, of whom two were men. To the later session only ten came, five from our own fellowship, of whom two were men. I was heart-sick and heart sorry for Jan Walkinshaw, AIM's

Scottish organiser, who had planned so long, so carefully and with such love for the day.

That evening I drove home to the Manse sad and grieved. 'So this,' thought I, 'is the climax of your ministry! This is how much your missionary enthusiasm has communicated itself!' Generally speaking, you see, people are simply not interested in missions. Perhaps they have a wrong image from the past as to what a missionary is and does. Perhaps they have been discouraged by some missionaries who came home with not much of a story to tell? Perhaps the uninterested ones don't believe in Jesus, in the manner of the above lady talking to her bishop? Perhaps even Christians have stopped accepting Jesus as God's final answer and word to sinners? Or perhaps they no longer appreciate that men and women without Christ are lost, here and hereafter, and go to hell when they die?

God knows and understands when He sees our lives filled with many lawful and needful busy-nesses. He also has compassion on those who have served their age well in earlier years and now are frail and find it a problem getting to meetings. Yet, when all allowances have been made, and all compassions bestowed, surely you will agree that these numbers are extraordinarily low? Would they be as low if we were to secure the services of Cliff Richard or Malcolm Muggeridge for a Saturday?

When Dorothy Fordyce organised Christian Aid among us she was distracted every year trying to find collectors to cover our parish area. Distributing and uplifting envelopes for the relief of the Third World is, of course, unromantic and ordinary. But few householders refuse to donate, and very few are rude and objectionable; and even if they were it would not matter, for the New Testament does tell of how worthy and honourable a thing it is to suffer abuse for the Name's sake. Dorothy's difficulties have now fallen on the heads of Alan Roberts and Katie Adam who are now distracted in their efforts to enlist help. They deserve all the more credit for seeing to it that £721 was raised this year. But Christian Aid tried recently to organise a Saturday half-day conference. In spite of appeals made for three Sundays, not one person came forward to volunteer.

While I was over in the States in May, Peter Chirnside was engaged in a TEAR Fund tour of Scotland under the title 'Hope for a Broken World'. A public meeting was arranged for the evening of Wednesday 28th May in the YMCA. So few came that the meeting was held in the small hall. On the following morning a meeting for local ministers and Christian workers was planned to convene in our own halls. Invitations were sent out over a wide area round our town. Only six said they would or could come. As matters turned out only four arrived, though our Guild ladies had prepared morning coffee for many more. Words could not describe my vexation for the feelings of Peter who labours so earnestly and so compassionately for the Lord's work in the Third World through TEAR Fund. People, you see, are not interested and choose not to know, care or share.

The North Africa Mission does heroic work for Christ in hard places, in Morocco, Algeria and Tunisia, reaching Moslems with the message of the Gospel of grace. Their local prayer fellowship (run, if you are interested, by Colin and Muriel Pearson) rarely rises to over five in number. Five pray-ers to cover all those millions of benighted souls!

The Overseas Missionary Fellowship also has a prayer group in town, organised by our elder Joe McKenzie. Around 20 attend, mostly from our own fellowship. Twenty pray-ers with a burden for the unsaved multitudes of the Far East!

Our own prayer fellowship is woefully thin at times in

spite of many appeals, exhortations, hints, warnings and encouragements. And, apparently, this is the state of affairs everywhere one turns. People name the Name, call themselves the Lord's people, but stand back from a living interest in His work. But I can now reveal that I asked for a sign from the Lord and made a vow some four years ago. I am anxious always to be the man God wants me to be, in the place where He wants me to be, doing what He wants me to do. I have no other ambitions. I asked for a sign from Him, a sign to indicate when my work here was finished.

Of course, it can be foolish and even dangerous to ask for signs from the Lord, as anyone knows who reads Scripture. Jesus had some hard things to say about sign-seekers (cf. Matt 12:39ff; 16:1ff; Jn 4:48). And the taking of foolish vows can be risky also (Eccl 5:1-6). I vowed to Him that, if ever there came an evening when there was not one male office-bearer at prayer, that would be the sign that my work had ended. The ministry is now of such a scope and dimension that it cannot be sustained without fervent prayer, public as well as private. I do not minimise the power of the latter.

That brings us back to my first paragraph, and to the question asked there: 'How does one get folk who name the Lord's Name, and who profess to be His people, to take a living interest in the Lord's work?' Will some kind soul help me with that problem? Will someone tell me where I have gone wrong, or what I have failed to do?

Yours sincerely,
THOMAS SWANSTON

19
COMMITMENT*

My Dear Friends,
I wonder if you know the droll tale of the chicken and the pig? One day, down on the farm, they were feeling dejected and depressed. 'All these prepacked breakfast cereals have robbed us of our usefulness,' they said as they walked down the road. 'No-one seems to need us any more.' Then they came to a transport cafe outside which there was a notice which read: 'EGGS AND BACON, only 95p.' 'Look!' called the chicken. 'We are needed after all!' 'Oh yes,' remarked the pig. 'But it is all very well and easy for you. You are being asked for only a contribution: what is required from me is total commitment.'

It is a telling story and the moral is plain. Much of the work of Christ struggles along because so many professing Christians have a 'contribution' mentality, and so few have the mentality of 'total commitment'. The chicken could lay a few eggs and depart: the pig had to stay behind and die. One cannot, after all, have bacon without dead pig. To have a 'contribution' mentality is undoubtedly less painful than having the mentality of 'total commitment'. The casual coin, the occasional cheque and the timeous donation are helpful enough in their own way but they cannot, in themselves, be necessarily identified with self-surrender. The heart-searching difficulty remains that none of us wants to die; yet until the beast in the story dies one cannot have eggs and bacon.

Something of the difference between the two mentalities may be seen in the careless way in which we use language.

*January 1988

We occasionally hear, for example, of someone being described as a 'born-again Christian'. But this is a needless use of words. What other kind of Christian is there? One cannot be an un-born again Christian. To belong to the generation of the once-born, to be born only of nature and of blood and of the will of man, is not to be a Christian at all. A man cannot be a child of God at all until he has been born twice and entered into a saving, evangelical experience of grace. Jesus Himself made this point plainly to a most religious man, Nicodemus, a leader of the Jews, a 'high heid yin o' the kirk'.

In the same way, just as 'born-again Christian' is a needless multiplication of words, so also is the description 'committed Christian'. What other kind of Christian is there? Can one be an 'uncommitted' Christian? Surely if a man is unsurrendered, unyielded and unavailable for the Master's will he has every right to question whether he is a Christian at all? God once said of the northern kingdom of Israel: 'Ephraim is a cake not turned' (Hos 7:8). We would say: 'Ephraim is a half-baked scone' - in other words neither cooked nor raw. But can one be neither cooked nor raw, neither saved nor lost, neither for Jesus nor against Him, and be a Christian?

There used to be a theory, popular in Christian circles some time ago, though one hears less of it nowadays, to the effect that receiving Christ is a two-stage process. At one point in time we accept Him as personal Saviour from sin; and at some other point in time we bow the knee to His lordship. Thus He becomes what He is, Saviour and Lord. But this is not how the New Testament speaks. Christ's saviourhood is implicit in His lordship, and His lordship embraces His saviourhood. It is because He is Lord of all that He is able to save sinners to the uttermost. It must follow from this that those who will not have Him as Lord cannot have Him as

Saviour. If we reject one we must, of necessity, reject the other. Therefore to speak of someone being an 'uncommitted Christian' is something of a contradiction in terms. What is asked for, and expected by, the Scriptures is the mentality of total commitment. We are either prepared to opt for it or we are not. The issue is as simple as that.

Certainly the church statistics of our time call for a high degree of consecration, and Christians who draw back from this level of commitment will have to face the fact that they personally are responsible for ministering and contributing to the prevailing decay and death. Dr. Callum Brown, a lecturer in history at Strathclyde University, made some challenging comments on this in the Open House column of *The Scotsman* on November 19th. Last year the communicants' roll in the Church of Scotland fell by 16,216, bringing the cumulative loss since 1956 to just short of half a million - a loss of 35 % of the membership in 30 years. The loss of active communicants since 1959 is 44%, of baptisms 60%, and of children at Sunday School 65%. In Scotland only 17% of the adult population attend worship regularly on the Lord's Day (in England it is 11% and in Wales 13%). Dr. Brown says: 'The truth is that Scotland has been secularising extremely rapidly since the 1980s... There is little evidence of open debate in the churches about strategies for survival. For, to be clear about the matter, survival is what the Kirk needs to think about very seriously. On the basis of present trends, the membership of the Church of Scotland in the year 2000 will be at least half what it was in 1960.'

We should not, of course, be preoccupied with the darkness; and one cannot share Dr. Brown's pessimism since there will always be a church on earth to glorify the God who never leaves Himself without a witness, however sombre the times. Yet the statistics stand as stark as they may, the 'chiels that winna ding' (i.e. facts which cannot be contradicted or knocked down), and they rebuke our carnal ease.

But perhaps it will take the pagans and atheists to teach us the lesson of glad abandonment and joyous surrender to a cause worth serving. I have been reading with great profit John White's book *The Cost of Commitment.* Dr. White is a psychiatrist practising privately in America, and he writes of the price of truly following Jesus in today's world. He cites a letter, written by an American communist in Mexico City, in which the man breaks off his engagement with his fiancee:

> 'We communists suffer many casualties. We are those whom they shoot, hang, lynch, tar and feather, imprison, slander, fire from our jobs and whose lives people make miserable in every way possible. Some of us are killed and imprisoned. We live in poverty. From what we earn we turn over to the Party every cent which we do not absolutely need to live.
>
> We communists have neither time nor money to go to movies very often, nor for concerts nor for beautiful homes and new cars. They call us fanatics. We are fanatics. Our lives are dominated by one supreme factor - the struggle for world communism. We communists have a philosophy of life that money could not buy.
>
> We have a cause to fight for, a specific goal in life. We lose our insignificant identities in the great river of humanity; and if our personal lives seem hard, or if our egos seem bruised through subordination to the Party, we are amply rewarded in the thought that all of us, even though it be in a very small way, are contributing something new and better for humanity.
>
> There is one thing about which I am completely in earnest - the communist cause. It is my life, my business,

my religion, my hobby, my sweetheart, my wife, my mistress, my meat and drink. I work at it by day and dream of it by night. Its control over me grows greater with the passage of time. Therefore I cannot have a friend, a lover or even a conversation without relating them to this power that animates and controls my life. I measure people, books, ideas and deeds according to the way they affect the communist cause and by their attitude to it. I have already been in jail for my ideas and, if need be, I am ready to face death.'

On some chilly wintry evening it would be a wholesome and profitable exercise to go through this man's letter and baptize it into Christian terms reading 'Christian' for 'communist' and 'Saviour' for 'Party' throughout.

To return to the chicken and the pig: the church is suffering from a surfeit of spiritual eggs. They have been donated by those with a 'contribution' mentality. We are somewhat short of spiritual bacon. The reason is obvious: in order to have bacon a creature must be led to the slaughter to die. No-one wants to die. But until you die how can you rise from death to serve God in the newness of Christ's resurrection life?

Yours affectionately, soldiering on but not unsmilingly,
THOMAS SWANSTON

20
CHRISTIAN LITERATURE*

Dear Friends,

'Of making many books there is no end,' said the Preacher somewhat dryly (Eccles 12:12). I wonder what he would make of the book scene today. The bookshelves throughout the developed world generally, and in western civilisation particularly, are groaning with literature of every conceivable, and inconceivable, description. It is a wonder that the earth's crust does not cave in under the sheer weight of print.

Christian literature also abounds in prodigious quantities, and it is of that that I wish to write, for I have reluctantly come to the conclusion that far too many books are being written and far too few people are reading them. This is a problem of epidemic proportions. It is not confined to Inverness or even to Scotland; it is like the sky - everywhere present.

My difficulty at first was practical: at the end of each month I go to the free section of the church bookstall and clear away all the out-of-date materials. In the space of a few months recently I thus disposed of some splendid, contemporary information on the Lord's work in Russia, Rumania and other eastern countries; on China and the state of the church there; on South America and its seething spiritual life; on Kenya and Upper Volta (now properly called Burkina Faso); on the sects and cults that proliferate in our society; on the drug scenes here and there.

Lest you think all of this too pious, too spiritual and other-worldly, there was much material on practical matters viz literature from IVOG (Inverness Voluntary Organisations

*October 1985

Group which keeps a caring and watchful eye on housing, alcoholics, unmarried mothers, single parent families and the like), and literature also on health concerns e.g. retinitis, muscular dystrophy, spina bifida, arthritis and multiple sclerosis.

Most of this free literature was dumped in the rubbish bin, unsought and unread. That is the problem and it disturbs the conscience.

We in the north are marvellously, perhaps uniquely, privileged from the standpoint of the availability of Christian literature. We possess a Church of Scotland bookshop on Fraser Street, The Scripture Union bookshop on Ardconnel Street, the Christian Literature shop at the top of Stephen's Brae and the Christian Literature Crusade on Castle Street. Is any other town of comparable size thus favoured?

Nor could it be argued that the failure of the Christian public to take advantage of these present blessings is due to the unacceptability or unreadability of the books to hand, for a broad spectrum of worthy literature is there, for the purchase price, from 'heavies' such as revived and reprinted Puritans, through commentaries by Inter-Varsity Publications, Zondervan and Grand Rapids, to lighter works of biography, testimony, evangelism etc. And still the difficulty will not go away: too many books are there for too few readers. One pities and sympathizes with bookshops that are struggling financially under such conditions. But how do we change the conditions?

Be it said, if negatively, that there are many church-going folk who are not interested in Christian literature because their interest in Jesus Christ is either non-existent or lies at a minimal level. They are interested in Him only in the way in which they are interested in golf, music-making, arts and crafts, holidays and like cultural affairs. He is essentially a fringe figure in their lives. They do not mind a little religion, but they do not know Him. It is absurd to expect such folk, dear as many are, to take an interest in the work of the Saviour through the medium of books. Their basic need is to be born again, to repent of their sins and self-righteousness and to come to Him for the abundant life that He holds out to sinners.

But, as for true saints, it needs to be said here that the spirit of the age, in this very business of reading, is against us. Our forefathers were prodigious readers. Many of the present day public libraries were conceived in the Victorian era and were products of the industrial revolution. Miners' Institutes included libraries, however modest, for the improvement of the working man. Working Men's Clubs were founded not primarily for entertainment and the consumption of alcohol, as they are today, but for the education and spiritual betterment of simple folk with promising intellects. But that has all changed. We prefer our truth today to be acted out for us, in colour on television. Truth for many is almost synonymous with drama. Movement is action; print is dead. The net practical result is that Christians read as little as possible, apart from the Scriptures; and when they do read for pleasure they often opt for material that can be less than worthy. A diet of the romantic fantasies (escape routes, actually) of Mills and Boon is not conducive to growth in the faith. And my heart failed recently to hear that Annie S. Swan was making a comeback!

My counsel is simple and hard: reading today is a stern discipline. You are either prepared to submit to the discipline or you are not. Lack of 'intellect' is not a good reason for not reading: it is an excuse. Experience suggests that it is astonishing what a simple mind can come to grips with, given the quickening power of the Holy Spirit. And a willing spirit works marvels, don't you think? Application, heart, zeal and fervour for Christ are all called for. Switch off the television set; banish the children from the room; let it be known that you are not at home to callers; pray for the light of God in Christ to shine on you and illuminate your understanding; knuckle down to it; become a scholar in the school of Him who Himself sat at the Father's feet in glad discipleship.

On the threshold of death, Paul wrote these words in a Roman jail: 'When you come bring the cloak... also the books, and above all the parchments' (2 Tim 4:13). One is fascinated by what the difference could be between books and parchments! Yet the challenge stands: if the blessed apostle, languishing in prison and about to pour out his life as a libation, stood in need of spiritual literature, do not we the more?

Yours very cordially,

THOMAS SWANSTON

PS: I reckon that over 80% of our congregation have yet to pay a visit to the Christian literature stall in the sanctuary.

21
AIMS OF MY MINISTRY*

Dear Friends,
My good brother and co-worker Rod MacKay, junior, asked me last year what the aims of my ministry were and what I hoped to achieve. I thought, therefore, that it would be right and useful, after these ten happy years, to set down the dreams on paper. 'Not that I have already obtained this... but I press on to make it my own' (Phil 3:12).

There are *three parts* to the vision:

The primary aim must ever be the building of Christian character, of one's own ('Physician, heal thyself') as well as that of others. And the reason for this must surely be obvious to all except those who are spiritually blind, deaf and dead: character is the only thing that survives death. Our bodies decay and return to the dust from which they came; our bank accounts all too soon evaporate; our properties and investments come, in the end, to nothing; our treasured possessions are dispersed; and even family lines and names disappear. Character alone, by which I mean the lineaments of what Jesus has done in us savingly and transformingly, through faith by grace, will endure.

Indeed, it could be cogently argued that character is what the glories of Heaven are exclusively about. This is undoubtedly one way of interpreting the imagery of the many precious stones of the Holy City in Revelation 21 - each with its own unique colour, many-faceted to show forth the lustrous beauty within. Heaven will be all Christ, and the little christs who are there, sinners purchased by His blood

*January 1982

and rescued by His grace, will be there to illustrate His praise. 'The Lamb is all the glory of Immanuel's land.'

Paul, too, saw this as standing at the heart of his mission. He speaks of 'Christ in you, the hope of glory. Him we proclaim, warning every man and teaching every man in all wisdom, that we may present every man *mature in Christ*. For *this* I toil, striving with all the energy which He mightily inspires within me' (Col 1:27-29). And the author of the Letter to the Hebrews shares the same dream: 'Therefore let us leave the elementary doctrines of Christ, and go on to maturity... and this we will do if God permits' (Heb 6: 1,3,). And it is staggering to consider what that writer reckons to be 'elementary doctrines' i.e. 'a foundation of repentance from dead works and of faith towards God; instruction about baptism and the laying on of hands; the resurrection of the dead and eternal judgment'. Notice that there are three pairs here: gospel truth, church truth and eternal truth which has to do with our final destinies. From *these* we are invited to move on to maturity. As Jesus Himself said, 'You...must be perfect, as your Father in Heaven is perfect'; by which He means not moral and sinless perfection, but balance and equilibrium of character, judgment, wisdom, maturity.

That people who are merely religious and churchy do not care for this ministry is not to be wondered at. But it is ever an occasion of surprise to find committed Christians who have no taste for these things. Some in our own fellowship would want me to take lower ground, preferring other ways and means, other attitudes; sermons, perhaps, rather than messages; or perhaps topical preaching. The last, in particular, was all very well and fine when men spoke to a Biblically-informed generation. But one could scarcely say that the majority of churchgoers today are Biblically informed! Some have only the vaguest idea as to what the gospel of

Christ is about; and for many others the Bible is a closed Book, literally and metaphorically.

But, as I often aver, it takes a whole Bible to show us a whole Christ; it takes a whole Christ to offer us a whole salvation; and it takes a whole salvation to make us whole men and women. Partial Bibles show us only a partial, fragmented Jesus; and such a Jesus can only partly save us; and if we are only partly saved, how can we be whole? Which, once again, brings us back to the subject of maturity.

I am committed, therefore, to expository ministry although I ask you to believe me when I say that I do try to make it as varied, as interesting, and as lively as a man may under God, given limitations of intellect and of personality. One resists, also, becoming hidebound exclusively by any one method, e.g. a series on the Apostles' Creed, or the Nicene Creed, or the Creed of St Athanasius (Yes, indeed! And very worthwhile it would be too!) or the Westminster Confession, might be welcome relief from dogged exposition. But all of that is dead and useless in itself, as indeed is all moribund, Spiritless and formal orthodoxy, unless it is anointed by the Holy Ghost and watered by the tears and prayers of the saints.

I am truly astonished that so many have failed to see the importance of corporate prayer in such a work as this. Perhaps you do see, but prefer not to take any serious or practical notice? Perhaps you turn away in embarrassment when I mention the essentiality and cruciality of prayer? Perhaps you may have discovered that you *cannot* pray; or that, in some sort of perverse way, you *will not* pray. Deep down and far ben there must be some explanation for such an alien spirit of non-cooperation from those who wave the evangelical flag, name the Name and profess to believe in the power of prayer.

All who read this know that I do not minimise the work of

private intercession. And I am a most compassionate and understanding pastor when it comes to matters such as personal shyness, timidity, nervousness or lack of fluency with words. But when a man says that he does not pray because he cannot, one questions where such a one stands with Christ and God. And when a true believer confesses that he will not pray, one wonders where he has gone off the rails with Jesus.

But there is a second dream: to breed a race of personal evangelists. And that, as far as I can see, is going to be a painful operation. We have relied so heavily in the past on special efforts, planned campaigns, mass evangelism and the like that we have almost lost the art of soul-winning - face to face encounter, man to man challenge, the eye to eye presentation of Christ to the lost. Here in the north the evangelism of one's neighbour has tended to mean taking him to worship to get him under the sound of the Word. The church gathering has thus become the place to 'get saved'. In other areas one meets groups of Christians who are waiting for the next special mission of outreach, the next visit of some travelling evangelist, waiting 'for the blessing'. But, I ask you, why not have the blessing *now*? Why not have souls for your hire now? Why postpone the days of good things?

I am aware, of course, that a few are a little sorry that I am less than keen on mass evangelism. But I have thought through my position here very carefully, both from the standpoint of Biblical principle, as well as from the history of the early church, and as well as from the history of the moving of God's Spirit in Scotland. But I also note that some of my gentle critics have yet to acknowledge their failure in this very matter of personal evangelism. Only a handful of folk have reached the stage of getting their unbelieving neighbour to attend worship. And the number engaged in leading souls to Christ ('hand-picked fruit' it used to be called) is microscopically small. And yet this will be the *evangelism of the future*. It is the evangelism that has kept the life of Christ alive in Russia and Eastern Europe these past 80 years. It is the only evangelism that is possible or fruitful in Islamic and other societies. Yet, perversely, we will not learn it. How many Christians have no unbelieving friends or contacts at all?

There is a third, and rather solemn, part to the dream: I am preparing men and women for the Great Tribulation. It is the universal testimony of the New Testament that towards the end of the Age the church will undergo a fierce and terrible phase of suffering, so much so that even some of the elect will be tempted to fall away. The love of many shall wax cold. The Man of Sin will be revealed, who will mesmerise and enchant multitudes and set himself up as God. There will come what is called the Apostasy - many renouncing Christ and giving up the faith they once professed. All these things are prophesied in Scripture. Forewarned is forearmed.

Certainly it cannot be denied that all over the world Christians today are under stress. European Christendom is no longer the centre of gravity for world Christianity. In Europe, and in Western civilisation generally, the churches are dying off wholesale. The spiritual movements of our generation are happening elsewhere, in Africa, in South America and under Marxist ideologies. Yet everywhere the pressures are on. Where Governments tend to polarise in their attitudes (as they do tend to do in a world of violence and extremes), whether to the far right or to the far left, the saints are caught in the middle. Christians, unfortunately, are always the odd men out, the odd bods, the people who do not fit in with any of the worldlings' socio-political schemes or dreams of man-made Utopias, and who dare to declare that

Jesus, being Lord of history, is above all the schemes of men, transcending them as an architect transcends his building, or an author his play.

Such, then, are my dreams. They are shared at least by some of those who read these words. They are also shared by my good and well-beloved colleague Bill Harrell, gradually trying to establish such a work in Immanuel Church, Virginia, after his spell of study at Aberdeen. I close with apposite and timeous words from the first issue of his Congregational Letter:

> 'The internal stimulus (i.e. the stimulus to the work of Christ) is God the Holy Spirit, working via His Word, the sacraments, and in response to prayer. We in Immanuel are committed to allowing the Lord to build us up primarily from within, so that less and less we will need to be like babes, who require external stimulation for motivation. That is why we are committed to a Bible teaching ministry, and why our prayer meeting is such a priority. Our ministry is simple by design, so that the glory and power of Christ may not be obscured, thus causing our holy self-motivation and resolve to be fractured and weakened. It may take those who visit us some time to see that what we offer is the opportunity for them to develop lasting fruit, and to build lasting individual and corporate Christian character. Nevertheless we press on, seeking to offer the gospel and ourselves to a needy and dying world.'

I say a hearty 'Amen' to all of that. Would you care to join me?

Yours sincerely, in that hope,
THOMAS SWANSTON

22
PREACHING THE WORD*

My Dear Friends,
In the early Church bishops and presbyters were set apart as men whose calling it was to defend the truth of the Gospel. It was soon realised that the best way to defend the truth was to preach it, and that accounts for the close connection between the defence of the Faith once for all delivered to the saints (Jude 3) and the preaching of the Word (2 Tim 4:2). There is therefore a sense in which evangelical truth, when it is properly and soundly preached, defends itself.

It need hardly be said that we find ourselves in a very different situation today. Not all bishops and presbyters live either to preach or to defend the truth, and some appear to find pleasure in publicly destroying it. During the course of the 'Honest to God' controversy some years ago (and how far off now seems that stormy affair, and how radically has the Christian scene since changed!) C. S. Lewis wrote an interesting letter to *The Times* in which he passed the dry comment that he could see no good reason why bishops should not be allowed to pursue their 'honest doubts' and their excursions into unbelief, relieved of their bishoprics and, of course, their salaries. For it is fundamentally dishonest of a bishop or a presbyter to accept a salary to destroy the Faith which, in fact, he is being paid to champion.

Why do I raise such issues here? Simply for this reason: if bishops and presbyters are appointed to preach and expound the truth of God, it disturbs me more than a little to detect, of late, in various Christian circles, a growing resist-

*October 1987

ance to teaching ministry in general and to expository ministry in particular. Christians in our generation prefer to be activists rather than disciples, to be doers rather than hearers, and seem less inclined to adopt the role of scholars in the school of Christ. No one doubts the necessity of Christian action and evangelical deeds: by them the world is to see our good works and glorify the Father who is in heaven. But our first and essential calling as Christians is to be taught by the Master. We are required to sit down at His feet and learn, for He Himself was a scholar at His Father's feet. 'Come unto Me,' He says, 'all who are weary and heavy-laden. Take My yoke upon you and *learn of Me, for I am meek and lowly in heart.*' The reference here is surely to the third of the so-called Servant Songs in Isaiah in which Christ, the Servant of Jehovah, is portrayed as a scholar, Himself a meek and lowly learner of the Father and of His ways:

> The Lord God has given me
>   the tongue of those who are taught,
> That I may know how to sustain with a word
>   him that is weary.
> Morning by morning
>   He wakens, He wakens my ear
> To hear as those who are taught.
> The Lord God has opened my ear,
>   and I was not rebellious. (Isa 50:4-5)

It needs to be said that teaching and expository ministry stand at something of a disadvantage in our age. Our generation is not lightly disposed to absorb preached truth. Men tend to believe truth when it is acted out before their eyes, preferably in colour, as it is on television. This is partly why the moral values and standards of what is projected from the screen have become the norm for the vast majority of common folk. What is on television is somehow thought of as right, believable, credible, acceptable or whatever, in much the same way in which people used to believe that everything that appeared in the public press was factually accurate and trustworthy. It is now quite some undertaking, therefore, to convince men that if God has said a thing it is true. Even if He says it only once it is true. Even if what He says appears to contradict the facts or the evidence of men's eyes, it is true. And it is true because He has said it.

To borrow the phraseology of Francis Schaeffer, nothing is more important than that the church of Christ should listen to the 'true truths' of God. It has pleased Him to encapsulate these true truths, to enshrine them, to inscripturate them in the Bible. From beginning to end that volume is the Word of God. It holds the *ipsissima verba*, the very words, of Him who sits on the throne, and all of this has been given by Him in grace for the salvation, the rescue, the nourishment, the edification, the upbuilding, the feeding, the equipment, the counselling, and the perfecting of His saints. To neglect the whole Word of God is thus to set oneself at a distance from what God has planned and given for our wholesome good.

Of course, expository ministry, the practice of preaching through books of the Bible, is only one way of communicating true truths. It has not always been so. The Reformers were, more or less, expository preachers. They had to be for they were speaking to a generation of men who had been kept in total spiritual darkness and ignorance by the heirs of the Mediaeval Church. The Puritans, in a later time, preached substantially from texts; and that is a strong tradition which has persisted throughout the years. The text would be stated at the outset and repeated frequently, and the sermon would be 'filled in' after each restatement. The virtue of this preaching method was that the worshippers went home remembering, at least, the text even when all else was forgotten. The Puritans, it must be said, were speaking to people who were Biblically informed. They knew the Scriptures and could set texts in their proper background. The Puritans were, when all is said and done, the inheritors of the Reformation. Today we are not a Biblically-informed age, and even many regular churchgoing folk have only a vague notion as to what the Bible is about and what constitutes the Gospel message of salvation. Textual preaching, therefore, seems to fulfil less and less of a useful function and the call is for some other way of communicating the 'whole counsels of God'.

I have, for my own part, tried to confine myself to expository preaching. There have been occasional departures from this from time to time. In my sixteen years as minister in Inverness we have covered series on the Miracles of Christ, the Gospel Parables, evangelistic messages on the miracles in John's Gospel, Basic Christian Doctrine, the Names of God in the Old Testament and the present series on the Seven Deadly Sins. Some day we must try to go through the Apostles' Creed or, better still, the Nicene Creed. We might even have the courage to tackle another, and more demanding, statement of faith - the Creed of Saint Athanasius, which you will find in the Anglican Prayer Book. Until then I am committed to the opening up of what God has said in His holy, blessed and absolutely trustworthy Word. And when I am urged and asked by well-meaning Christians to move on to something else... perhaps something more trivial, more superficial, less insistent and taxing mentally, more easy to absorb... I can only remind them of two realities. The first is that God has not yet asked me to change: when He does so I will gladly and obediently do so. The second is that this is, to date, the only method which God has honoured in me and through me. All the folk who have been won for the Saviour and thoroughly converted to Him, and all who have gone into full-time service of the Gospel, have been won and have gone under the sound of the expository ministry entrusted to me. Why should I depart from ways which have proved God-anointed and God-honouring to take up other schemes and lesser ploys to which I have not been called?

At the risk of wearying you let me state the principle again: it takes a whole Bible to show us a whole Christ; it takes a whole Christ to offer us a whole salvation; and it takes a whole salvation to meet all our needs and make us whole again in the spirit of the Gospel. This is the hope which garrisons my service in the ministry. It is my dream and vision. Come, share it with me.

Yours sincerely,
THOMAS SWANSTON

23
PUBLIC INTERCESSORS WANTED*

My Dear People,

I want to speak, as plainly and as faithfully as I may, to the growing minority of people who are developing something of a guilty conscience about the failure of their prayer-life, private and public, but especially the latter.

But firstly let me dismiss the foolish, empty opinions of those who say that they 'do not believe in prayer meetings'. Such talk is worthy of Turks and infidels, and is the sort of language one expects to hear from the Great Unwashed, the generation of the once-born, those who have never truly been converted to Christ. Perhaps, like me, you react to the word 'meeting' in the way in which we tend nowadays to react to relics of the Victorian age. I do prefer to speak of 'prayer fellowship' or of 'the prayer family'. But if you 'do not believe in prayer meetings', surely the time has come for you to ask yourself in what sense you believe in Christ? Prayer meetings were good enough for Jesus and the early church, and they ought to be good enough for us. Unless, of course, we now set ourselves up as superior to both Him and it? The early church turned the world upside down, which is more than can be said about those who 'do not believe in prayer meetings'.

One looks for characteristics and features of the prayer-life of the church today, and can describe them only in terms of non-appearances; the non-appearance of men, of office-bearers, and of 'grand church workers'. Facts are chiels that winna ding, and these are facts beyond dispute; men in gen-

*July 1975

eral, elders and office-bearers in particular, and good kirky folk especially, simply do not meet together for corporate prayer, but are conspicuous by their absence. This is not something peculiar to our own situation here, but may be seen everywhere. Go almost where you will, this phenomenon is like the sky - it is universally present. Must we press for an answer to that most ultimate of all alternatives: 'Don't because you won't, or don't because you can't?'

Almost proverbially, men will do anything but pray. They will organise sales, raise money, and work their fingers to the bone; they will visit the sick and needy, and care for widows; they will discuss Christ and talk endlessly about religion and church affairs; they will even preach or enter the ministry. But they will not pray. The cause is not far to seek: men may engage in all of these activities and still, at heart, be radically uncommitted to Christ. One may do all of these things and not be a Christian at all.

Deeper reasons, too, may be sought and found. We are all temperamentally different, and some are more shy, timid, reserved and fearful than others; and there are undoubtedly the considerations of age, of convenience, and of pressures of time. Perhaps we do not give God the credit for His wondrous patience with us in our weakness, for He understands us and cares for us beyond our wildest dreams. 'He knows our frame, He remembers that we are dust.' One concedes that for some Christians prayer is a long, hard struggle. It is curious, nevertheless, how those who plead reserve can have so much to say on almost every conceivable topic under the sun. How talkative and garrulous the prayerless can be when they choose! If I were to suggest a way out, could not a few words of prayer be written on paper and read, to help overcome the surprise at hearing one's own voice? There can be no compromise in that and, in a warm, tender-hearted, loving fellowship, why should this not prove a happy release for those who long to pray?

More deeply and searchingly, prayer presupposes belief in an eternal world - that other dimension of the spiritual with which our natural life is shot through, and under whose judgment our natural life stands. Unfortunately, so many church people believe in a spiritual world only in theory. It has little practical bearing on real life, being considered remote, unreal and the province of those professional clergymen who, to preserve their priestly power, have not encouraged their congregations to pray. It is small wonder that so many churchy folk describe prayer as 'carrying religion a bit far'.

Deeper still, prayer has a disarming way of revealing where the pray-er stands spiritually, what he is in his inmost heart. Prayer tears away the veils, the sham, the hypocrisy, the facade, and exposes the man as he is. Many do not pray, therefore, because they suspect that if they are out of joint with Christ or living a life of double standards, their juvenility or immaturity will immediately be exposed. Have you heard the story of the young minister who was visiting a lady for the first time? As he rose to leave she put her hand on his arm and said: 'Before you go you will say a word of prayer. I want to see where you stand with God.' A little daunting for the young man, perhaps, but shrewd of the lady, and a timely message for us all.

There are even deeper problems. There are the major ones of folk who do not come to prayer fellowship, or who come only when the minister is away, or who can find grace to pray only when he is not there. To my mind this is evidence of a spirituality that is sadly agley, or of a profound form of psychological sickness that may need years of the Great Physician's therapeutic touch for healing. I wonder if this attitude may not be traceable to bad relationships with authority-figures in childhood? I think of some Christians who do not get on well with adults generally, and suspect that this is due to an unhappy youth in which they were unloved and uncared for, perhaps in some graceless, callous, unfeeling home. For better or for worse, a minister is an authority-figure, and the silence of some in prayer (or their non-appearance) may have something to do with wrong attitudes, resentments, harboured from early years, or grudges against power never fully resolved in Christ.

This is partly the attitude represented by those who say that they do not pray because 'they can't pray like the minister'. But who would want you to? Certainly not the minister. He is not the perfect pray-er. The Perfect Pray-er is in heaven, and He sends His Holy Spirit of intercession into the hearts of all who believe and who mean business with Him. Pray like yourself, inspired by that Spirit. Be your authentic, genuine, best self for Jesus and never mind the critics; for, if you do not seek deliverance from this form of bondage (and that is what it is) you may find that your religion is built on a man and therefore on corruptible flesh and you will, by having tried to ape another, have brought upon yourself all sorts of diseases and maladies of soul. It is not important that you should adopt certain styles or mannerisms. It is not even important that you should be able, as some are, to quote the Authorised Version at great length in prayer. It is important that you should be transparently, and candidly, and without hypocrisy, real for Jesus.

One appeals vaguely to those who have 'made a decision for Christ' and who would claim to be conservative, traditional and evangelical. I think particularly of those whose spiritual roots lie in groups such as Scripture Union, Crusaders, the Mission Hall Movement, the Christian Brethren and the Free Church. Representatives from all of these come round us. Surely you cannot be unaware that these associations and societies have always insisted on the priority of corporate prayer in the onward march of Christ? Whatever may be the case now, there certainly was a day when a man's absence from prayer raised all sorts of questions - his consecration, his sanctification, his spiritual and psychological health, or even his basic salvation. It is not a light thing to trifle with such matters and I wonder where your excuses will be when you look into the kindly but searching eyes of Christ, the God with whom we have to do, on the Great Day? What explanation will you give Him for your isolationism, your insularity, and your failure to participate? Or perhaps you want to read new meaning and content into the word 'evangelical'? It is flattering and kind that you should approve of a Biblical ministry, but where do you stand with Christ and where are you in relation to the present ministry? By the blood of the Cross, by the mercies of the Gospel which you profess, by the intercession of the Spirit, I beseech you to turn again and think again lest you be mistaken.

The organised church in our day, certainly in Western Christendom, is under the judgment of God. God is bringing her to a historic end for her infidelity and unbelief. Only the churches that pray together will survive the coming holocaust. God is doing a New Thing amongst us, here in Inverness as well as in Scotland generally. Those who are not aware of this must be as blind and as deaf and as spiritually dead as any can be. But such a ministry cannot survive without prayer. Without prayer the people, the money, the power and the blessing will depart.

None of what I have said denies the value of private intercessions. May God bless and multiply the secret prayers; but I want public intercessors and I want them quickly.

Prayer is a Christian's life. To be a Christian is to pray. Prayer is what God made us for. It is His own breath in us returning to its home and source. But is it easier to release your breath or to hold it in forever? The man who holds in his breath forever is the man who dies. Perhaps he never had any breath in him at all? Perhaps this man of silence, who never speaks to God, never lived at all? But if we have the breath and hold it in much longer I cannot believe that God, in this day of His power, will fail to hold us guiltless.

Yours, as soberly as ever I wrote,
THOMAS SWANSTON

24
CORPORATE PRAYER*

Dear Friends,
Surely our first words this month must be of thanks to the Lord for His goodness to us during the weeks of the UCCF Mission. Original fears, that perhaps too many of the students were young and inexperienced, proved groundless, and many have confessed to a real warming of heart. Certainly there was a new response to the challenge of the Gospel, and an impact has been made on careless and indifferent lives, hitherto heedless of grace.

We record our gratitude to the Cameron and Main families in Scorguie for the generous way in which they opened their homes for meetings, and to the many who handed in good things by way of material help at the halls. It was obvious that there had been much Mormon activity throughout the scheme prior to our visitation, and a minority of homes were inclined to give us short shrift, weary of more 'religion'. One visiting pair was plagued all evening, receiving little response and sullen looks - until they discovered that they were trailing permanently, a few doors behind a team from the local Conservative party. The householders thought that we were Socialists!

It is inevitable that such a Campaign should show up our strengths, both as a fellowship, and as part of the national church. There is still, for example, a great openness to the Gospel. Men and women are still willing to sit down and listen, provided Christ is offered to them in a new and living way. The majority have little time, by and large, for the

*October 1977

organised churches which they consider irrelevant, lifeless and out of date. Such attitudes should make Christians all the more bold to attempt great things for the Saviour. We are too timid by half!

We are grateful to the local YMCA for cancelling their regular after-church meeting to allow Free Presbyterian and Free Church young folk to come to our Youth Rallies. It was quite a spectacle to see our upper hall thronged with nearly 200 folk in their mid and late teens, singing God's praise and hearing the Good News with rapt attention. And it was also quite something to behold such crowds in our own place, expectant upon God. The singing was an experience, don't you think?

It is inevitable, too, that the Mission should show up our failures. Of these let me speak briefly. I do not know what is to be done about the various homes that are sealed against the Lord Christ. I do not mean unbelieving homes, but homes that glory in being Christian and evangelical. I will address you now. You are sealed! Sealed against usefulness, against blessing, against fruit-bearing. Sealed against all inconvenience and sheer 'bother' of being a living witness in today's secular society. You are barred against 'alien' life, as if you were mediaeval castles in a state of siege. But how will you appear when you look into the eyes of the Son of Man who, in the days of His flesh, had not so much as a place whereon to lay His head? How will creature comforts come to your help on that Great Day when we all have to answer for the many kinds of stewardship committed to our charge?

Many are near the kingdom and that is a fact. My concern is that you have been near the kingdom for years, in some cases for almost a lifetime. Perhaps you are waiting for the *curum* (Gaelic for anxiety about sin, conviction of sin) to fall on you? You want the sky to open and something to 'happen' to you? You want deep anguish to come upon you, almost a physical outworking of years of accumulated guilt? Believe me, these may have been features of past reawakenings, but for you the sky will not open. There will be no rending of the heavens, no new revelation. God has spoken His last word to you in the man Christ-Jesus. He has nothing more to say. He cannot add to that perfection of manhood, life, character and death. If you are waiting for the *curum* you will wait in vain, and so be lost for ever. I believe that your waiting is simply another excuse for evading the real issues - your need to be 'near the kingdom'. But 'near the kingdom' and 'not far from the kingdom' are also 'almost persuaded' (Acts 26:28 AV); and 'almost persuaded' is lost. That is the risk that men take when they gamble with eternal things and fool around with Jesus. As John Bunyan reminds us at the end of *Pilgrim's Progress*: 'Then I saw that there was a way to hell, even from the gates of heaven, as well as from the city of destruction.'

I had thought that perhaps the Mission might have brought out a few new faces to public prayer. A vain hope! It was not to be. No new faces appeared. No, not one. Prayer is, it appears, the last straw that breaks the back of the Camel Ecclesiastic. Prayer is 'carrying religion a bit too far'. It is the great non-starter in church circles. It is the Cinderella of all activities. It is the last resort. Kirky folk will do anything but this: buy, sell, organise, knit, sew, fry, bake, cook, talk, go to the mission field, scrub, discuss - anything but pray!

And the reasons are not far to seek: prayer is inclined to reveal where we stand spiritually. It sorts out the boys from the men, the Christian soldiers from those of the merely chocolate variety. Without prayer, the churches are fast declining into religious clubs, patronised by elderly ladies of both sexes. 'Ladies of both sexes,' did I say? Why, of course! Every male is not a man. A 'male' is a person who is not a 'female'. 'Male' has to do with gender, with sex. 'Males' may be mice, but 'man' has to do with character. A 'man' has stamina, courage, moral and spiritual fibre. He is not ashamed to stand up and be counted for Jesus. The churches are suffering from a surfeit of males, and from a dearth of men. Who will be a man for God and the Gospel?

All of that is put rather bluntly, I concede. Forgive my foolish, crusading zeal! I know of no other way of awakening slumbering consciences. But please do not smother the challenge beneath a feather bed of qualifications. Surely you get the message? There was a day when calls for prayer were dismissed by haughty, churchy folk as belonging to the 'lunatic evangelical fringe'. That is no longer the case. Moderators from about the time of Professor J S Stewart have sent out repeated appeals, down to this very day under Dr. Gray of Dunblane Cathedral. And until the church turns to this, the churches generally will continue to minister to 'baptized unbelievers' - the phrase is Emil Brunner's, not mine - sans Bibles, sans understanding, sans Jesus, sans tithes, sans hope (sans is the Elizabethan English for 'without') and sans, very often, interest.

Without prayer, without more pray-ers, nothing more can happen. This is the God-appointed way to blessing. Without it there can be no reviving of the church's brightness. All new life begins, continues and is ended in prayer. That is how God has ordained things. If the church does not believe this I am afraid that she cannot have Him for her friend, and if He is not her friend what, then, is He?

Yours in hope, waiting, looking, longing,
THOMAS SWANSTON

25
PRAYER*

Dear Friends,

'Lord, grant that all our good works, having begun in Christ, may also be continued and ended in Him, to the praise and glory of Thy Name.' So runs an ancient prayer. The beauty and worth of its sentiment is that it distinguishes 'works' from 'works... begun in Christ'. Not all good works begin, continue and end in Him; and, far from being done to the praise and glory of God's Name, many are done to the praise and glory of self!

We are, then, as Christians, to see to it that our deeds of evangelical virtue both start in Jesus and are carried out and ended in Him for the Father's praise. And here is one further daring thought: our good deeds started in Jesus must also start in prayer. However simple or obscure the work, however influential or far-reaching the effects, the deed must start in prayer.

I was recently asked by Rutherford House, Edinburgh, to write a short tract on 'Prayer', and I thought that it would be good to reproduce some of that material, slightly modified, here:

'Prayer is one of the major disciplines and exercises of the Christian life. *By* it, *in* it and *through* it the believer speaks to God through the mediation of Jesus Christ, the only mediator, or middle-man, between God and man' (1 Tim 2:5).

It needs to be emphasised at the outset that prayer is speaking *to* God. It is not speaking *about* God to some audience, real or imaginary. There are Christians who, in a

*October 1982

spirit of mild dishonesty and opportunism, take advantage of prayer and use it as a means of preaching to present company. But to sermonise is not to pray! Prayer is speaking to God and that may be, and is best, done in childlike simplicity.

Prayer is the simplest form of speech
That infant lips can try;
Prayer, the sublimest strains that reach
The majesty on high.

It follows from the above that a Christian, by his essential nature, is someone who prays. Prayer is what Christians were made for, and to be a Christian is to pray. It is the hallmark of the person who, by grace through faith, belongs to Jesus Christ. 'Behold, he is praying!' was said of Paul after his conversion to Christ (Acts 9:11). But what was special about this? Had not Saul the Pharisee all his life 'said his prayers'? What was special in Saul of Tarsus converted? Before he came to a saving knowledge of Christ he 'said his prayers'. After he came to know Christ he *prayed*. There is a world of difference between 'saying prayers', in a formal duteous lifeless way, and *praying*. The difference between the two is sometimes the difference between heaven and hell.

Prayer is the Christian's vital breath,
The Christian's native air,
His watchword at the gate of death;
He enters heaven with prayer.

Prayer is the contrite sinner's voice,
Returning from his ways;
While angels in their songs rejoice
And cry, 'Behold, he prays!'

In the beginning man was made to speak to God, his Maker and Providence. In the opening chapters of Genesis Adam is portrayed as the crown of God's creation, the finest and most marvellous being ever fashioned by Him. Adam, in Genesis chapter 1, sits atop the pyramid of creation; in Genesis chapter 2 he stands at the centre of the Garden. In both pictures all things are put under his feet (Ps 8:5,6). He is, under God, Lord of all.

As crown of creation and Lord of all, Adam, of all creatures, had the power to commune with God in speech. But sin, having entered the world through Adam's first transgression, erected a tragic barrier between God and man. Man was no longer on speaking terms with God and Earth had become, in the words of C. S. Lewis in his Dr. Ransom trilogy, 'the silent planet', having no parley with its Maker, estranged and speechless before God. This is part of the judgment and condemnation of sin.

But Christ, the everlasting Word of God, broke savingly into that dreadful silence. In Him God spoke to man that man might again speak to God. In the fullness of time, and as the climax and goal of His mission, Jesus gave His life's blood to open up a royal road between man and God. He offered Himself freely, a willing sacrifice, for the forgiveness of sins, for the cleansing of the foul, for the empowering of the impotent, for the healing of the wounded and *for the giving of speech to the dumb*. Therefore the man who trusts in Jesus is the man who, through Jesus, has access to God in speech.

A fine word is used in New Testament Greek for such 'access'. It is the word *parresia* which, in the Authorised Version, is translated as 'confidence' in 1 Jn 2:28; and 3:21 and 5:14, and as 'boldness' in Eph 3:12; Heb 10:19 and 1 Jn 4:17. The fundamental ideas behind the word are of liberty of speech and of freedom to be heard, especially in the presence of some exalted personage. Jesus died to purchase such frankness, such outspokenness, for sinners in the sight of a holy God. Therefore a Christian is someone who, having this *parresia,* speaks to God.

The Bible, it need hardly be said, is strewn with many encouragements to Christians to exercise this liberty of speech before God. Great men who made an impact on their generation for God and for righteousness are held up to us as examples worthy to be followed. Moses (Ex 32:7-14; Num 14:11-20), Samuel (1 Sam 7:8-10, 13 and 12:18-23) and Elijah (Jas 5:17-18) were all men of prayer and lived lives of prayer, and it should not be doubted that prayer lay at the heart of all their endeavours. The secret of victory is victory in secret!

Nothing, however, is more encouraging to a Christian than the knowledge that, when he prays, the entire Trinity of love and power is galvanised into action. When prayer is heard and answered each person of the Godhead is at work. We pray *to* the Father, *through* the Son, *by* the Spirit. The Father Himself plants the prayers in our hearts by the Spirit, and the Spirit wings those prayers to the throne of grace through the mediation of Christ. And when our inner beings are too disturbed for words, and when our emotions and griefs are filled with conflict, the Spirit bears our voiceless and unvoiced prayers to the Father (Rom 8:26-27).

Prayer is the soul's sincere desire,
  Uttered or unexpressed,
The motion of a hidden fire
  That trembles in the breast.

(In the Rutherford House tract there are some paragraphs here on the different sorts of prayer: worship and adoration, confession and supplication, intercession.)

But prayer subdivides yet again into the *private* and the *public*. Private prayer, along with the study of the Word, is a necessary part of the secret devotional life of everyone who names the Name of Christ. By such intimate prayer the pray-er is himself changed since prayer, being one of the 'means of grace', puts sweetness into the soul, refreshes and fortifies the spirit, and binds the believer more closely to his Lord and Saviour. Nor is there any need to confine private prayer to some special place or time, in the manner of the worship commended in Matthew 6:5-6. Private prayer can be engaged in all the day long, and a life of prayer, instant to know God's will, to serve and to obey, is a glorious reality.

Public prayer is a more serious issue for the reason that it is most often the most shamefully neglected. By 'public prayer' is not meant prayers heard when the saints assemble for worship, but rather prayer-fellowship prayers. Jesus taught that there is exceptional blessing in such prayers when God's children come together collectively as a family (Matt 18:19-20). When saints are multiplied faith too is multiplied, and prayers offered believingly from Christians together, as distinct from Christians individually, carry weight with God and move the hand that guides the universe.

It should be noted that a Christian's faithfulness in prayer is a matter of *duty*. This does not primarily have to do with consecration, or with pious feelings, or with sanctification, or with 'laying oneself on the altar'. A Christian's presence at prayer-fellowship may be an *expression* of these realities, but presence at prayer is firstly a matter of duty and of obligation. Christians sound in wind, limb and heart, should join together in communal prayer: it is their *duty* to do so and failure to do so is little less than dereliction of duty and is, partly at least in many cases, a refusal of the challenge of discipleship, of the way of the Cross and of radical commitment to Christ.

When allowances are made for the frailty of our natures, for advancing age, for sickness and indifferent health, for shyness and personality problems, for family commitments and the like, absence from prayer is normally associated with (1) plain unbelief, (2) secret and not-so-secret backsliding, (3) spiritual indifference, and (4) attitudes of rebellion, independence and non-cooperation.

On the other hand, incentives about to draw Christians to pray together: (1) the plain teaching of the Bible (1 Thess 5:17; 1 Tim 2:8; James 5:13-16), (2) the example of Jesus (Matt 14:23; 26:36; John 14:16; 17:9,15), (3) the practice of the early church (Acts 1:14; 6:4; 12:5), and (4) centuries of evangelical tradition. None of these can lightly be set aside or cast away.

O Thou by whom we come to God,
The Life, the Truth, the Way,
The path of prayer Thyself hast trod;
Lord, teach us how to pray!

(The verses quoted above are from James Montgomery's hymn, *Prayer is the soul's sincere desire*.)

Yours sincerely,
THOMAS SWANSTON

26
NEED FOR PRAYER*

Dear Friends,
When are the churches of Christ going to learn that prayer is the answer to all their present problems? And when are we in Scotland going to learn this in our own denomination? If you think of the church pictorially as a vessel sailing in high state through the seas of history, our progress since the turn of this century is marked by a wake of abandoned gimmicks, of fruitless ploys and of efforts and antics which owe more to human ingenuity and cleverness than to Biblical spirituality. If all else fails - and all else so far has - should we not at least try that which is patent from Scripture, the discipline, duty, responsibility and pleasure of prayer? Why do we, in a spirit of perversity, seek out obscure and untested methods when the proven and divinely-acknowledged lie to hand?

There was a day in the not so distant past when Christians who sought out other believers for prayer fellowship were thought of as belonging to the lunatic fringe of the church. These were designated hotheads, enthusiasts, the unco guid and over-pious, the holy brigade tolerated only because we in the Church of Scotland prided ourselves on being a 'broad' church. The 'real' life of the church was held to go on apart from, and in spite of, peripheral activities such as prayer and the study of Scripture. But all that was yesterday, and since then the paganising of the church has proceeded apace. The truly interesting thing is that calls to prayer are now addressed to us not by weird, out of the way, intransigent fundamentalists, but by distinguished Moderators, by General Assemblies

*January 1989

and by the committees of the church in Edinburgh. But while the calls may well be addressed to us the challenge is basically unheeded. It is certainly true to say that there are now more praying folk and prayer groups in Scotland than there have been for many, many years; yet they are still a microscopic minority and are viewed with some suspicion by traditional churchgoers. The recent Lifestyle Survey, organised by the Board of Social Responsibility, reveals that a majority of church members, including elders and office-bearers, do not read the Bible on a systematic, regular basis, and seldom pray. I have spoken with several ministers who admitted that they never prayed except on formal occasions such as funerals, weddings and divine worship.

Yet prayer is what the church was made for. In C. S. Lewis' trilogy on the Dr. Ransom theme, the imaginary spiritual beings on other worlds call Earth the *Wounded Planet* and the *Silent Planet.* It is the world which no longer speaks to God. The communion has broken down and the intimate face to face fellowship has been marred. Man and God have nothing to say to each other; they are no longer on speaking terms. The irony is that man was made for speech with his Maker and with his fellow men; he was born for verbal converse. Only the wounded and the silent maintain their distance from God, and from their fellows, and so perpetuate the estrangement. It is part of the Good News of the Gospel that the work of Christ has reversed this tragic state of affairs. The man in Christ, therefore, is the man who speaks with God. To speak with God is prayer; prayer is what the church was made for; and prayer is the answer to all our present problems.

'All?' you ask. 'Is that not too naive and simplistic? Can it be the answer to kirks closing by the dozen annually; to the plummeting numbers of men and women entering full-time service; the praiseless praises; to the deadness and moribundity; to the departure of our young folk from true religion and its ways?' Well, naive and simplistic the answer may be, but it is the naivety and simplicity of Christ. He was born in answer to the prayers and cries and longings of the human heart for a Saviour. When He came His life was a life of prayer. He taught men 'to pray and not to faint'. He not only prayed privately, He encouraged His followers to pray both privately and collectively on the principle that faith is multiplied when believing saints come together. He died on the Cross in an attitude and spirit of prayer. Why, therefore, will we not be like Him? Why are we so slow to imitate Him here? When is the church going to learn?

Some have asked me gently why I have not, for some time, issued strong challenges with regard to corporate prayer. My answer is this: it is my suspicion, founded on experience, that such diatribes and public invective do little good and are subject to the law of diminishing returns. Some listen in wonder and total incomprehension. Others merely become angry and resentful. Others depart laden with spiritual guilt. But, besides all this, it is also my conviction that there is something in such repeated challenges that is degrading to the Name and honour of the Lord Jesus Christ. The impression is given that His is some tenth-rate, hard-up, down-at-heel cause in need of our support to keep it going. That is a view of Gospel work which I abominate. His kingdom will advance and grow with us or without us. If we choose to cooperate, to respond and to consecrate ourselves in His service, ours will be the privilege and His will be the glory. If, however, we choose to keep our lives to ourselves and to refuse to let Him interfere, ours will be the loss and the shame.

Many, of course, do not pray at all, largely, I suspect because the whole world of the Gospel and of other-worldly religion is alien and foreign to them. Others confess that they cannot pray for reasons that are moral, personal, psychological or spiritual. Others can pray but, in a spirit of stubbornness, do not. Others, yet again, have declined from prayer for the simple reason - observable to all save themselves - that they have allowed themselves to lapse into a backslidden state. The geography of prayer, the lie of the land, is fairly complex! But mark my words, until Christians turn again to this holy exercise, the decline in the churches will continue. The institutional places of worship will go on closing; official church membership will become more and more elderly; the pews will continue to empty; the monies will dry up; the number of candidates coming forward for the ministry will thin out; and church unions, linkages and mergers will abound. And the greater part of the responsibility for all of this will lie not with atheists, humanists, Marxists or our late twentieth century pagans, but with the prayerless and unbelieving inside the churches' walls. Hear the voice of God in these Scriptures:

> 'If my people who are called by my name humble themselves, and pray and seek my face, and turn from their wicked ways, then I will hear from heaven, and will forgive their sin and heal their land' (2 Chron 7:14).
>
> 'Again I say to you, if two of you agree on earth about anything they ask (i.e. in prayer), it will be done for them by my Father in heaven. For where two or three are gathered in my name (i.e. in prayer) there am I in the midst of them.' (Matt 18:19-20).
>
> 'Therefore lift your drooping hands (i.e. hands no longer lifted up in prayer)... so that what is lame may not be put out of joint but rather be healed' (Heb. 12:12-13).

Yours cordially, for the Saviour's cause,
THOMAS SWANSTON

27
TWO FEARS OF GOD*

My Dear Friends,

I want to write to you about the two fears of God: the false and the true, especially about the former, for I am increasingly dismayed and appalled by what false fear can do to people's personalities, by the havoc and disaster it can wreak in Christian service, and the damage it can and does do to believers. For it is by its sour, sad fruits that this base-born, unholy dread is best known. I am thinking especially of sensitive, shy souls who have been intimidated, browbeaten and hurt by an abject fear of the Lord, an irrational terror of Him, which in fact owes nothing to Him since it does not come from Him, does not minister or add to His praise, and brings Him no pleasure. There is a fear of God that God immediately disowns and abominates. This alien emotion produces three sorts of person: first of all it breeds people who are hardhearted, callous, unfeeling, and legalistic; secondly, it can breed folk who are timid, frightened, nervous, strained, and full of unnecessary fears; and thirdly, it breeds hypocrites whose inner beings remain quite untouched, unmelted and unmoved by the love of Jesus. The whole evangelical wing of the church is littered with such legalists, such fear-ridden souls, and such hypocrites. 'An enemy hath done this.'

I am not thinking here of the man who does not make any religious profession - the natural, once-born man. His tragedy is that he has, in himself, no fear of God of any kind. The very idea of God as Judge does not enter into his reck-oning. He has no thought that one day he must stand at the bar of God,

*July 1972

at the divine Tribunal, to receive a recompense for the deeds done in the body. So he sins carelessly, heedlessly, even gaily, and he does these things because 'there is no fear of God before his eyes' (Ps 36:1 and Rom 3:18 in context). Like Esau he is a profane person. But it is of professing Christians I write.

Can we set aside the well-intentioned, but misguided, advice of those folk, especially child psychologists who tell us that fear is a wrong motive and that it is futile to try and plant it into adults, and wrong to inculcate it into children? Fear is, perhaps, not the highest of motives. Love is the highest. But at least fear is a motive, and a rather powerful one at that, as can be seen from the moral state of a world which has stopped believing in it and has cast off fear's restraints. You do not want your child to play with fire? You do well. It would be ideal if you could simply tell him not to do so, out of sheer love for you. But children are thrawn, stubborn and perverse. Sin is born in them. Therefore you teach your child to fear fire. Is that wrong? 'Perfect love casteth out fear' (1 Jn 4:18), not all fear, but wrong fear. There is a healthy fear that is right, strong and good. 'The fear of the Lord is clean, enduring for ever' (Ps 19:9). Will you not be made clean and whole by its energies? Besides all this, it was gentle Jesus, meek and mild and harmless, who taught men the holy dread of God. Will you not listen to Him, and sin no more? 'I will forewarn you whom you shall fear,' He says. 'Fear Him who, after He has killed, has power to cast into hell. Yea, I say to you: Fear Him' (Luke 12:5).

But where should the Gospel emphasis lie in a life that fears God? In the North of Scotland we are familiar with the motto of Aberdeen University: *Initium sapientiae, timor Domini*: The Fear of the Lord is the Beginning of Wisdom. This piece of counsel occurs twice in Proverbs (1:7 and 9:10), and the stress is on the moral quality of a man's life: to fear God is to live a life of integrity and righteousness. 'The fear of the Lord is to hate evil' (8:13). But there is another, and strangely less popular, verse: 'The fear of the Lord is a fountain of life' (14:27). This speaks of the vitality, the dynamism, the living-ness of the man who fears God. Any fear of God, therefore, which stultifies and paralyses Christians, and leads them to inertia, wooden-ness, or dullness and deadness of soul, is not a fear that comes from God. It is false fear. Real fear, godly fear, emerges as care for others, as compassion for human need, as concern for their souls and wellbeing; and fear that does not blossom, sooner or later, into burden-bearing, is not the true fear of God. 'Knowing the terror of the Lord, we persuade men' (2 Cor 5:11). The fear of the Lord is nothing if not evangelical.

Where, then, does the false fear come from? It comes from Satan, who rejoices to see useless, fruitless Christians. It is one of his triumphs in our generation that he has taken God's holy Law and has thrust it into Christian hearts, and has twisted it and used it to produce a wrong fear of God, so paralysing and unnerving the most promising of God's children. Legalism is the curse of the evangelical church of our day, and it is a measure of the success of the demonic strategy that so many Christians live as though God were a ringmaster, whatever they confess Him to be with their lips. It is all wrong: wrong because it is Satanic, and wrong because it wounds and crushes men, and brings them into a bondage of shibboleths, of rules and regulations; into lives without liberty, without joy, without grace, without fruit. Circumscribed lives, hedged in, restricted, screwed up and chewed up. Lives without vision, without horizons. Little lives. Un-spacious lives.

If you have time, read the speech by Eliphaz in Job 4:12-5:1, in which he almost boasts of a vision he had by night, a nightmare experience in which a 'spirit' passes before his face, and fills him with terror and dismay. But is this horrific visitation from God? Does the fear it engenders come from Love Himself? The speech is true. It is the spirit behind the speech that is false, through and through. True words, spoken by a liar, even by the father of lies! (Jn 8:44).

More and more, therefore, I have come to suspect and distrust religion whose fear, however piously or even soundly expressed, is not the mainspring of care for the needy and the lost. Why is it that Christians have such a struggle to find words at the Prayer Meeting? It is not that they do not want to pray, for they do. Are we so overwhelmed by the majesty and power of God that we are struck dumb? It is beyond dispute that Satan can take even the greatness of God and use it to subdue us. It is paralysis that he is after! Or why do we have to suffer so much humbug, cant and unnatural solemnity in worship? Why is it that Christians find it so hard to relax and be their best selves in God's company? It is because there is an enemy of souls, who hates Christ, all who love Christ, and all who mean business with Christ. His goal is impotent Christians, and he is not fussy how he achieves his end, be it by legalism, tyranny or hypocrisy.

Take these words, and God will give you His Spirit of liberation and grace to make them your very own:

> 'God has not given us the Spirit of fear, but of power and of love and of a sound mind... Stand fast, therefore, in the liberty with which Christ has made us free, and do not be entangled again with the yoke of bondage... You shall know the truth, and the truth shall set you free... If therefore the Son shall make you free, you shall be free indeed!' (2 Tim 1:7; Gal 5:1; Jn 8:32,36).

Yours affectionately,
THOMAS SWANSTON

28
RIGORISM NOT FROM GOD*

My Dear Friends,
I could not begin to tell you how dismayed I get to see so many joyless, inhibited Christians in the world. I have in mind particularly some of the most progressive and careful souls in whom I have begun to see signs of a certain intensity and strain. Even when you eliminate all the normal causes of disaster in a saint's pilgrimage - demonic attack, or the legacy of uncrucified and lawless desires, or the guilt-laden heritage of unconfessed sin, or the harvests reaped from secret back-sliding - there still remains even in some earnest, well-meaning and consecrated lives, a rigorism that cannot come from God. Paul would have described it as a 'zeal for God... but not according to knowledge' (Rom 10:2). There can be, in an evangelical testimony, a drive, a pulse, a false dynamic that is not heaven-born at all, and whose ultimate aim is the destruction either of a believer's pleasure in Christ, or of his fruitfulness. Usually both.

I think especially of a young lad who has ruined himself, perhaps almost beyond repair, trying to be someone whom God never intended him to be. He talks a language, and apes evangelical modes and mannerisms, all quite alien to his true, natural nature. The result is that he has become a nervous, strained, mirthless, legalistic puppet; a caricature of what Jesus wants him to be. It will take years to heal his hurts. He has failed to learn what some others are failing to learn: that the grace of Christ has to operate within the limits of fallen human personality.

*January 1973

It is an arresting fact that our basic characters are formed early in life, long before we find Christ. Even for those who are saved in early or mid-teens, change can be hard; for salvation involves, at least in part, the undoing of the havoc wrought by sin in tender and impressionable years. It is much harder, on the other hand, to change later on in life. By the time we reach middle or old age we settle down to a comfortable existence that does not care for interference. Our characters have more or less hardened and, sad to say, our destinies are, by and large, fixed. So-called 'death bed repentances' are the exception rather than the rule, and understandably so. Once our attitudes and thinking have calcified and turned to stone, once our minds have become closed to new truth, there is little hope of salvation. Generally speaking, men die as they live. 'As the tree falls, so must it lie' (Eccles 11:3). I am not saying that folk cannot be converted in later years. I am saying that it is not for nothing that the Bible tells us to prepare for eternity and Judgment when we are still of a sensitive spirit. 'Remember now thy Creator in the days of thy youth, while the evil days come not...' (Eccles 12:1).

Both the Jesuits and Hitler realised the importance of these critical, formative years. ('Give us the child for the first five years and we will make him a Roman Catholic/Nazi for life.') It is here that the old Nature-and-Nurture controversy comes into its own. We are born into the world with a certain rudimentary genetic equipment (Nature) and this is unalterable, built in, inescapable. It may be shaped and modified, however, by our upbringing, our environment, schooling, home circumstances, associates (Nurture). Often it is the Nurture that determines what is to come out of the Nature - what is to be dominant in a man's personality, and what recessive and unexpressed. But the Gospel says that there is a third factor that breaks through into the Nature/Nurture set-up. It is the grace of Jesus, and brings salvation. Yet the salvation has to work within who and what we are constitutionally.

You will surely not now think that I, above all men, am trying to set boundaries to the power of God. The Bible does speak about a miserable generation who 'limited the Holy One of Israel' (Ps 78:41). They took it on themselves to decide what He could and could not do. Indisputably it is unbelief that normally hedges God in and prevents miracles. 'He could not do many mighty works there because of their unbelief' (Matt 13:58 and Mark 6:5). Some religious people expect nothing from Christ, and He answers their prayers! But I am not speaking about unbelievers, but about believers who do expect great things from Christ, but who expect too much by way of liberation and emancipation, and hurt themselves in the process. The 'full salvation' that we sing of can never be truly 'full' while we live in mortal, corruptible bodies. As the dry old worthy said: 'There's naethin' wrang wi' ony o' us that canna be cured by the General Resurrection.'

Here is how the Westminster Confession put it, in the chapter dealing with our becoming holier men and women: I will modernise the language:

> Those who are effectively called and given new natures, having a new heart and a new spirit created in them, are further made holy really and personally through the power of Christ's death and rising, by His Word and Spirit dwelling in them. The lordship of the whole body of sin has its sting drawn, and its various desires are more and more weakened and caused to die; and so Christians are more and more made alive and strong in all saving graces.

> The purpose is the practice of true holiness, without which no man shall see the Lord... This being made holy extends through the whole personality, but it is not perfected in this life. There still remain some remnants of corruption in every part of the personality, from which arises a ceaseless war-without-truce; the flesh warring against the Spirit, and the Spirit against the flesh.'

Or, consider this parable: when Jehovah took Israel into the Land, He promised to drive out their enemies 'little by little' (Ex 23:30), lest they should think that it was by their own carnal might that the salvation had come. Should this not help to take the tension out of our over-zealous, unrelaxed lives? A man with a bad speech defect cannot automatically expect to be cured of his stammering overnight simply because he happens to have found Christ. Only with sympathetic pastoral care and gentle oversight may he come to see that his stammering is possibly an escape mechanism he can afford to do without. There is a better Refuge!

Take a more serious case: here is someone with a major personality disorder: his life is distracted, demented, deranged and domineered by some frightful psychological condition. What Jesus offers such a man is deliverance in measure, compassion, room in which to breathe, and the power to be his very best twice-born self in the world of grace.

Or here is the man who has come up through a shocking, loveless, graceless childhood. He has been so crushed, bruised and bawled-at in his home that, in manhood, he has to shout at others, and be aggressive to be a 'somebody'. He has to fight in order to be heard, and any authoritative figure becomes his sparring partner. Of course the man is sick. Jesus offers him understanding, grace to overcome, and a love that accepts men in the context of Christian fellowship, prayer and care. Why not? Jesus saves actually as well as potentially.

Let this moving paragraph from C. S. Lewis have the last word, and comfort all who have ears to hear: in *Beyond Personality* he says:

> If you are a poor creature - poisoned by a wretched upbringing in some house full of vulgar jealousies and senseless quarrels - saddled, by no choice of your own, with some loathsome derangement of personality - nagged day in and day out by an inferiority complex that makes you snap at your best friends - do not despair! He knows all about it. You are one of the poor whom He blessed. He knows what a wretched machine you are trying to drive. Keep on. Do what you can. One day (perhaps in another world, but perhaps far sooner than that) he will fling it (your body) on the scrap heap and give you a new one. And then you may astonish us all - not least yourself: for you've learned your driving in a hard school. (Some of the last will be first, and some of the first will be last).

Have you got the message? I hope so. Be gentle with yourself. I will be looking for a few changes.

Yours most affectionately,
THOMAS SWANSTON

29
VOCATION IN YOUTH AND OLD AGE*

Dear Friends,
I want to speak to two anxious groups, at either end of the age scale - firstly to young Christian folk who suspect that God is passing them by in the choice of a life's partner, and then to older people who, by reason of age alone, feel set-aside, useless and 'ill'.

Much needless hurt has been caused by the improper and careless use of the word 'norm'. One hears of marriage described as the 'norm'. But this is not the case. It is not the will of God that all should be married, no more than it is His will that all should be single. Marriage is certainly more common than celibacy, and it is good that this should be so since without marriage the world would come to an end. But 'norm' is not the same as 'normal', and is the wrong word to use. Was Jesus 'abnormal' and only half a man because He was not married? Marriage is the 'norm' for those who are called to be married, as celibacy is the 'norm' for those called to be single. The norm, therefore, for a Christian is, in the first instance, neither marriage nor celibacy; the norm is the will of God. For some it is His will that they should be married; for others it is that they should be single. Man's chief end is not to find a partner, but to 'glorify God and enjoy Him for ever'. Some can do this married, and others can do it single. The question: 'Should I be single or married?' thus resolves itself into: 'Is the will of God on the throne of my life?'

Failure to appreciate these simple, elementary truths has opened up a highway to many errors. From time to time there

*January 1976

arise, often among the young, foolish cults and fashions in which celibacy is exalted - almost as if it were somehow a more sanctified state than marriage. The spiritual pride, which is the harvest reaped from the soil of such 'vain imaginations', would surely fill many barns in hell! Celibacy is no more sanctified than marriage if it is outside the will of God for a Christian's life. There is nothing 'holy' about remaining single if, in fact, you are called to be married; and there is nothing 'holy' about getting married if you called to be single for Christ's and the Gospel's sake. As Christians we have to discover who we are, and part of this involves knowing the strength and limitations of our personalities and the borders within which grace has to work. But once the Lord's will has been ascertained, there is no room at all for pride or superiority. 'Who are you to pass judgment on the servant of another? It is before his own master that he stands or falls. And he will be upheld, for the Master is able to make him stand... Why do you pass judgment on your brother? Or you, why do you despise your brother? For we shall all stand before the judgment seat of God' (Rom 14:4,10).

Jesus did speak about those who refrained from marriage for the kingdom's sake, adding that this saying would not be acceptable to all men (Matt 19:12). And Isaiah, too, tells of the special blessing reserved for the single and separate who keep God's sabbaths, assuring them that God will give them a name 'better than sons and daughters' (Is 56:5). But a Christian needs to be very sure indeed before committal is made to such a vocation. One cannot but give honour and credit, in this context, to those devoted souls (usually womenfolk) who, for the love of their own flesh and blood, and often for the sake of Jesus, have sacrificed prospects of marriage and of family life. I dislike the expression 'old maid'. One cannot help being 'old'. We are 'old' because we happen to have been born at a particular time; we have no choice in the matter. And since when was virtue ('maid') a fault and occasion for ridicule? Are the testimonies of the Mary Slessors, the Florence Nightingales and the Gladys Aylwards of this world to count for nothing?

For the impatient and frustrated my counsel is this: commit your case to the Lord. Entrust your plea with Him. Whatever He has in store for you will be His very highest for your life. He will not offer you second-best. He loves His children, and delights to bless with His richest and sweetest for their lives. His will for you, whether it be celibacy or marriage, will never be anything other than 'good and acceptable and perfect' (Rom 12:2). It is no profanity to suggest that, for your own peace of mind, the will of God for your life is not your concern but His. 'Cast your burden on the Lord.' 'Casting all your care upon Him, for He cares for you.' Sanctified patience such as this brings its own rewards in pleasurable and God-honouring service.

What, then, does Jesus have to offer? For most, marriage; for the rest, celibacy; for all, chastity. We are called either to chaste celibacy or to chaste marriage, the one as pure and as Christ-centred as the other. True-hearted celibacy, or true-hearted marriage - these are the alternatives, for all men.

To the older folk let me say this: age is not a disease. It is simply another stage in life and has a beauty and usefulness all its own. Of course, we do tend to slow down a little when we get on in years! There are certain things we cannot do simply because the organism will not cope. Here, as in many other airts, the spirit is willing but the flesh is weak. But you are not 'ill' just because you are old. In fact, there are many elderly people who - in terms of mental outlook and good spirits - are far healthier than some youngsters. Well-being has really little to do with age: it is a question of attitudes to life, and especially of relationship with Jesus. It is because the lie is believed (age=disease) that so many lapse into apathy and helplessness, and become needlessly pitiful. They begin to neglect personal appearance, or fail in domestic duties, or stop coming to worship ('I'm not so able now'). In some cases the reasons are genuine; but in many, I fear, folk have fallen victims to the lie.

The Scriptures have a word of hope addressed to this very situation. 'They still bring forth fruit in old age... to show that the Lord is upright' (Ps 92:14,15). 'And your life will be brighter than the noonday; its darkness will be like the morning. And you will have confidence, because there is hope; you will be protected and take your rest in safety. You will lie down, and none will make you afraid' (Job 11:17-19). 'Even to your old age, I am He, and to grey hairs I will carry you. I have made, and I will bear; I will carry and will save' (Is 46:4). Can it be therefore, that there are people who really come into their Christian own, and so be their evangelical best, only when they enter 'retirement'? Fruit-bearing in old age - there's a word of promise! In its light, have you yet found your ministry?

The Lord's own loving-kindness and grace be on you in 1976.

With affectionate esteem,
THOMAS SWANSTON

30
FRUITFULNESS IN OLD AGE*

My Dear Friends,
It is a striking fact of life these days that the generations are living to riper and fuller years. This is witnessed to by the mushrooming, in our society, of specialised homes and hospitals for the care of the aged, the geriatric and the confused elderly. While the State tries to handle this area of concern as best it may, private nursing homes also multiply to help cope with the problems brought on by gathering years and frailty.

The problems are occasioned by the reality that not only are we, in general, tending to live longer, but old people, in particular, are surviving into more advanced years - a very different problem! For better or for worse, by the skills of science and the expertise of modern medicine, life is being prolonged more and more. As Christians we must acknowledge that this has happened under the good providence and the wise permissions of God.

But how are we to approach the problems? A Christian gentleman in my last congregation often told me how he prayed every day that the Lord would save him from ' a cantankerous old age'. But old age need not necessarily be cantankerous; nor need it be fruitless or useless for Christ. We are told that when Moses came to his latter end he was very active, vital and alive at one hundred and twenty years! 'Moses was a hundred and twenty years old when he died; his eye was not dim, nor his natural force abated' (Deut 34:7). In our 'declining years' we are not obliged to decline and lapse

*March 1988

into becoming pathetic souls. On the contrary, as Christians we ought to encourage ourselves to lay hold on what the Word of God has to say about advancing, and advanced years.

Some of the most precious words in the Bible have to do with old age, and some of the most cherished and hopeful promises are given to the elderly. And there is good reason for this: in Scripture a value and a worth are set on age that are not set on the young. The compiler of Proverbs expresses the sentiment so: 'The glory of young men is their strength, but the beauty of old men is their grey hair' (20:29). Job touches on much the same idea when he says: 'Wisdom is with the aged, and understanding in length of days' (12:12). This does not mean, of course, that we do not find foolishness in the old; nor does it mean that wise heads cannot be found on young shoulders. Better a mature eighteen year old than an eighty year old who has refused to grow up! Experience does show that there are many old fools as well as youthful sages. But Scripture suggests that, on balance, the elderly who have had the gumption to learn wisdom in the hard school of life are to be offered respect, homage, reverence and worship. Therefore God gives loving and beautiful words of assurance and comfort for old age. Consider the following verses.

Upon thee I have leaned from my birth;
thou art he who took me from my mother's womb.
Do not cast me off in the time of old age;
forsake me not when my strength is spent.
O God, from my youth thou has taught me,
and I still proclaim thy wondrous deeds.
So even to old age and grey hairs,
O God, do not forsake me,
till I proclaim thy might
to all the generations to come (Psalms 71:6,9,17-18).

The righteous flourish like the palm tree,
and grow like a cedar in Lebanon.
They are planted in the house of the Lord,
they flourish in the courts of our God.
They still bring forth fruit in old age,
they are ever full of sap and green,
to show that the Lord is upright;
He is my rock,
and there is no unrighteousness in Him (Psalm 92:12-15).

Even to your old age I am He,
and to grey hairs I will carry you.
I have made, and I will bear;
I will carry and will save (Isaiah 46:4).

In the light of such precious promises it is dreadfully wrong that age should be associated, in many minds, with futility and emptiness. Not all old folk are Christians, of course. Yet it can truthfully be said that even some Christians fritter away their last years in vain pursuits - reading little, watching inane shows on television, obsessed with health, preoccupied with crosswords and taken up by trivia. The truth is that our spacious years of retirement have been given to us by God for a purpose. They ought to be the best years of our lives in terms of usefulness for Christ in quality service.

Think of the Levites who ministered in holy things in the tabernacle. They retired at the age of fifty; but they did not retire into indolence, vacuity and nothingness. 'And the Lord said to Moses: 'From twenty years old and upward they shall go in to perform the work in the service of the tent of meeting; and from the age of fifty years they shall withdraw from the work of the service and serve no more... to keep the charge...'

(Num 9:23-26). The last phrase can mean 'to keep watch' or 'to keep guard'. I am persuaded that God gives us these extra years in order that we may become prayer warriors 'keeping watch' over the work and 'keeping guard' over the service of Christ from the mountain top, as Moses prayed on high while the battle with Amalek raged below in the valley.

Consider how many dejected ministers and struggling congregations could be blessed beyond measure by such intercession! Think of how many struggling servants of Christ on mission fields, at home and abroad, might suddenly find their workload lightened, the pressures eased, the battle grow less intense... and all because the work of mediatorial prayer had been multiplied! Fruitbearing in old age is no idle dream but rather a heart-warming and glorious reality. But let the sweet singer of Israel have the last word, both of promise and of invitation:

Those that within the house of God
 are planted by His grace,
They shall grow up, and flourish all
 in our God's holy place.
And in old age, when others fade,
 they fruit still forth shall bring;
They shall be fat, and full of sap,
 and aye be flourishing (Metrical Psalm 92:13-14).

Yours affectionately,
THOMAS SWANSTON

PS: For the ignorant, old age is as winter, for the learned, it is a harvest (Jewish proverb).

31
ADOLESCENT SEXUALITY*

Dear Friends,

On Wednesday 5th July of this year (1978), Dr. James Hemming, an author and educational psychologist, spoke to a conference of teachers and youth workers in London. The event was sponsored by the Brook Advisory Centre and Dr. Hemming's theme was the constantly recurring one of our need to come to terms with adolescent sexuality.

In the course of his lecture he maintained that if adults fail to accept that adolescents are likely to become sexually active as they grow through teenage years, the sexual development of the growing young is likely to become distorted. 'If adolescents are not allowed to develop responsible love relationships with one another during the late teenage years,' he said, 'the alternative will not be chastity and assiduous application to school work but fantasy... and an obsession about sex.' Our failure to accept adolescent sexuality has induced a sideslip away from reality towards deviation, substitution and disillusionment. Child assault... and other sexual deviations were the result of a society ill educated about sex. 'This is not a call to wild permissiveness. The morality of sex starts with its acceptance. Once we bring sex into the open as a desirable part of human experience we are in a position to develop the real values of sex: honesty in relationships, sensitivity, self-respect, concern for one another, and responsibility for seeing that no children are conceived before a stable, happy home has been securely established for them.'

*January 1979

He went on to aver that 'the no-sex-before-marriage enthusiasts' were in a 'completely untenable position'. 'Old-style sexual inhibition has a very bad track record. We have around us today not only high figures for divorce but also hosts of frustrated marriages, sexless marriages and emotionally cold marriages, which need never have happened if the partners had had a chance to achieve sexual maturity by the natural processes of growth and development.' It was now accepted by most people that students at university and in colleges were likely to be sexually active, but an equal acceptance was denied to young adults at school. It was necessary to reverse that attitude, and for schools to provide information and support.

What truly appals the Christian spirit in such an approach to the problems of adolescent sexuality is the failure to introduce any absolute standard of moral conduct, the failure to appeal to any final court for arbitration. We certainly have come a long way from the Ten Commandments here! I wonder if Kierkegaard and Jean-Paul Sartre, the high priests of the 'existential' thinking that laid the foundations for today's permissive morality, ever supposed that their philosophies would come thus far? And I wonder if the worthy Karl Barth, the theologian and churchman who put existential thinking into religious clothes, ever intended that matters would end like this? I am not concerned to attack any one man for, in fact, such views are widely held nowadays; if one could scratch a little beneath the surface of the teachings of some humanistic educationists and child psychologists, one might find much the same sort of outlook, viz. there are no 'absolutes' in morality. Extra-marital sex is not necessarily wrong, and may be all right if conducted within 'responsible' relationships, or if carried on in the 'context of meaningful love'.

But even the most avant-garde and advanced of views

leave us with even greater problems for, if you allow that young people develop in different ways and at different rates, who will say when an adolescent is 'responsible' enough for love? And who will determine the marks of a 'responsible' relationship? And who will judge when youngsters have fallen into 'meaningful love' with each other? Surely the evidence of Christian history suggests that true love is a much 'harder' thing than is dreamed of in some of these new-fangled, high falutin' systems? Real love is often hard to come by and, once won, has to be soldiered and weathered through many a battle and storm. And this is amply testified to in the New Testament which says that: 'Love does not insist on its own way; is not irritable or resentful; does not rejoice at wrong, but rejoices in the right. Love bears all things, believes all things, hopes all things, endures all things' (1 Cor 13:5-7). One appreciates more and more how superficial and shallow folk who 'fall in love' can just as easily fall 'out of love' again, for what they found was not love at all. The truth about true love is deeper and stronger and fiercer and harder than is to be plumbed by decadent, effete, do-as-you-please moralities. It is best seen by eyes that have been opened to the beauty of Him who was Love Incarnate, Love made flesh, among us; Love made man; and Love made sin.

And it is a little strange to find Hemming speaking of adults failing to accept that adolescents are 'likely to become sexually active' throughout teenage years. Surely grown-ups are, almost to the point of distraction, all too aware of the difficulties? And surely no generation has had matters of sexuality so thoroughly aired? At worst we are besieged by sex - from billboards and hoardings, from advertisements in which luscious ladies commend to us the unlikeliest of products, and from the magic box with its endless succession of indifferent 'comedy' shows with their filthy talk, their low innuendo, and their salacious double-entendres. How could any adults fail to notice adolescents 'coming alive' to sex in an environment so saturated with it? And at best sexual counsel is being given, sometimes with surprising sympathy and tact and discretion, in senior schools as well as in the home (the proper place for it) by wise and compassionate parents.

Of course, some parents are careless, and are either so neglectful that they fail to school the young through the difficult years of puberty, or else are so embarrassed by their own sexuality that they shelve the matter and pass the responsibility on to others. And also, of course, the schools may fail. But, succeed or fail, we cannot doubt that adults are aware of the growing powers latent within their sons and daughters. Surely the most primitive societies, with their scrupulous oversight of initiation rites, should teach us how careful and guarded adults generally are over the years of 'growing up'. More harmful is the suggestion that the sexual aberrations of our time come from ' a society ill-educated about sex' i.e. that the root of the problem is ignorance and poor education. Since the answer to ignorance is enlightenment, it should follow that when men are enlightened and educated the problems will disappear. But none of this reckons with the darker recesses of human nature. We are not, by nature, morally neutral; nor are we born virtuous and good and requiring only some education to 'lead us out'. Our trouble is that we are biased towards the evil; a man may be, as C. S. Lewis reminds us, a well-educated devil. And youngsters who are well-informed on matters of sex are not automatically thereby balanced, mature, responsible and caring for others. I have known 'informed' adolescents, infinitely practised in erotic affairs, who were also cold and hard, callous and without consciences, consumed with illicit and unbridled lust. Enlightenment and knowledge of themselves do not secure virtue! It takes Jesus Christ to do that, for only New Men, born again of the Spirit of God, men with new natures can live life as God meant it to be lived - abundantly and cleansed by the Blood of Christ.

I have been taken with a review recently published in *Voice,* a student outreach paper, in which Ron Shammotto gives a critique of two 'X' certificate films - *Shampoo* and *Last Tango in Paris.* Both films present a serious view of the seventies' obsession with sex. The audience for *Shampoo* may well settle back and prepare itself for a giggle at a sexual romp on a 'higher level' than some of the *Carry On* films. But *Shampoo* has a sting in the tail and portrays the disillusionment, the ashes, the disenchantment, the bitterness that are the invariable harvests reaped when people are used as 'objects', and when sex is treated as only a vehicle for personal pleasure. 'The end of the film is effectively unsettling, leaving the audience with the tragedy of misused sexual freedom... these films present the tragedy of a cheapened view of sex, but *prescribe no positive answers*...Christians view sex as the physical seal on a permanent relationship between man and woman - not as a cheap source of pleasure or escape. For the Christian, love leads to a permanent commitment between man and woman, of which sex is both the symbol and a crucial part...such a view means that in practice, the cheapness, heartbreak, frustration and often tragedy of depersonalized sex is avoided.'

And how odd to find so responsible and senior a man saying that the 'no-sex-before-marriage enthusiasts' are in a 'completely untenable position'. Was Moses wrong after all? And God before him unto all eternity? And Jesus, and Paul, and Augustine, and Luther, and Calvin? And all the Christians of every communion of all the ages? Are they all wrong and in a 'completely untenable position'? Does not the devil in Hemming go too far? And there is no evidence to suggest that 'old-style sexual inhibition' does anything but good when energies are channelled into worthwhile, caring activities. There is not much sign of a 'bad track record' in the lives of such folk as Florence Nightingale, Mary Slessor and Gladys Aylward! And what of the marvellous Henry Martyn who sacrificed marriage for the Gospel's sake, and whose biography *My Love Must Wait* by David Bentley-Taylor is a classic, and compulsory reading for Christian adolescents?

Shampoo and *Last Tango in Paris* are said to 'prescribe no positive answers'. But Christians do have a Book which not only faces honestly the problems of human sexuality, problems brought upon us by nature and by choice, but which also gives answers - and in those answers opens up a whole new world for the questing, seeking young - a world of vistas and avenues of hopeful, positive, creative, clean living. Seemingly few of the smart-Alicks at the top today will call unlawful sex by the old names - fornication and adultery.

But the Bible does not fear to call sin, sin. All that Jesus offers to anyone, man or woman, is a life of chastity and devotion to Himself. We are either chaste and single, in which case we are celibate; or else we are chaste and married. There is no middle way with our great and glorious and uncompromising Saviour. In either case, chaste and single or chaste and married, He offers us His best for us, since He cannot give less than that to those whom He loves so well. And in either case, single or married, it is for the edifying of the church, for the building up of His Body, for the feeding of His sheep, for the good of our fellows and, in all of this, for His own praise and glory.

Herein is divine simplicity. Herein are health, love, laughter, bliss and life eternal - rich and unfrustrated. Herein is wisdom. Take it, and be free.

THOMAS SWANSTON

PS: 'Existentialism' in its early days, was a way of looking at life; it was a philosophy of 'existence'. However, it tended to move away from the idea of 'revealed' religion. Morality, therefore, was not an absolute affair, handed to us and required from us by God; it was an 'ad hoc' business, i.e. you made up your morals as you went along. What was right for one situation was not necessarily right for another situation. Hence the well-known phrases 'permissive morality' and 'situational ethics' i.e. ethics you think up for the situation in hand. On the secular side existentialism moved into humanism and atheism. On the religious side it moved into the sort of thinking about the Bible advocated by Barth who said that the Bible was not the Word of God; it only *became* the Word of God when it registered on the heart. This, of course, raises serious problems, for who is to say what parts of the Bible are the Word and what are not?

32
LONELINESS*

Dear Friends,
Several years ago in America a study was made of the theme of loneliness in modern society. In answer to the question: 'What, for you, is the loneliest night of the week?' a significant majority answered: 'Saturday'. One does not normally associate Saturday evening with loneliness. That is traditionally a night for company, good or otherwise, for public entertainment and mirth. It is an evening consecrated to dining out and socialising. Yet this group of interviewees thought that that was the evening when loneliness most overcame and overwhelmed them.

I am not speaking here about the 'good' loneliness of which Hubert van Zeller writes thus: 'The soul hardly ever realises it but, whether he is a believer or not, his loneliness is really a homesickness for God.' That longing, the ache for one's true home and lasting country, has been planted in the heart by God. By it deep calls unto deep. The only 'answer' to that aloneness is the Beatific Vision, the sight of God and of Him who is 'distinguished among ten thousand' to the yearning soul (Song of Solomon 5:10). 'Your eyes will see the king in his beauty; they will behold a land that stretches afar' (Isa 33:17). Homesickness can be cured only by home.

Of the 'bad' loneliness much can be said, and it appears that ours, par excellence, is a generation that has bred just such desolation. The paradox - and a maddening and tantalising one it is - is that we tend more and more to live together in crowded communities. Towns and cities grow hideously

*January 1983

larger year by year; multi-storey flats and tenements compel men to huddle together in close proximity; and schools, under the banner of comprehensiveness, are expanded to Gargantuan proportions. Yet the loneliness persists. It is the secret pain that will not go away.

There is a word on everyone's lips these days: it is the word 'alienation'. Twentieth century man is alienated from his fellows and from God. Children are alienated from their parents, as many parents are from each other. Man is alienated from his work since he rarely sees the end-product of his labours. Overwhelmed by secularism and materialism, and gorged by instant pleasure and entertainment, man is estranged from any sense of eternity, of another world and of his answerability to God.

Such aloneness, in a sense, is a primary mark of the human condition. Life is, after all, a series of separations. At birth we are separated from the safety and security of the womb. As ancient Time devours the years we are sundered from infancy, from childhood, from youth, from middle age and from life itself. Death divides us from dearest loved ones, and strips us naked to stand before the Throne. There is a touching pathos in the words of Thomas Wolfe: 'The whole conviction of my life now rests upon the belief that loneliness, far from being a rare and curious phenomenon, peculiar to myself and to a few other solitary men, is the central and inevitable fact of human existence.'

And the loneliness comes at us persistently in all sorts of ways. One thinks of the desolation of the single lass who, eschewing marriage, has given her life to caring for aged parents. One thinks of the aloneness of those with deep, intractable psychological and emotional problems. One thinks of folk blighted by the curse of inadequate personalities, ceaselessly struggling to cope. One thinks of the forlornness of those stricken by grief in the passing of loved ones. John Milton wrote well when he said that loneliness is the first thing which God's eye named 'not good' (Gen 2:18). It is one of the scourges of our age and few are exempt from its ravages.

'Essentially loneliness is the knowledge that one's fellow human beings are incapable of understanding one's condition, and therefore are incapable of bringing the help most needed. It is not a question of companionship - many are ready to offer this, and companionship is certainly not to be despised - but rather one of strictly sharing, of identifying. No two human beings can manage this, so, to a varying extent, loneliness at times is the lot of all' (Hubert van Zeller).

For my own part I confess that I speak from a position of weakness: I do not know the meaning of loneliness. I am never alone and never feel that I am alone. This is partly due to a self-sufficiency, a stalwart independence, even an insularity, which I inherited from my mother's family. But it is also partly due to the fact that I have always found life to be far too short for all the things I want to do, the books I would like to read, the places I would like to visit, the people I would like to meet. Long before desolation has even begun to gnaw at my peace, my wellbeing and integrity, I simply dander off and do something creative or useful - cook a meal, work at a tapestry, read poetry or write a new hymn tune. These ploys are not escapism. I am not running away from loneliness. There is simply no need for me to do so.

One would wish also to separate loneliness from solitude, the two being very different. The delights of the latter are among God's richest boons to man, taking in the pleasures of reflection and self-examination, the leisure to commune intimately with Jesus, and the luxuriant, holy joys of the quiet place. As Paul Tillich puts it finely: 'Language has created the word 'loneliness' to express the pain of being alone, and the word 'solitude' to express the glory of being alone.'

There are, of course, lonely people who are responsible for their condition. They are among the most tragic and pitiful souls in all creation. The lady who has been brought up by her parents to believe (often without much foundation!) that she is a cut above the other girls and superior to them, and who has been foolish enough to believe that this is really the case, cannot seriously complain when she is shunned and ignored for the snob that she is. The man who makes success his idol, and who ruthlessly brushes out of his way anyone or anything that stands between him and the fulfilment of his ambitions, is destined for an old age of loneliness and ashes. He may have made a great deal of money; he may have been awarded a peerage; he may surround himself with business acquaintances; he may (and probably will) have compassed himself with various luxuries. But he will be on his own.

The neurotic who is utterly incapable of projecting himself into someone else's problems, but who endlessly talks about himself, his family and his woes, is simply isolating himself from the sympathy and true love of his fellows. Why should such a person lament when no-one ever calls on a basis of friendship, when the telephone never rings and when no invitations arrive? Such folk are like Bunyan's Mr. Cumberground: they are a weariness to the earth.

How responsible are we for our loneliness? There is undoubtedly a massive blindness in all of us, a blindness to our true selves and to our motives. We often see only what we want to see, hear what we want to hear, and admit what it is convenient for us to admit. Yet man is not totally blind, and God has left us with some insights. This being so, what has been refused in this matter of loneliness is nothing less than a radical death to self. 'The Lord turned the captivity of Job when he prayed for his friends.' In order to be free and fulfilled the Ego must die. Every Christian is summoned to enter into that death to self which Jesus died, once for all, for every believer. To be a Christian at all, according to the New Testament, is to have died thus with Him, and to have risen also with Him to newness of life, to life abundant.

I am persuaded that there is no final lasting 'cure' for loneliness in this world. To seek for such is to pursue 'a vain thing, fondly imagined'. I am equally as persuaded that friendship with Christ - rich, intimate and satisfying as this is - is the nearest we shall ever get to assuaging the pains and the imperious anguish of being alone. Like all worthwhile relationships this needs to be worked at, in private and in public, as well on one's own as in the society of His other friends.

I close by asking some of the fringey, peripheral 'evangelicals' among us: 'Have you noticed that Jesus has other friends in our congregation?' And if, as Joseph Fort Newton observes: 'People are lonely because they build walls instead of bridges', has the time not come for you to start becoming a pontifex (bridge-builder)? If you do precisely that there is no good reason why Saturday night should be lonely or, for that matter, any other night of the week.

Yours affectionately,
THOMAS SWANSTON

33
INADEQUATE PERSONALITIES*

Dear Friends,

It is possible for societies to survive without Gospel grace: Buddhist and Moslem ones have been doing so for centuries. No society, however, can survive without law, whether spiritual, moral or civil; and it is our present British tragedy that we have renounced both grace and law as touchstones of, and guides to, healthy living. We will not have the world of grace (mercy, salvation, forgiveness, and so on), nor will we have the world of law (the fear of justice, submission to authority, personal honesty and integrity etc.). The inevitable end-product of such a society is personal chaos.

When the foundations of any culture are shaken, when the basics are questioned, when the ground beneath men's feet is taken away, when the standards of sound judgment are removed, the last bitter fruits are broken lives, unhappy hearts, homes ruined by drink, lust and violence; shattered hopes; morals breached in the name of liberation, and bodies abused and spoiled by sin.

It is, perhaps, almost inevitable that such a society, grace-rejecting and law-rejecting, should throw up increasing numbers of inadequate personalities. Practically every fellowship has, in measure, its share of problematic folk, many of whom find difficulty in coping with life. It is, of course, no more possible to 'define' an inadequate personality than it is to define an adequate one, but the causes are fairly standard and long recognised: the loveless, joyless childhood; heartless and insensitive parents who have no deep,

*January 1988

trusting relationships with their children; a spirit of bullying in the home, when the impressionable young are chivvied around as if they were mere objects.

Inadequate personalities, coming out of all of this (and out of much more), are in the unfortunate position of being in a kind of no-man's land. They are not so sick that they need specialist care; nor are they so healthy that they can fit in with other people, and lead a 'normal', constructive, helpful existence. They are in a sort of limbo, a shadow-land, an in-between country where they have neither found nor lost their true selves. On the whole they have sad lives, laden with various kinds of unhappiness, and they rarely seem to rise above their personal struggles, emotional instability and 'nerves'. They tend to live underneath circumstances rather than above them. And even when they come to know Jesus as Saviour and Friend they often fail to enter into that fullness of life abundant which is His promised bounty to all who trust Him.

It is important to realise that an inadequate personality has one aim in life - to achieve importance by becoming 'somebody'. Somehow he has to compensate for his private weaknesses, and all sorts of devices are used to that end. We are all familiar with the leather-jacketed young man of a former generation, plastered with badges ('Keep the Pope off the moon' and 'It is wrong to eat people' and 'Love me for my own sake'). The lad is looking for an identity. He is really going around asking the world: 'Who am I?' He is also trying hard to hide his frightened little self beneath his armour of leather gear and brass studs!

The malingerer, too, whose life is a dreary recital of back aches, headaches, and 'off-days' and who 'enjoys' poor health, is trying to cover up his personal inadequacies behind a mask of feigned sickness. The last thing he desires is to be well. Sympathy is what he wants, to minister to his egocentricity.

But there are other less innocent ways of achieving importance. Inadequate personalities often become inveterate, consummate gossips. The real strength and triumph of the tale-bearer is that he (but substitute 'she' throughout if you wish) knows something that the other does not. That is his strength. If the other party has already heard the tit-bit, the gossip's strength is gone unless he takes the original tale and adds to it, embellishes and adorns it. And once the story becomes general knowledge the whisperer lapses into unimportance; he becomes a nobody again.

I am not suggesting that all gossips are fundamentally inadequate personalities. The reasons why folk turn to talebearing are legion. Some women, for example, turn to gossip because they are secretly disappointed with marriage, or because they find their husbands boorish, or because they are bored to distraction with the humdrum nature of domestic life. But every gossip, at heart, is a failure in one way or another.

Inadequate souls are also known for the way in which they try to cultivate the friendship of 'stronger' personalities. Ministers, doctors and other professional people are regular targets, I am sorry to say. The point of the exercise is that failures and shortcomings can be hidden underneath the umbrella of the 'stronger' friend. Social-climbing and status-seeking are by-products of this urge. Name-dropping, too, is a mark of inferiority allied to this. But people who have found their true selves and who, like Jesus, can be at home and at ease in any society, do not need to drop names in order to achieve importance. They already are important by virtue of the fact that they have found their true selves in Christ. In my judgment and experience such friendships (and they often start by being too fierce, too hot, too sudden, too soon) are doomed not to last. How could they last, or be of God, when they are not built on a sure foundation? How can a relationship endure when one party is constantly possessed, and the other is a possessor frantically seeking fulfilment?

The point is well illustrated, though with a different relationship, by C. S. Lewis in the story of Mrs. Fidget. She 'lived for her family'. You could tell by the hunted looks in their eyes! If ever, pleasure-bent, they went out for the evening, mother always sat up waiting for them, no matter how late the hour, her sad, wan, dedicated face acting as a kind of rebuke. Personal liberty was a luxury they were never allowed, for their lives were utterly possessed by Mamma. Then she died. 'The Vicar said Mrs. Fidget is now at rest. Let us hope she is. What's quite certain is that her family are.'

Again, there is the flight into the world of 'Christian service'. Many men and women go into Gospel work to escape their true selves. Perhaps the truth is that they have never found out who they are, and hope to do so in 'service'. They are trying to become 'somebodies' in the world of 'doing' rather in the world of 'being'. But I should have thought that the first area in which the servant of God must find and prove himself is prayer.

Stephen, you will recall, was one of the deacons in the early church. He was a worker, a serving man. But the Bible tells us that he was also 'full of faith and the Holy Spirit... full of grace and power' (Acts 6:5,8). He already was a somebody in himself, in Jesus, before he became a somebody for others. A man who puts his 'service to the church' before prayer is simply shirking his spiritual responsibilities; he is evading the challenge of the truth.

Was this what was wrong with Demas? He forsook Paul 'in love with this present world' (2 Tim 4:10) and went to

Thessalonica. But why Thessalonica? Certainly there had been a mighty moving of the Spirit there. Was Demas going to Thessalonica to hide his secret bankruptcy behind a facade of Christian business? And is the church of the living God not already too full of prayerless busybodies?

But what is to be done with inadequate personalities? I am sorry if this sounds a little hard but, first of all, inadequate people have to be kept strictly but lovingly in their place. They are not to be allowed to exercise their petty, private tyrannies within a fellowship; they are not to lord it over others; they are not to domineer and boss their fellow Christians around. There is no aggression in the world quite like that of a possessive, inadequate soul! It is utterly wrong that an immature, half-developed few should ruin the joy and harmony that ought to be found within an integrated church. Inadequate folk must be contained, if that is not too strong a word, and that for their own good as well as for the good of others.

Only then can the second process begin: such folk must be shown exceptional Christian care and treated with loving patience. The Gospel, by its very nature, is bound to attract poor souls, which is partly why there are so many needy folk in Christian fellowships. And if we are inclined to criticise and censure, we should think of how dreadful they would be without Christ! It could be argued that the message of Jesus, almost by definition, is for the 'poor in spirit', and comes as 'glad tidings of great joy' to the inadequate. Everyone in heaven will have confessed to bankruptcy at some point or other, but Paul suggest that God has allowed inadequate souls into the church for a very special reason and almost of necessity: 'the parts of the body which seem to be weaker are indispensable, and those parts of the body which we think less honourable we invest with the greatest honour, and our unpresentable parts are treated with the greater modesty, which our more presentable parts do not require. But God has so adjusted the body, giving the greater honour to the inferior part, that there may be no discord in the body, but that the members may have the same care for one another. If one member suffers, all suffer together; if one member is honoured, all rejoice together' (1 Cor 12:22-26); but the whole passage from v14 onwards is a lesson on Christian care.

Contained and cared-for, that's the recipe for the inadequate, but especially the latter, for it is marvellous what can be achieved when, with dignity, we learn to face the limitations of our personalities and so, within the strictures imposed by sin, live fruitfully and with good cheer. It is all summed up in the kinds of peace we have in the once-for-all death of the Peace-maker: we are reconciled to God, to each other, and to ourselves. What Shaloms are there for those who care to explore!

Yours very affectionately,
THOMAS SWANSTON

34
THE MIND IN THE LIFE OF A CHRISTIAN*

Dear Friends,
The part played by the mind in the life of the Christian has always fascinated me, and I want to write of that now.

Few would, or could, doubt that the theme is of some urgency and importance in our time. We are the children of an age in which the emphasis in Gospel work is on 'spiritual experiences', 'happenings' and inner feelings rather than on any thinking approach to the faith once for all delivered to the saints (Jude 3). 'The trouble with you Calvinists,' as someone said to me, 'is that you are far too interested in truth.' Too interested in truth? Can such a thing be? If God is the God of truth, if His Son, Christ Jesus, is truth incarnate and if the Holy Ghost is the Spirit of truth, can we afford not to be too interested in truth? I am happy to see that John Stott has a fine address on this very subject, entitled simply: *The place of the mind in the Christian.* But if few would doubt the urgency of the theme equally few could question the insistence of Scripture on the primacy of the use of our intellectual faculties in both the absorbing and imparting of the Gospel.

Consider the following verses. They are far from exhaustive and have to do with mental application and activity:

> 'You shall love the Lord your God with all your heart, and with all your soul, *and with all your mind*' (Jesus' summing up of the second table of the Law in Matt 22:37).
> 'Do not be conformed to this world, but be transformed *by the renewal of your mind*' (Paul's call to Christian surrender and consecration in Rom 12:2).

*October 1988

'Let everyone be fully convinced *in his own mind*' (Paul urging the need for discernment in 'doubtful things' in Rom 14:5).
'We have received not the spirit of the world, but the Spirit which is from God, *that we might understand*... The unspiritual man... *is not able to understand*... But we have *the mind of Christ*' (1 Cor 2:12,14,16).
'I will pray with the spirit and I will pray *with the mind also;* I will sing with the spirit and I will sing *with the mind also'* (1 Cor 14:15).
'Do not be children in your thinking; be babes in evil, but *in your thinking be mature'* (1 Cor 14:20).
'Do not be quickly shaken *in mind'* (2 Thess 2:2).
'Be renewed *in the spirit of your minds'* (Eph 4:23).
'Set your minds on things that are above' (Col 3:2).
'By faith *we understand*' (Heb 11:3)
'Gird up *your minds!'* (1 Pet 1:13)
'We know that the Son of God has come, and has given us *understanding to know* Him who is true' (1 John 5:20).

I can recall how forcibly I was struck by this neglect of the mind in Christian circles when I addressed a gathering of educated and highly qualified professionals some years ago. Within their own disciplines many of these men and women had reached the top in their careers, and the majority were monumentally skilled and gifted. But private conversation revealed that although these experts had applied their intellects to some success in professional matters they had somehow, and for some reason, set aside their intellects when it came to the things of the Spirit. On the Gospel message some had views which could be judged to be incredibly naive and simplistic. It was almost as if there were some blockage and hindrance to Christian growth, maturity and advancement. The 'simple Gospel' was seen by many to be merely a part of the Bible. The idea that the whole of Scripture is, in one way or another, Good News, did not appear to have entered their heads. But Jesus said: 'Man shall not live by bread alone, but by *every word* that proceeds from the mouth of God'. Every word? Yes indeed - every word, without qualification! Could it really be the case that because they had been moderately successful in one area of life i.e. the academic, the scholarly and the professional, they mistakenly imagined that this automatically qualified them in another area i.e. the spiritual?

The issue arose recently in a discussion which I had with my brother minister, David Easton. We talked of people's motives in churchgoing. He pointed out, shrewdly, that nowadays many worshippers tend to go to church to be soothed, comforted, to find wholeness and meaning, and to bathe in what the Victorians would have recognised as 'the odour of sanctity'. Sermons are expected on the themes of 'courage to face the challenges of today', or 'hope for tomorrow's world' or 'uplift for your personal problems'. But in former generations worshippers went to church to be informed, instructed, taught, disciplined, subjected to the Word of God and armed for spiritual warfare. What has happened is that the activity of the understanding has been set at a discount. The mental grasp of the propositional truths of the Gospel has been put aside, and feelings and inwardness and personal reactions have taken its place. It is now man who occupies the stage rather than God. Even in our religion we can be consumed with self-centredness!

Take, for instance, the traditional division of our personalities into mind, heart, conscience and will. The 'mind' is the cognitive part: it absorbs the truths, facts and data that are fed to it. It has to do with understanding and apprehension. The 'heart' is the feeling part. With it we love, treasure affections, move and are moved and exercise compassion, care and tenderness. The 'conscience' is the fearing part of our natures. It is the secret alarm clock installed by God to be sensitive to the approach of sin. With it we are conscious of righteousness, of the holiness of God and of the fundamental difference between what is right and what is wrong. It is essentially the sentinel in the citadel of Mansoul. The 'will' is the doing part. With it we respond in practical ways to the Word and will of God. With it we bow the knee to Christ in action and service for Him and for the cause of the Evangel of grace.

Modern psychologists would, of course, challenge and question this understanding of man's nature. The approach taken today tends to be 'holistic', seeing man as a single unit, a living soul with separate but integrating parts. But the primitive picture of mind, heart, conscience and will still holds good, for all its faults; and Scripture teaches that the first appeal of the Gospel is to our minds. It has pleased God to make Himself known to us in propositional truths, in statements that are true in themselves. In Schaeffer's words, these are the 'true truths' of God and are true whether they are supported by evidence or not. They are true simply because God, the God of truth, has spoken them. He cannot lie! 'Understandest thou what thou readest?' asked Philip of the Ethiopian eunuch as he read the scroll of Isaiah 53. Philip could well have said: 'How do you react to this passage? What are your personal feelings when you read this?' But he asked no such things. He was anxious to find out if the man had grasped *with his mind* what the prophet was saying.

I am not suggesting that the Gospel word is first and foremost a word to the educated. In fact Christian consecration and devotion have, in themselves, very little to do with a person's intelligence quotient or even with his schooling. I am bound to confess here that some of the greatest disappointments in the course of my ministry have been folk with university and college educations who promised so much and evidenced so little. Nor do I suggest that the appeal and challenges of the Word should end, as they begin, with the mind. From the mind the truth must per-colate downwards to the heart, there to be loved and held in affection. 'Oh, how I love Thy law!' sang the psalmist (Ps 119:97). 'While I was musing, the fire burned!' (Ps 39:3).

Nor, yet again, does the truth stop here. Truth is to be feared as well as loved; we are to tremble before it as well as rejoice. Therefore truth must percolate further down to reach the world of conscience. And from there it moves to the will, to bend it, to bring it into accord with the will of God, to lead the believer forth into a life of service and soldiering.

A religion that is all 'mind' soon degenerates into a barren intellectual exercise, as so much religion has done in Scotland in past generations. A religion that is all 'heart' and little else, tends to become an affair of sentimentality and emotionalism. A religion that is all 'conscience' is a grim assemblage of sundry paralysing fears and dreads. A religion that is all 'will' can all too soon develop into the tedious drudgery of good works without faith, service without love and the awful barrenness of a busy life. But take mind and heart and conscience and will together and you will have, under the good providence and grace of God, the elements and makings of true religion and a Gospel worthy of the name.

Martin C. D. D'Arcy said: 'There is no salvation save in truth, and the royal road of truth is by the mind.' John Henry Newman said: 'Almighty God influences us and works in us through our minds, not without them or in spite of them.' Galileo said: 'I do not feel obliged to believe that the same God who has endowed us with sense, reason and intellect has intended us to forego their use.' Well spoken, all three!

Yours sincerely,

THOMAS SWANSTON

35
LOVE*

Dear Friends,
The time has come for us to think of love and to practise it more fervently, although such a time is ever and always urgent upon Christians. One thinks especially of the divine love, of His for us, rich and immense, saving and free as it is, reaching its glory and climax in the message of the Gospel of grace. From there one moves naturally to thoughts of our love for Him, poor, unworthy and limited though that is, yet marvellously possible because of His love for us (1 Jn 4:19). And, inescapably, one is thereafter drawn to our love for others, fragile, cool and stunted though that also can be for a whole variety of reasons.

Love, of course, is what God is in Himself (1 Jn 4:8), and all our thinking about love must start at the heart and essence of His Godhead. Love is not simply something that God does; Love is what God is. It is the quintessential fabric of His nature and stands at the core of His very Being. He can never, therefore, cease to be love since that would involve Him in the dethroning and undeifying of Himself. Were He to cease to be love the very universe would disintegrate.

It is the glory and hallmark of all true love, whether divine or human, that it chooses never to remain alone. Love that stays alone is like a life that keeps itself to itself - eventually it withers and dies. True love, living love, like true life and living life, reaches out for the loved-one. Love's way is ever to give and not to count the cost, and what Love gives is Love's self.

*July 1984

This does not mean that the beloved is necessarily worth loving, or lovely, or even immediately lovable. We are not by nature either lovely or lovable, and God does not love us because He thinks that we are worth saving. There are no 'deserving cases' in His economy! He loves us as we are, rebels by birth and by choice, at war with Himself, at war with ourselves, at war with our fellows, unattractive and unbeautiful, and He showers upon us 'love to the loveless shown that they might lovely be'. He dresses us up in the beauty of Christ His Son, decking us in the holy garments of another's righteousness, another's virtue, another's strength and loveliness. Only thus arrayed are we fit to 'worship the Lord in the beauty of holiness'. As Saint Augustine said, 'He loved us foul that He might make us fair.'

In this reaching out for the beloved we see true love's patience and long-suffering. Love can lay siege to fortresses long held fast in the sullen grip and bitter bondage of the Enemy. Love can assail the grim barricades of the unyielded heart year after year with tireless fortitude and unwearying resignation. Love can wait a lifetime for surrender. Love stands undeterred by the raised portcullis, by broad moats which bar Love's advance, by shuttered windows, locked doors and ramparts lined with men beseeching Love to go away (cf. Matt 8:34).

First reactions (and second and third and more) to Love's overtures and pleas may thus often be neither hopeful nor encouraging. Yet Love endures buffetings. She is not much moved by being rejected. Love waits and weeps, and while she weeps she calls on men to heed the eternal things that belong to their peace. By the word of truth, by the agonies of the Saviour, by the wounds of the Crucified, by the shame of His borrowed grave, by the splendours of His rising, by the throne of His heavenly reign, by His intercession on high, by the certainty of His coming again to be our Judge, Love preaches, prays, urges and invites men to hear, believe and live.

We ought all to bless God more and more that love is not easily cast down and is awesomely unwilling to take 'No' for an answer. True love, His for us, is not readily rebuffed by our evasiveness, our perversity, our dreadful insularity, our excuses and by our desire to run our own lives without Love's interferences. Love stoops to conquer and while she stoops she waits and weeps.

Love is strong as death; its zeal for the beloved is as powerful as the grave. Many waters cannot quench its flame, nor can floods of adversity, hardship or trial drown it (cf. Song of Solomon 8:6-7). But what, you may ask, are we to make of hell and the New Testament teaching on everlasting punishment? Can this be a denial of the love of God? Hell, as Tom Torrance has said, is God's hell. It is not outside His kingdom but is the creation of a love which foresees that heaven would be a far worse torment than hell for those who have never bowed the knee to the Lordship of Christ. An unconverted person in heaven would be a stranger in a strange land, whose music was anathema to him and whose songs he could not sing. Hell, Love's hell though it be, was not originally founded for men at all but was 'prepared for the devil and all his angels.' If men choose to side with that fell crew not even Love, however patient and gentle, can save them.

To love such a God who loves us so is to love Love Himself, the mighty and determined Lover of our souls. To love Him is the first and greatest commandment, summing up the first tablet of the moral law of God. To be in Him is to be inside Love, surrounded by it, bathing in it, luxuriating in it, upheld and strengthened by it, sustained and carried forward by it. To be in Him is to be involved in the greatest, the most exciting and the most romantic of all love affairs. But, as is the case with all love affairs, the relationship must constantly be worked at and involves effort, determination, heart-searching and prayer. All true love, on the debit side, must be ready to suffer pain and loss: loss of money, loss of the esteem of others, loss of prestige, loss of success, loss of time, loss of convenience, loss of pride and loss of independence. Since true love, and loving God, can be so costly it is important that we should find out who Love is.

We do not need to seek far, for Love has told us what He is like. He has spoken in His Word and shown us in His Son. Yet, though Love is thus available and accessible to us, learning at Love's feet can be hard, demanding work. This, incidentally, is why some Christians give up the struggle to grow at a comparatively early stage, so depriving themselves of a universe of richness and sweetness, to say nothing of denying themselves salvations beyond description or compare.

We are to love Love in His majesty and in His meekness, in His grace and in His judgments, in His power and in His weakness, in His almightiness and in His impotence, in what Love can and in what Love cannot do. In wind, rain, sunshine and high gale we are to love Love Himself. We are to love all of Him. We are to love Him in storm, in tempest and in calm. In spiritual warfare and in days of peace we are to love Love for Love's sake. This is our privilege, our highest duty and our everlasting joy.

It is a matter of observation that there are forlorn souls who find it hard to accept God's love, to commit themselves to it, to surrender to it or even to believe in it at all. It is not that they do not trust in Christ for salvation. Their basic faith is not in doubt. They are truly born again of the Spirit and belong to

Him. Yet they cannot believe, in their heart of hearts, that the Lord loves them as He says He does. There is in them an inability to respond to Love's overtures in any tender and affectionate way.

Experience suggests that the suspicion for such a sickness, and the blame for it, must lie at the feet of loveless parents. Countless Christians appear to have been reared in the most loveless homes in which they were denied 'tactile love' that intimate, self-giving, affectionate form of tenderness which is so essential if a child is to grow up feeling wanted, cherished and cared for. One young man confessed that he never at any time in his life heard his parents confess their love for each other openly, nor did they ever show it except perhaps in some perfunctory way. How afraid some fathers and mothers are to demonstrate grace and gentleness to their bairns! And with what enthusiasm can such parents reserve their energies and emotions for other pursuits, e.g. expensive holidays, sports, hobbies and cultural affairs!

The Lord knows and understands the grim desolations of a loveless childhood. He weeps for the inner wildernesses produced by early years starved of the milk of human kindness. Yet we are surely under some kind of obligation to rise above such handicaps and avail ourselves of the resources of the Holy Spirit. The Lord loves you without reserve or qualification, whatever your childhood may have been like. You need more and more to relax in His love for you. You are precious to Him, of infinite worth and dearer to Him than all the suns and stars of space. He loves you as you are, and whether you believe it or not. To love Him in return, however feebly, is both the minimum and maximum of what He requires of you. The requirement is so simple that even a child can engage in it. Indeed, perhaps a child can engage in it best of all.

To translate God's love for us and our love for Him into loving our fellows (which is the summary of the second tablet of the moral law) is a lifetime's discipline and a great spiritual art. Learning to love the people whom we do not happen to like, loving the loveless, the unattractive, the neurotics, the inadequate souls, the tedious; the boring, the pathetic, the immature...all of this summons and commands us to consecrated endeavours and sanctified imaginations.

The solemn thing is that there is an alternative to this kind of loving. The option is always open to us to withdraw into ourselves, to cherish the 'self life' to sew ourselves up tight in a cocoon of ego-centricity in which we are 'safe' from the hurts and pains which will surely come if we love as Jesus loved. The late C. S. Lewis puts it very finely and searchingly thus:

> To love at all is to be vulnerable. Love anything, and your heart will certainly be wrung and possibly be broken. If you want to make sure of keeping it intact, you must give your heart to no one, not even to an animal. Wrap it carefully round with hobbies and little luxuries; avoid all entanglements; lock it up safe in the casket or coffin of your selfishness. But in that casket - safe, dark, motionless, airless - it will change. It will not be broken; it will become unbreakable, impenetrable, irredeemable. The alternative to tragedy, or at least to the risk of tragedy, is damnation. The only place outside Heaven where you can be perfectly safe from all the dangers and perturbations of love is Hell.

Yours, with growing affections,
THOMAS SWANSTON

36
THE NEW BIRTH

Dear Friends,
When an acorn falls into the ground there is a sense in which its future is predetermined and can take only one course. Given the proper conditions and the appropriate environment a healthy acorn can do no other than grow into an oak tree. Oak trees grow only from acorns. They do not grow from apple seeds. Apple trees grow from apple seeds. That is the way God has ordained things in nature. The acorn's destiny, therefore, is - to use an overworked word these days - encapsulated within its shell. The life, the basic germ of vitality and growth, is in the acorn. If a living oak tree is seen to be growing, that is sure evidence that an acorn was sown. If no living oak appears, bearing the proper characteristics and features of a true oak, either no acorn was sown in the first place i.e. there was no primary germ of life there at the start, or else something has aborted and gone wrong in the acorn's sowing.

The Christian life, too, has its beginning. It is called the New Birth of the Spirit, or being born again. That is the acorn from which the oak grows. In the New Birth it is Christ Himself, by the Holy Spirit, who is the primary, native, original seed of life in the believing man. If that 'acorn' of essential life is not there, there can be no hope whatever for an 'oak' of Christian possession, or of victory, or of vital fruitbearing. Only oaks grow from acorns, and only acorns produce oaks. Being born again constitutes a man a Christian, and Christians are men and women who, by their very essence,

*October 1989

have been born again of the Spirit. This New Birth, in its reality and power, is the sine qua non of being a Christian, and is that without which Christianity ceases to exist. The New Birth stands before all else: before repentance and sorrow for sin, before faith and conversion, before sincere profession, and before prayer and service.

I have often said that the God and Father of the Lord Jesus Christ, is a generous God. He is expansive in His desire to save. 'The Lord is... not wishing that any should perish, but that all should reach repentance' (2 Pet 3:9). Something of that largesse of heart, that generosity, that liberality, can be seen in the different ways in which He tries to communicate to us the wonder, the necessity and the inner meaning of the New Birth.

In the prologue to his Gospel, John divides mankind into two categories. There are those who are 'born of blood, born of the will of the flesh, born of the will of man' (Jn 1:13). He is obviously referring here to natural birth. We are all born once of our natural mothers, born of human blood, of human will and of common humanity. But John also speaks of a second category. They too have been born once, but they have also been born twice. 'children of God who were born... of God' (Jn 1:12-13).

In our Lord's famous encounter with Nicodemus, the New Birth is described in a different way. Jesus said: 'Truly, truly, I say to you, unless one is born anew, he cannot see the kingdom of God' (Jn 3:3). William Hendriksen, in his commentary on John's Gospel, translates it thus: 'I most solemnly assure you, unless one is born anew, he cannot see the kingdom of God'. The sentence in the original Greek actually begins: 'Amen, amen I say to you!' But what can Jesus mean by being born 'anew'? What is 'anew'?

The Greek word is *anothen* and, in the rest of John's

Gospel, means 'from above' or 'from the top'. In 3:31, John the Baptist describes Jesus as 'the man from above' (anothen) or 'the man from the top', the One above all. Facing Pilate in 19:11 Jesus speaks of 'power from above' (anothen) available to Him for the asking. In 19:23 Christ's tunic is described as seamless, 'woven from top (anothen) to bottom'. To be born anew therefore, is to be born from above, to be born of a heavenly birth. Jesus, as it so befell, was astonished that Nicodemus, this 'teacher of Israel', this earnest and diligent churchman, was ignorant of the New Birth, for the need to be born again was not some new teaching introduced by Jesus. It is not exclusively New Testament doctrine, but is found in the Old Testament and stands at the heart of the New Covenant (Jer 31:31-34; 32:39-40).

The New Birth, indeed, is older still and is suggested in the first chapter of Genesis. The heart of sinner man, outside Christ, without God and without hope in the world, is like that first creation 'without form and void', a place where 'darkness' covers 'the face of the deep' (Gen 1:2). That is a description of the heart of the unsaved man, and his heart remains in that case until the Spirit of God 'moves on the face of the waters' and the sinner is born again and becomes a new creation in Christ. 'If anyone is in Christ he is a new creation; the old has passed away, the new has come' (2 Cor 5:17). That is what it means to be born again. In the previous chapter of 2 Corinthians (4:6), when Paul wants to describe the New Birth, he goes precisely to Genesis and to the creation imagery there. 'It is the God who said: "Let light shine out of darkness", who has shined in our hearts to give the light of the knowledge of the glory of God in the face of Jesus Christ'. Only when God shines into the sinner's heart savingly, only when the Spirit of God moves over the face of the darkened waters, can men claim to be Christians. Oak trees grow only from acorns. Without acorns it is not possible to have oak trees at all.

But, of course, oak trees can be imitated. One could, I suppose, plant a forest composed of plastic oaks, artificially manufactured. From a distance they might pass as the real thing. Tourists, speeding past in their fast cars, might comment on what a fine forest of mighty oaks stood here! But plastic oaks, as we all should know, do not grow from real acorns. Real acorns with their essential germ of life, produce real oaks. Plastic oaks are made by men, and come from factories. The difference between plastic trees and real trees is this: if you slice through the trunk of a plastic, man-made tree, you will find nothing but solid plastic all the way through. If, however, you slice through the trunk of a real tree, you will find rings in the wood; and the rings tell you that this tree is alive and growing.

Most great experiences, like great men and great events can be imitated. Real gold is mimicked by brass; real silver by ghastly chrome; real diamonds by French paste; real flowers by hideous, plastic monstrosities; real silk by synthetic fabrics; real brothers in Christ by false brothers; the real Christ by pseudo-Christs; true prophets by false. The New Birth, too, has its imitations. In the forefront of the imposters one finds religion without Christ, devotion to church traditions, Sabbath piety and unctuous religiosity, churchianity and the love of buildings and properties set far above love for the Lord, kirky pride, middle-class morality, decency and respectability. Brass, however, is not gold; nor chrome, silver; nor French paste, diamonds; nor silk flowers, garden blooms. There is no convincing substitute whatsoever for the New Birth. 'You *must* be born again,' said Jesus. Must! It is a matter of urgency and necessity.

But why Christ's insistence on the New Birth? Can we not

get past God with a modicum of religion? Will our money, our good works and our prayers not suffice to please Him and move His hand to open the door and let us in? I recall having a lively conversation with a believing brother on this theme. I was on my way home from a trip to Hungary and had called to see him and his family. Came the evening, the supper and the verbal exchanges! We discussed what Paul meant when he said: 'You He made alive, *when you were dead* through the trespasses and sins in which you once walked... God, who is rich in mercy, out of the great love with which He loved us, *even when we were dead* through our trespasses, made us alive together for Christ' (Eph 2:1-2, 4-5). The point at issue was: 'What is the nature of this 'death' in man before he becomes spiritually alive in Christ?' My friend was of the mind that Paul here was using symbolic language and that the death was not real but metaphorical. I argued that this was rather dangerous thinking since one could, in the same way, argue that the New Testament imagery for hell is 'symbolic' and that perhaps, therefore, hell is not real but a metaphorical idea. Thus did our sallies go, well into the night. My last word was this: 'If the 'death' of the sinner before he comes to Christ is not 'real', why does Scripture use such powerful and awesome imagery to describe it?'

It is the universal witness of the Bible that men without Christ are dead in their sins, dead to the living God, dead to His knowledge, dead to grace and to prayer, dead to the Lord Jesus Christ and dead to the person, work and power of the Holy Spirit. However religious, devout and pious the sinner may be, however thorough a churchman, he is dead (he does not have the life of God), dumb (he does not, and cannot, speak), deaf (he does not, and cannot, hear) and blind (he does not, and cannot, see). And it is the essential mark of such a man that he can do nothing to help himself. Help, therefore, has to come from the outside. What a dead man needs is not encouragement to pray (how can the dead pray for themselves, or, indeed, for others?); not a word telling him to come alive again (how can he come alive again since he has never been alive in the first place?); not an exhortation prodding him to pull himself together (how can a corpse pull itself together?)... but a Saviour, an Emancipator who will raise him from fundamental death to newness of life in Christ. What a corpse needs is not revival but a resurrection.

Major Mark Fillingham, writing in *OCU Contact*, the magazine of the Officers' Christian Union, says this: 'To be spiritually alive is to be in a loving, harmonious relationship with God; to be spiritually dead is to be separated and estranged from God, the source of spiritual life... It (the regenerating action of God in the New Birth) is an intervention by Almighty God. As such it is accomplished by a direct work of the Spirit of God, the Holy Spirit, in the person of the convert... A man may be helped to faith by reason, insight or argument, but the whole exercise is spiritual from first to last.' Only God can raise the dead! 'By God's great mercy,' says Peter, writing to the Christians scattered throughout the Empire, 'we have been born anew to a living hope through the resurrection of Jesus Christ from the dead, and to an inheritance which is imperishable, undefiled and unfading, kept in heaven for you' (1 Pet 1:3-4).

I am convinced that if the New Birth were more faithfully preached in our pulpits (there are churches where it is scarcely, if ever, mentioned), and its truth and reality more zealously known by church-going folk, our denomination in Scotland would be transformed beyond recognition. When the former Bishop of Woolwich in his book, *Honest to God* said that he confessed himself to belong 'to the generation of the once-born', he was, in fact, telling the world that he was not a Christian. One simply cannot be a Christian and, at the same time, be once-born. As Horace Bushnell puts it: 'There could be no growth if there were not something planted... Until the new man is born, or begotten, the soul abideth in death, and therefore cannot grow.' Oak trees come from acorns, and only acorns produce oaks. Plastic oaks do not come from acorns; they are made by men and come from factories. Only God makes real acorns which grow into real oaks. And when the real oak grows it is a sure and certain sign that an acorn has been planted. 'Amen, amen, I say to you, unless one is born anew, he cannot see the kingdom of God' (Jn 3:3). That is both a solemn warning and a cordial invitation. Is it too much to hope that I might live to see its fruits fairly soon?

Yours cordially,
THOMAS SWANSTON

37
CHRISTIAN ASSURANCE*

Dear Friends,
This letter may not be to everyone's taste. It may not even meet everyone's present need. But, for the comfort of some, if not of many, I sense that something needs to be written about the subject of Christian assurance. How, in other words, may any sinner, who is also a true Christian, be absolutely sure that he is saved and a true child of God?

For my own part I confess that I speak here from a position of weakness. I have never doubted my salvation, any more than I have ever doubted the fact of God. Even in my wildest days of wandering, far from Christ and love and home, I never questioned God's existence. Only a fool (Ps 14:1; 53:1), I had been taught from childhood, would do that. To question the unquestionable, to challenge omnipotence, to doubt the obvious, to undermine the very ground of *my* existence seemed to me then, as it seems to me now, to be a form of madness.

I also knew in those crazy years that, had I died, I should have gone to hell and been lost for ever. God's goodness, wisdom and love I often viewed with scepticism, especially when life seemed to have no meaning for me or for others. But God's essential life, His simply being there, I did not at any time mistrust. In exactly the same way I have been sure of being a Christian from the moment of the second birth. Wayward, disobedient, thrawn and unbelieving I have often been, and all these things are to my shame, condemnation and confusion of face. But they did not persuade me to suspect

*March 1981

that I was a damned soul. The salvation of any man, whether he is a Christian or not, does not depend on his religious or moral performance but on the decree of God. God makes a pronouncement from the Throne. He gives a verdict, a ruling, a judgment, and that is the only ground of salvation. 'Justification is an act of God...'

Yet there has always been in Christian circles something of a fashion for doubting one's salvation. In some areas of Scotland this thing is almost a fashion, a religion, a cult in which a man's spirituality is virtually gauged by the depths of his doubt - as if unbelief and anguish of spirit were measures of holiness! The real tragedy is that these doubters are so informed in the claims of Christ and the teaching of the Gospel. On either side of them stand two very different groups.

On the one hand there are those who say that a man can never know for sure that he is saved until he dies. The hopelessness and despair of such a position are immediately obvious. Is it not a rather risky and daring enterprise for a man to leave such a serious issue unsettled until he dies? Would it not then be too late? 'It is appointed for men to die once, and after that comes judgment' (Heb 9:27).

On the other hand there are those who hold that it is 'presumptuous and wicked' for any sinner to claim to be saved in this fallen world, so riddled with error and delusion, to protest that his sins are forgiven and that he enjoys fellowship with God. The answer to this is plain: God has spoken in His Word. What He says there is true. He does not need to say a thing many times over for it to be true. If He says it once it is true, and it is true for ever. His truth was true once, is true now, and will always be true. Therefore this group must be asked other questions, 'Do you believe the Word of God? Do you trust what God has said? Are you prepared to commit yourself to it, lean on it, to order your life, here and hereafter, by its precepts?' It is precisely because men do *not* trust God's Word, or take it at its plain face value, that they doubt their salvation. It would be truer to say that it is more 'presumptuous and wicked' to doubt what God has said than to question one's salvation. For to doubt God's Word is to call Him a liar.

> 'He who believes in the Son *has eternal life,* and he who does not obey the Son shall not see life, but the wrath of God rests on him' (John 3:36).
> 'By this we *may be sure* that we *know* Him, if we keep His commandments' (1 John 2:3).
> 'We *know* that we have passed out of death into life, because we love the brethren' (1 John 3:14)
> 'Let us not love in word or speech but in deed and truth. *By this we shall know* that we are of the truth, and reassure our hearts before him (1 John 3:18-19).
> '*By this we know* that we abide in Him and He in us, because He has given us of His own Spirit' (1 John 4:13).

These are not the personal opinions of the apostle John: they are infallible, inerrant, trustworthy words of assurance from One who has told us that He cannot err (Heb 6:18). To doubt what He says - about sin and its cure, about man and his destiny, about righteousness and holiness, about consecration and assurance - is infinitely more heinous a sin than to question whether one is saved or not. For the principal standard by which we may judge whether or not we are saved is the standard of the Word itself.

Some who read this may belong to that group of timid, shy, fearful folk whose consciences are genuinely over-given to being exercised by such questions. Such must be on their guard against the Evil One who, knowing that he can never steal their salvation from them (Jn 10:28-29) will try to rob them of their basic peace of mind (Isa 26:3), their power to bear fruit (Jn 15:2,5,8), and even their very sanity (Eph 6:17). 'We are not ignorant of his devices,' says Paul. He loves to play on our feelings, of unworth and guilt, of uselessness and unhappiness. Therefore, at the end of the day, we cannot rely on our feelings. Our final reliance must be only on what God has said.

I hope that this will not weary you, but let me close with some quotations from the Larger Catechism. The Larger Catechism's little brother, the Shorter Catechism, is more famous, having been designed for the instruction of those who were 'of weaker capacity' in spiritual matters, i.e. baby Christians or simply enquirers. The Larger Catechism was for those who had made 'some proficiency in the grounds of religion' i.e. who had made some progress on the road to spiritual maturity. Three of the questions in the Larger Catechism deal with the issue of Christian assurance and I reproduce them here, changing the language a little to make it more contemporary:

> Q 79: *May not true believers, because of their imperfections, and because of the many temptations and sins by which they are overtaken, fall away from the state of grace?*
> A: True believers, because of the unchangeable love of God, and because of His decree to give them (a) perseverance, (b) their inseparable union with Christ, (c) Christ's continual intercession for them, and (d) the Spirit and seed of God abiding in them, can neither totally nor finally fall away from the state of grace, but are kept by the power of God through faith unto salvation.

Q 80: *Can true believers be infallibly assured (a) that they are in a state of grace, and (b) that they shall persevere in it unto salvation?*
A: Those who truly believe in Christ, and strive to walk in all good conscience before Him may, without extraordinary revelation (e.g. spiritual 'experiences', inner reassurances), (a) by faith rooted in the truth of God's promises and (b) by the Spirit helping them to see in themselves the graces to which the promises of life are made, and (c) by the Spirit bearing witness with their spirits that they are the children of God, be infallibly assured that they are in the state of grace, and shall persevere in it unto the end.

Q 81: *Are all true believers at all times assured (a) of their being present in the state of grace, and (b) that they shall be saved?*
A: Since assurance of grace and salvation are not of the essence of faith, true believers may wait long before they obtain it. And, after enjoying it (i.e. the assurance) they may have it weakened and disturbed through various moods, sins, temptations and betrayals. Yet they are never left without such a presence and support of the Spirit of God as keeps them from sinking into utter despair.

In short, can we not trust our heavenly Father's promise? And, if we are true children in His house, would it not be strange if He withheld from us for ever the reassurances and tokens of His tender care? Perhaps you need to be persuaded all over again just how much - how infinitely much - you matter to Him?

Yours affectionately,
THOMAS SWANSTON

38
THE HOMELINESS OF GOD*

My Dear Friends,
There are few Biblical themes that I love quite as much as that of the homeliness of God. Time and again I catch my breath to discover and rediscover what can only be termed, at the risk of being misunderstood, as the vulgarity of God. There's a commonness about Him, a domesticity, a blunt and practical streak, a bluff and forthright way of doing things. His other-worldliness is sometimes all too this-worldly, too painfully so for our comfort. And it puts to shame, and calls into question, so much of the over-starched, stiff, cold, unctuous formalism of much of our religion. Do you understand what I mean?

I do not mean, of course, that God is crude, or even rude; although there is a bit in Him that loves to scale us down to our proper size, and knock the windy pride out of our puffing sails. And He does this with the most gracious of smiles on His face, and all in the most good-humoured way. He has too great a respect for human personality to do things otherwise. There is courtesy in Him, but it is not a pose struck for effect; it is not a show designed to take people in, as our mannerisms can be. It is part of the fundamental reserve and decorum of His nature. Do you know, then, what I mean by the vulgarity of God?

Jesus, the Lord of Glory, converts 120 gallons of dirty washing water into the finest wine, and so makes, and saves from disaster, the wedding feast. It was not normal drinking water, but the stuff that stood in jars at the door for the use of

*January 1972

weary, dust-stained travellers. Before He dies, Jesus girds Himself with a towel, and stoops to wash the feet of the twelve. This is why Peter tells us to 'put on the apron of humility' as Jesus did at the Last Supper (1 Peter 5:5). We are to climb down, and as unobtrusively and as unostentatiously, as He did. After He rises from the dead, we find Him on His hands and knees blowing up a charcoal fire on a beach, cooking, with those fearful scarred hands, a resurrection breakfast for men who had given up the Kingdom's work and had gone back to their fishing. Jesus is always the servant. He is the down-to-earth God; the practical, caring, saving One. He is not afraid of what the modern theologians call 'involvement'.

Paul walks through the streets of Ephesus, and men touch his 'sweat rags' and are healed of their diseases. Sweat rags, forsooth, and not the best Irish lawn scented with ecclesiastical eau-de-cologne! The Authorised Version is too polite when it speaks of 'handkerchiefs' (Acts 19:11,12).

To crown all, the Gospel teaches the Resurrection of the Body, not the Immortality of the Soul. The body, mark you: so that heaven, and hell, will be solid places. The word 'glory' in Hebrew, means 'weight, heaviness'. But surely you have the message? Christianity is the most materialistic of all religions. The Word was made Flesh and dwelt among us.

The stable is exposed, bare and unsheltered, shaming our affluence. But God is not uncomfortable in it. Tradition has it that Jesus was born in a cave where animals were kept, now the grotto under the Church of the Nativity in Bethlehem. But men - trust them! - have ruined the primitive simplicity of the place, decorating it with silver stars, and lamps and holy ornaments. So robbing God of His earthiness. Can God be so domestic? So Homely? Can meekness really be might? Is such humility really a demonstration of power? The way down - is it the way up? Someone has spoken of the Incarnation as the Divine Scandal. And so it is: that Spirit should become Flesh; and the Eternal a mortal man. God became a baby, to save you.

Born to raise the sons of earth,
Born to give them second birth.

This is Christmas. 'The grace of God, that bringeth salvation, hath appeared unto all men' (Titus 2:11). 'Ye know the grace of our Lord Jesus Christ that, though He was rich, yet for your sakes He became poor, that ye through His poverty, might be made rich' (2 Cor 8:9).

My dear congregation, whom God has given to me to shepherd in grace, many of your homes have been shadowed and darkened by sorrow this year, as loved ones have passed to their rest. Will Christmas be lonely and empty without them? Bereaved heart, in the Baby's eyes are tears reserved for the grave of Lazarus. The shortest verse in the Bible is: 'Jesus wept'. Friend, lift up your sad heart to Him! Jesus makes no mistakes. His ways are perfect. He is silently planning for you. He knows. He loves. He cares.

We greet the suffering ones with special tenderness. Some of you have battled for many years against weakness and pain, depression and discouragement. Your courage and patience are a standing rebuke to us healthier folk. God be with you this Christmas. Christ is Immanuel: God with us. May He gladden your home, and lighten your load.

After many centuries of longing and preparation, Jesus has come. Into your bondage, sorrow and night; into your shameful failure and loss; into your fear and dread of the tomb, Jesus has come. Precisely for you.

To all members and friends who support our work by their

devotion and prayers, I send Christmas Greetings with all the love I can command. The signs are not lacking that God is doing a new thing among us. There is a fresh spirit at work, a spirit of enquiry, of service, of learning, of searching the Scriptures. May this grow increasingly, and may we be blessed in the Gospel, and made a blessing to others in this our needy town and nation.

May the Saviour's presence and joy be yours.

Yours, with growing affection,

THOMAS SWANSTON

39
LORD'S DAY OBSERVANCE*

Dear Friends,
This letter is, inevitably, rather long. I hope that you will be patient and read it carefully. A fair section of the Christian public has been dismayed by a recent article on observance of the Lord's Day. It first appeared in last September's issue of the Christian Graduate, the quarterly journal of the Graduate's Fellowship wing of Inter-Varsity Fellowship, and was later reproduced, uncritically and without comment, by Scripture Union. In it, writing under the title: *Sunday, puzzling Sunday,* the author, Rev John Wesson, questions the church's traditional understanding of the Lord's Day. Mr. Wesson is chaplain to a Polytechnic college, and is associated with various evangelical endeavours in England. The thrust of his argument is simply this: nowhere in the New Testament is the Lord's Day called the 'Christian Sabbath', and it is now high time for Christians to remove from the Lord's Day all the negative, prohibitive practices which derive their sanction and authority from the Old Testament Sabbath. He describes the straight tie-up between Old Testament Sabbath and New Testament Sunday as 'something of a theological confidence trick'.

It is sad, and indeed, extraordinary, that in so slender a piece of writing Mr. Wesson should question and impugn the honesty of no less a scholar than the late E. J. Young who, until his death, did so much to raise evangelical scholarship of the Old Testament to a level of credibility and acceptance. If you know of, or have heard of, or have read any of Prof-

*July 1974

essor Young's major works you will recognise that he must be a brave man who dares to throw down the gauntlet to him, who was a godly and gracious soul in his day with a fine, perceptive mind. Yet Mr. Wesson does so. But his words have not passed unchallenged, and cannot do so.

It needs to be confessed that, superficially, his argument is convincing: nowhere in the New Testament is Sunday called anything other than 'the Lord's Day' or 'the first day of the week'. It does not, on the surface, have much connection with the Jewish Sabbath, and is certainly never called the 'Christian Sabbath'. What are we to answer to these claims?

Many Christians today, especially the young, are confused by the subject of Lord's Day observance, or are embarrassed by it, or else are quite disinterested. It is always a revelation to see who attend meetings of the Lord's Day Observance Society. Christian witness there is largely from one end of the spectrum: mostly Free Presbyterian and Free Church, with few from the Church of Scotland, and fewer still from evangelistic, fundamental groups. Yet all the denominations who could reasonably be expected to show concern (though their absence denies what they profess with their lips) would nominally commit themselves to the authority of God's Word. They would also be the first to rise to defend God's moral law, enshrined and summed up in the ten commandments, as a revelation of Himself and of His will for men.

It is the awful hypocrisy surrounding the day that appals. Most churchgoing folk, including office-bearers, do not observe the Lord's Day at all, but keep the Lord's half-day, giving a casual nod in the direction of God at worship, and smartly scurrying off to enjoy themselves and find pleasure, as best they may in a litter of newspapers and a miasma of tenth-rate films. I am inclined to wonder where the Lord of the Sabbath fits into such lives, if He fits in at all. The words of James are timely here: he reminds us that they who offend in one commandment offend in all. This can only mean, that, in the sight of God, those who profane and make light of the day, are guilty along with adulterers, liars and thieves. Of course, you can earn yourself a bad name by telling lies and committing adultery. And you land in jail for murder or stealing. Yet you may violate the Sabbath and be perfectly accepted by civilised society. But God is not mocked.

Sometimes a wedge is driven between 'moral' and 'ceremonial' law in the ten commandments. It is claimed that the law on Sabbath observance is really 'ceremonial', and belongs to the Jewish set-up along with other specifically Jewish things: therefore it has been done away in Christ, along with animal sacrifice, special food taboos, and temple liturgy. But is it not unnatural to claim that the laws against lying stealing, etc., are 'moral' while the Sabbath law is 'ceremonial'? Nine of 'moral' and one of 'ceremonial' is surely an odd combination? It puts a false construction on the commandments. Is it not easier to think, as the Westminster Confession of Faith does, of the commandments as being four plus six: the first four, including the Sabbath, being Godward, and the second six being manward?

'But why should Jewish law,' it is asked, 'be foisted on a 20th century society that doesn't want it? We live in a post-Christian era; why should we be shackled either by Christ or Moses?' But these are illegitimate questions. The Sabbath is not particularly either Jewish or Mosaic. Several heathen nations also had sabbaths in the dawn of mankind's history; and the Biblical Sabbath dates from before Moses (by whom the law was given), and even before Abraham, father of the Jewish nation. The Sabbath, along with marriage and work, is a *creation* ordinance, and is part and parcel of the moral structure of the universe (Gen 2). These three are basic to man's wellbeing as a creature made in God's image, therefore to tamper with or violate these laws, built into the very fine fibre of things, is to challenge the God-appointed order and court disaster. Marriage, work and the Sabbath have, in our generation, disintegrated. Yet the fact that men want these ancient institutions changed or removed in no way weakens their abiding validity. The voice of the majority is not necessarily the voice of God!

What should the voice of the minority be saying? One primary message is that God is, in Himself, a Sabbath for men. 'In the beginning God created... and on the seventh day God ended His work... and He rested... and blessed the seventh day and set it apart' (Gen 1:1 and 2:2,3). Before and after the world was made, God was and is His people's Sabbath. In the Trinity, the blessed Godhead of Father, Son and Holy Spirit, there is not the remotest suggestion of confusion. In the heart of the Eternal there are no storms, but only a great calm. The God of peace is without contradiction or conflict. The 'rest' of God on the seventh day, therefore, is not the 'rest' of exhaustion. He did not stop because He was tired! God faints not, neither is weary, and could have created universes for ever, effortlessly willing and dreaming them into existence. But He loves to be Himself, therefore He saw His handiwork that it was good and sat back in His everlasting throne to enjoy the 'rest' of self-fulfilment.

Men, too, in this frantic and frenetic age, need to be still. We should 'rest from our labours as God did from His' (Heb 4:10). The Sabbath is thus a picture and parable of justification by faith or conversion. We need to give up our works, good as well as bad, in order to be saved and enter the rest that remains for God's people (Heb 4:9). Church folk, above many others, sadly need to learn this. We have to renounce our virtues, as well as our vices, in order to be saved. Our consciences must be purged from 'dead works' before we can serve the living God (Heb 9:14). We cease from our labours to enter into the finished work of Christ.

It is often stated that Jesus 'liberalised' the Sabbath, as witness His walking through the cornfields with His disciples. But in fact this was permitted by the law (Deut 23:25). He lived and died perfectly, and so safely, and those who are saved are saved into a law-abiding Christ. And to no less an end than that the righteousness of God's moral law might be filled to the full, and lived out, in us (Rom 8:4). Every believer has in his heart the fullness of Him who came to do His Father's will by keeping the Father's law, Sabbath included.

Our age has, generally speaking, ceased to believe in an eternal world. Men live and die without much reference to eternity. Yet it is this age that has rejected the Sabbath and that is scarcely to be wondered at, for the Sabbath is a portrait of the Canaan of final rest, the victorious rest, of heaven which is the heritage of all who die in the Lord. John Donne, in one of his famous sermons on Eternity, speaks of glory as 'a Sabbath flowing into a Sabbath'. Then, and only then, will Christians truly 'rest from their labours'. The Lord's Day, the day of resurrection, *is* the Christian Sabbath. On it Jesus set behind Him His works, notably His passion, and entered into His triumphant rest and reign. He sat down (Heb 1:3).

Too much anti-sabbath propaganda is founded on the wretchedness caused by the Sabbatarianism still prevailing in some isolated parts. Sabbatarianism without grace, tenderness and love *can* be a desolating phenomenon - as if all true religion were balanced on that one fine point of law! Sabbatarianism *can* embitter and harden men's hearts, and alienate them from Christ. Nevertheless the commandment remains, and I fear that the liberalising of Sunday is only part of a much larger movement aimed at the abolition of the Lord of the Sabbath. As has been pointed out: in any revolution the rebels do not first start with the king, but with his counsellors. They change his laws. Only at the last is the king himself executed.

'Be watchful and strengthen the things that remain, that are ready to die,' said Christ to the church in Sardis. Our land is bracing herself at this time for another summer of Lord's Day charabanc tours and drunken bus-party sprees. In what sense can many of these Sabbath activities be called re-creation? But where do you, personally, stand in relation to the Lord of the Sabbath? And, if you so far have observed only the Lord's half day, what will it profit you if you gain countless imagined freedoms, and in the process lose not merely your God and Gospel, but also your own soul?

Earnestly yours,
THOMAS SWANSTON

Westminster Confession of Faith, on the Sabbath. Chapter XXI
Section VII. As it is of the law of nature that, in general, a due proportion of time be set apart for the worship of God: so ii His Word, by a positive, moral, and perpetual commandment, binding all men in all ages, He hath particularly appointed one day in seven for a sabbath, to be kept holy unto Him: which, from the beginning of the world to the resurrection of Christ, was the last day of the week: and from the resurrection of Christ was changed into the first day of the week; which in Scripture is called the Lord's Day, and is to be continued to the end of the world as the Christian sabbath.
Section VIII. This sabbath is then kept holy unto the Lord when men, after a due preparing of their hearts, and ordering of their common affairs beforehand, do not only observe an holy rest all the day from their own works words and thoughts about their worldly employments and recreations; but also are taken up the whole time in the public and private exercises of His worship, and in the duties of necessity and mercy.

40
FINAL AUTHORITY*

My Dear Friends,
I hope that you will not find this a dry letter although, in the nature of things, it is bound to be a little long. The theme, if somewhat abstract, is of perennial interest to Christians, and its practical implications for this world (with its more solemn implications for the next) are obvious. The theme is: final authority in matters of religion.

I was intrigued that this should be so much an issue in America in these days where the 'Defence of the Bible' movement is acquiring momentum. The immediate issue over there was a public accusation that the redoubtable Fuller Theological Seminary had moved from its basic position on Scripture, especially with regard to inerrancy and infallibility. When, therefore, a Christian in the States wants to know where you stand spiritually he asks: 'Do you believe in the inspiration, inerrancy and infallibility of the Scriptures?' Here in Scotland we tend to answer such questions by asking the questioner to define his terms. Is he thinking of any particular version of the Scriptures - Authorised Version, or Revised Version, or Revised Standard or what? Does he mean 'Scripture as originally given', thus allowing for Biblical and scholarly research? How does he distinguish inerrancy and infallibility?

Such questions may seem remote from the world in which Christians have to live and testify to the Lord's salvation. But if we ignore the questions they will not go away and when the worldlings, or the worldly churchlings, challenge the Chris-

*July 1977

tian and ask: 'Why do you hold the things you hold, say the things you say, and do the things you do? What is your authority? What is your last court of appeal? Why do you stand where you do?' - what are we to answer?

It may encourage us to remember that Jesus Himself had to face such hard questions. 'By what authority are you doing these things, and who gave you this authority?' asked the priests and elders (Matt 21:23). The word here translated 'authority' is a rather special word. It means: delegated influence, power handed down from a superior, jurisdiction or right. Throughout His life Jesus insisted that He was not acting on His own. 'I can do nothing on my own authority,' He said (John 5:30). Jesus was no mystic loner, preoccupied by some independent private cause. His true authority was objective and lay outside Himself. His ministry had the accreditation, the blessing and the approval of God.

At another time He could say: 'I have not spoken on My own authority: the Father who sent Me has Himself given Me commandment what to say and what to speak' (John 12:49). Jesus, of course, did not have to look far for testimonies to all that He was and did. John the Baptist bore witness of Him that He was the Christ (John 5:33). The mighty works done by His hands proclaimed to the world who He was. 'The works which the Father has granted Me to accomplish, these very works which I am doing, bear Me witness that the Father has sent Me' (John 5:36). But more, the Father had honoured His ministry (John 5:37); and yet again, the Old Testament Scriptures bore witness of Him (John 5:39).

Churchgoers, tragically, do not share Jesus' confidence and are sadly divided over where the last court of appeal really is. In a general way all Christians believe that the final authority is Christ Himself. 'He is Lord of all,' said Peter (Acts 10:36). But *how* do Christ's lordship and authority reach the church? There are three sources, generally speaking, of authority: these are not mutually exclusive, but surely we need to have an order of priority? The first authority is that of *human reason:* this is the position of liberals in the church. The second is that of the *church* and Christian tradition: this is the position of Roman Catholicism and also of Eastern Orthodox churches. The third is the authority of *Scripture:* this is the position of evangelicals. Let us think of these.

The authority of reason is, superficially at least, attractive and impressive. Man is, after all, a thinking being, a creature of mind and intellect. Any insult to him here is an insult to his whole being. In a sense, therefore, the miracles of Christ, the 'mighty acts of God' (and the existence of a supernatural world at all, a dimension of super-nature) are an affront to man's dignity as a 'rational' being. It is simply not reasonable that a child should be born of a virgin, as Joseph knew full well when he thought to divorce Mary privately. If we are living in a 'closed universe' water simply does not turn into wine. It is simply not possible to feed 5,000 people with a few loaves and fishes. Storms do not cease suddenly. Such stories are an insult to natural man and his 'rational' nature.

The assumption is that reason is infallible, that it can be trusted implicitly and without qualification. But there is little either in history or in human psychology to support such a view. When Calvinism speaks of the Doctrine of Total Depravity it does not mean that we are all as bad as we can be, since that is obviously not the case. It simply means that every department of our personality has been invaded, infected and poisoned by sin. We respond wrongly to the claims of the Moral Law of God because our *conscience* has fallen. We do the things we should not do, and we do not do the things that we should do, because our *wills* are fallen. Our loves are hopelessly in the wrong order, and our affections riotously confused, because our *emotional life* is fallen. Our thinking too is wrong, because our *reason* is fallen. 'Trust in the Lord with all thine heart and lean not on thine own understanding.'

One of the saddest of all spectacles in the church today is that of those whose religion is little more than a collection of their own ideas. The final court of appeal for such folk is that of Personal Opinion. I wonder if such appreciate the absurdity of their position? Can we imagine what it would truly be like at a meeting for public worship if the religion of every man and woman was simply a collection of personal opinions? In such a gathering no opinion of any man or woman would be better or worse than the opinion of anyone else. Such a scene would be rather like the Tower of Babel after the event! But the deepest grief of all is that in Hell such people will have all eternity to reflect on how terribly wrong they were. There will be no atheists in hell, nor will anyone there doubt the authenticity of the Word of God.

When we come to the church and Christian tradition we are marginally on safer ground, for does not the church go back to Christ Himself and have not His teachings been handed down from age to age? Yes. But, as the Reformers were not slow to insist, the councils and assemblies of men - Popes and General Assemblies not excluded - have erred even on fundamental doctrines. For the church is not called to be the judge of God's Word, but the Word's servant. The church did not bring the Word into being, but was herself brought into being by the Word. The Word makes Christians, and not the reverse! And it is to the loss of the church in history that men in their assemblies have added to the Word, and in doing so have subtracted from its glory. For as soon as you add to perfection you immediately diminish it. Traditions, therefore, cannot be entirely trusted since they are the products of the minds of fallible men. We should all reckon with Christ's scathing remarks to the church leaders of His day who had cluttered up the simplicity of the Word with their accretions and addenda. 'You make void the Word of God with your traditions,' He said. And even the best of us may fall into this snare. 'We do this because it has always been done like this here; it is the custom! Our fathers always did it in this way; it was good enough for them and so it is good enough for us.' The assumption is that our fathers, with their traditions, were right. But were they?

There is only one sure court of appeal, and that is the Word of God itself, 'which lives and abides for ever'. God has spoken to us in His Word. All other ground is sinking sand. He needs to say a thing only once in order for it to be true. God has spoken. We are at liberty, of course, to discuss what He has said but, in the end of the day, when the smoke of the battle has cleared and the sound of argument has ceased, God's Word is to be obeyed without qualification and without reserve.

We hear a good deal in our time of the old Latin tag: 'Ecclesia reformata sed semper reformanda' - the church has been reformed but always stands in need of reformation. But if the church is to be reformed she must be reformed not by the vacuous imaginations of men but by the cleansing, the washing, the disciplines and the precepts of God's Word revealed to us in the propositional truth of Scripture. Christians must constantly be betaking themselves to the Scriptures, to the Judgment-Bar of God's Word. 'If they speak not according to this Word it is because there is no light in them.' If what is said is in the Bible then it is true. It is true even if there is no external evidence to support its truth. It is true *because God has said it.* It is true even if it is an affront to our rationality. It is true even if it appears to be absurd, for the absurdities of God are wiser than the clevernesses of men.

Why all this concern over the theme of final authority? My fear is that in many areas of the evangelical world Christians are drifting from the authority of Scripture - inspired, inerrant and infallible. In some quarters lip-service only is paid to the authority of the Word; whole passages of Scripture are never read, expounded, digested or used; and even specific Biblical doctrines are rejected outright. If I may end by quoting some fine words of Francis Schaeffer from his address to the Lausanne Congress on World Evangelisation in 1974:

> 'There is no use of Evangelicalism seeming to get larger and larger if at the same time appreciable parts of Evangelicalism are getting soft at that which is the central core, namely the Scriptures. We must say with sadness that, in some places, seminaries, institutions and individuals who are known as evangelical no longer hold to a full view of Scripture. The issue is clear. Is the Bible true truth and infallible wherever it speaks, including where it touches history and the cosmos (world order), or is it only in some sense revelational where it touches religious subjects? That is the issue...
>
> The issue is whether the Bible gives propositional truth (that is, truth that may be stated in propositions) where it touches history and the cosmos and this all the way back to pre-Abrahamic history, all the way back to the first eleven chapters of Genesis, or whether instead of that it is meaningful only where it touches that which is considered religious...
>
> Martin Luther said: 'If I profess with the loudest voice and clearest exposition every portion of the truth of God except precisely that little point which the world and the devil are at that moment attacking, I am not confessing Christ, however boldly I may be professing Christ. Where

the battle rages there the loyalty of the soldier is proved and to be steady on all the battlefront besides is mere flight and disgrace if he flinches at that point.' In our day, 'that point' is the question of Scripture.

Holding to a strong view of Scripture, or not holding to it, is the watershed of the evangelical world. The first direction in which we must face is to say most lovingly, but clearly: Evangelicalism is not consistently evangelical unless there is a line drawn between those who take a full view of Scripture and those who do not.'

Yours earnestly,
THOMAS SWANSTON

41
ORDINATION OF WOMEN*

Dear Friends and Fellow-workers,

Episcopalians are under the rule of bishops; that is the meaning of 'episcopacy'. We are under the rule of elders; that is the meaning of 'presbyterianism'. But sometimes another expression is used: we are said to be ruled by 'conciliar government'; this simply means 'government by councils'. The four 'councils' by which we are governed are immediately recognisable: they are Kirk Sessions, Presbyteries, Synods and the General Assembly. In a sense, what we in the Church of Scotland are caught up into is a kind of pyramid structure. The 'many' at the bottom (in congregation and Kirk Sessions) are ruled by the 'few' at the top (the General Assembly meeting once a year). But, of course, there is much coming and going in between, with Sessions being held responsible to Presbyteries; Presbyteries, in turn, being held responsible to Synods; and the whole being held responsible to the Assembly.

On the whole the system works, even if the pyramid sometimes becomes top-heavy and looks more like a mushroom on the verge of collapse! One blessing of the 'system' is that the stronger are encouraged (and, indeed, obliged) to help the weak; thus richer congregations are duty-bound to support those that are financially less viable. And every man, theoretically, is entitled to have his say, and can come forward with a complaint in the proper way.

But why am I raising these rather formal issues? For a good reason: every minister, at his ordination, is required to

*July 1980

acknowledge the Presbyterian system of government to be 'agreeable to the Word of God' and is committed to taking his 'due part' in the courts of the church. He must also promise to be 'subject in the Lord to Presbytery'. This is a difficult phrase, for one may ask, 'What does 'in the Lord' qualify? The minister's subjection? Or the decisions of Presbytery?' If 'in the Lord' refers to the minister's subjection, one may answer that the Scriptures do not allow us to be subject to the decisions of men *without qualification.* The decisions of men are to be tested and taken to the judgment-bar of the Word of God. If 'in the Lord' refers to the decisions of Presbytery, one may take the stand of Martin Luther who claimed that the councils and assemblies of the church had often erred and, indeed, had frequently contradicted each other. For the question arises, 'What is a minister to do if he is persuaded that a decision of Presbytery is not "in the Lord"?' Sooner or later these issues will rise to the surface, particularly in the cases of men who feel that they cannot, for conscience sake, and in the light of their understanding of Scripture, ordain a woman either to the eldership or to the ministry.

The issues are both simple and complex. A number of years ago the General Assembly ruled that a woman could not be excluded from ordination to eldership simply on the grounds of her sex. She could be excluded (as may any man) on the grounds of her life or doctrine i.e. if her Christian testimony left much to be desired, or if her beliefs deviated from the Christian norm. It was inevitable that the opening-up of ordination to the eldership should lead to the opening-up of ordination to the ministry. And that is where the church stands today.

The church, on the whole, has responded lukewarmly to the Assembly's ruling and permission and there are, comparatively speaking, few women elders or ministers. Perhaps the Scots are too conservative. Perhaps we are hesitant to make such a drastic break with some 1900 years of Christian tradition. Yet, theoretically, it would now be possible for any church to have an exclusively female Session under a lady Moderator. Indeed, there is nothing now to prevent the General Assembly being exclusively composed of women, with a distinguished woman minister in the chair. But such days seem very far off.

More problematic is the large number of men in the ministry who feel that they cannot proceed to the ordination of women. It may well be that test cases are already in the pipeline, and it may take such test cases to settle the issue one way or another.

According to church law, if a minister refuses to ordain a woman to the eldership, the Session has the right to take him to Presbytery. He may there be charged with 'contumacy' (which is thrawn-ness or stubborn-ness) and brought to trial. No doubt it would take a somewhat militant and aggressive Session to go thus far, since the issue would create a great deal of public interest; but there are such Sessions in the land!

If a minister stands trial, what then? It goes without saying that he will be obliged to muster a convincing set of facts and arguments for the pleading of his case. But what then? According to church law, one of five things may then happen. The minister may be admonished, rebuked, temporarily suspended from office, permanently deposed from office or excommunicated from the church. If the minister wishes to appeal against the decision of the Presbytery he can take his case to the Synod. If the Synod condemns him, he can appeal against the decision of the Synod and go to the General Assembly, there to plead his case at the bar.

My own suspicion is that none of this controversy would have arisen if the church's view of revelation had not changed. For all the years of church history Christians have believed that God speaks, and reveals Himself, in His Word. Christians have always believed that God speaks in other ways - in creation, in history, in conscience and, supremely and savingly, in Christ. But we can approach creation, history, conscience and Christ only *through the Word.* What we know of Christ and what we know of the voice of God in creation, history and conscience come *through the Word.* All this has changed now. Apparently God now reveals Himself to us in 'our understanding of the Word inter-reacting with and interrelating to contemporary movements in history'. It seems too complicated to be true! And how can it be true? And how can anyone believe this and not expose himself to the charge of being subjective, i.e. of using this new theory to give expression to his own private opinions? For how are the contemporary movements (e.g. Women's Lib, Gay Lib, Black Power, Leftism in politics) to be judged except by the Word? What has happened, I suspect, is that theologians have seen a contemporary trend (e.g. Women's Lib) and have taken this to be the voice of God speaking to the church. They have then gone back to the Bible and have tried to integrate this with Scripture. Unable to integrate it, they have re-written the Scriptures. Therefore Paul was anti-feminist; the early church was paternalistic, patriarchal and male-dominated; the Pauline teaching on women is 'time-bounden' i.e. is confined to that period, and is not true for all the church age. And so on and on!

(Incidentally, there is not a vestige of evidence in the New Testament that women are inferior or second-rate. On the contrary, both Jesus and Paul rescued womankind from the low-esteem and degradation of their age. The Gospel of Christ, far from being 'hard on women', dignifies them and lifts them to their true, God-appointed and honoured station.

Men and women, are, in the sight of God, equal in status but different in function. What could be simpler, more sweet or more acceptable to either sex?)

Yet there is tragic irony in the cases of men who may yet be brought to trial over the issue of ordination. For who, one may ask, are to sit in judgment on these men? I know ministers who are perfectly prepared to ordain women, yet whose own personal spiritual beliefs could virtually be written down on the back of a postage stamp. I know men who deny the deity of Christ, the Virgin Birth, the resurrection, the Last Judgment, the Second Coming, the atonement and the very fundamentals of salvation - yet who continue in the ministry. Are these men to be allowed to remain, while others who hold to the tenets of historic, apostolic Christianity are unfrocked? Surely the church, if such were to happen, would expose itself to charges of shame and infamy? Or is it the case that in the Church of Scotland we now have only two definite statements of fundamental belief: (1) thou shalt not be baptized a second time, and (2) thou shalt not refuse to ordain a woman? For the rest, may men believe what they wish?

Perhaps wise and sympathetic statesmen at the top need to be approached with a view to introducing an element of reconciliation. Perhaps the Assembly will have the good sense to introduce a new 'conscience clause', allowing men liberty in this matter. Perhaps Presbyteries ought to allow ministers, other than those being brought to trial, to perform the ordination ceremony on condition that the ladies involved are freely admitted to the Session. Perhaps, and perhaps and perhaps. But my own position is well known. I can not, and will not, ordain a woman either to the eldership or to the ministry since, in my judgment, it is: (a) against the Word of God; (b) against 2000 years of Christian tradition (are the Apostolic Fathers and the Church Fathers, and the Reformers and all Greek and Russian Orthodox Christians, not to mention Roman Catholics and Anglicans, wrong?); and (c) against the psychology and nature of womanhood. And who will argue rationally, spiritually and Scripturally against these four unanswerable propositions viz. that God is the Head of Christ, that Christ is the head of the church, that the husband (in marriage) is the head of the wife and that the man (in the church) is the head of woman?

Yours, contending for truth,
THOMAS SWANSTON

42
COVENANT BAPTISM*

My Dear Friends,

I cannot recall, at any time, having had much interest in the well-known controversy between those who believe in infant baptism (paedo-baptists is their grand name) and those who hold to 'believer's baptism' (commonly known as Baptists or 'immersionists'). Between the baptism of infants by the sprinkling of a little water and the immersion of adults in a large amount of water there lies another position: in some Eastern churches infants are immersed! I understand that the fonts are deep and that the water is lukewarm! Other Christians believe in an intermediate practice somewhere between sprinkling and immersion. It is called 'affusion' and involves pouring water over the candidate for baptism. Yet another group of Christians subscribes to the reformed teachings of Calvinism, as we do, yet declines to baptize infants on the grounds that one can believe in a covenant God without administering a covenant 'sign' such as sprinkling, to little children who are incapable of personal faith. These Christians are sometimes known as Reformed or Calvinistic Baptists.

Early on in my Christian life, while pacing such a minefield, I learned that devout, godly and mature saints held varying views on the doctrine of baptism and I have tried to respect, ever since, the opinions and convictions of those from whom I differed in this matter. I decline, on principle, to allow water, whether in small or large quantities, to separate me from wholesome, spiritual communion in Christ

*January 1987

with a fellow believer. Life is too short, and the needs of our darkened generation too urgent, to allow of such public squabbles. It is right that we should talk of such issues, for Christian discussion can stimulate and sharpen the mind; but it is equally as right that we should talk, and differ if need be, in the holy love of Jesus. I personally am fully persuaded as to the rightness and scripturality of the sprinkling of infants, and that for this good reason: it is part of what is known as Covenant Theology. It is of that, and its implications, that I now wish to write.

We in the Church of Scotland, as in Presbyterian churches generally, are committed to Covenant Theology. The Westminster Confession of Faith, which is our subordinate, or secondary, standard of faith (as the Bible is our first) is really an interpretation of Scripture. It offers a way of looking at the Bible through Covenant Theology spectacles.

Adam, for instance, is viewed not as a private individual acting for himself: he is seen as the Covenant Head of the old, lost, unregenerate, once-born humanity. When Adam sinned he sinned not only for himself: he sinned for all the progeny of which he was the natural father. That is why Paul can say that 'in Adam all men die'. There is no point in protesting that we were not in Eden when Adam sinned and therefore cannot be held responsible for his action. That is not how Scripture thinks. We were in the Garden when he sinned because we were 'in Adam'. In that sin he not only dragged down the entire race to come, he also, since he was the caretaker of God's Garden, corrupted the whole universe. 'The stars are not pure in His sight.'

In the same way, Jesus Christ, the Redeemer of God's elect, is seen as the Covenant Head of the new humanity, the brand new race of men and women brought into existence by His death and resurrection. They are the twice-born, begotten again from death to newness of life to serve the living God. When Christ died He did not die for Himself: He died for His family of bairns yet unborn. He acted not for Himself but for them. When He died they died; when He lay in the grave they also lay there with Him, dead to sin; and when He rose again on the third day, the church rose with Him.

The Bible in such a scheme is a covenant book given to a covenant people. Israel in the Old Testament was the covenant nation of God. The blood of the Passover lamb was covenant blood, and its shedding presaged that great and awesome, yet wondrous, day when the blood of the Lamb, the covenant Son of God, was spilled for the forgiveness of sins and the cleansing of sinners. The Gospel of Grace is a covenant message destined for covenant ears. The salvation that it offers is a covenant salvation sealed in the blood of the Lamb. And heaven, at the last, is a covenant place for a covenant people purchased under the grace of a loving, covenant Father-God.

Not that there are two covenants, old and new. There are two 'testaments' in our Bible, but they are not a testament of law set over against a testament of grace. There is no suggestion anywhere in the Old Testament that men could then be saved by keeping the law or by doing good works. When God says in the Old Testament, 'This do, and thou shalt live', or, 'Keep my commandments and live', He is not saying, 'This do... keep my commandments... and be saved'. He means this, 'This do... keep my commandments, and you will live life to the full, spiritually, satisfyingly and richly.'

There is, in fact, only one way to be saved, and that is by the grace of God through the exercise of personal faith. The Old Testament saints were saved by Christ as we are, they by prospect and we by retrospect. Abraham rejoiced to see Christ's day and was glad! Thus the Cross casts its shadow backwards into the Old as well as forwards into the New. And there is only one covenant, that of grace. In the Old Testament it is seen as law; in the New it is seen as Gospel. The covenant signs in the Old Testament were circumcision and the Passover: in the New they are baptism and the Lord's Supper. And there is a marvellous naturalness in that arrangement for, if the God of the Old Testament is a covenant God, it would have been unthinkable for Him suddenly to change His nature and ways at the coming of Christ.

What am I trying to say behind these arguments? Simply this - that for a number of years I have felt that the present youth structures of the Church of Scotland are very nearly a disaster area. The structures are, and have been for a long time, rather fruitless and unproductive. Theoretically young folk are supposed to be channelled upwards, through various groups, into church membership through a commitment to Christ as Saviour and Lord. But that is not happening. It is not happening anywhere.

I suspect that in older days it happened rather mechanically. Young folk in their later teens 'joined the church' to please their parents, or because they were leaving home to work elsewhere, or because they were going up to university, or because it was 'the right thing to do', or because one day they hoped to be married in church, or because they had reached a certain age. None of these is a proper reason, or a right motive, for associating oneself with the Lord's people in communicant membership. We have now reached a situation in which not only do the young folk from our organisations not join the church, what is more serious, very few join themselves to Christ for salvation. Coming to church, as we all ought well to know, is one thing; coming to Christ is another.

In practice, therefore, we are losing the young people of

our churches. They drift away, and the vast majority are seen no more. There was a day when at least some of the blame for this state of affairs could have been laid on poor leadership. How committed to Christ, in any personal way, were some of the leaders in the old days? How many were truly regenerate of the Holy Spirit? How many were tainted by liberal, broad-minded theology? How corroded were they by the acids of modernity? How many were persuaded and had a clear grasp of basic evangelical doctrine?

Thus far the old. But that was yesterday. We now have today a more dedicated, more consecrated and better informed leadership than we have had in the churches for many years. And still the losses persist. The failure, apart from the youth structures in church work, surely lies in the homes, many of which have abrogated their responsibility to communicate Christ to growing sons and daughters. The most natural persons in the world to teach Christ to the young are not Sunday School teachers, however well qualified, nor yet Bible Class leaders, nor yet the leaders of youth organisations, whether uniformed or not, but the parents. Sunday Schools, in any case, were never intended to be the principal centres for the education of church children. They were originally intended for the evangelisation of children from non-church homes and their aim was to bring them to Christ. It was taken for granted that in Christian homes there would be worship, prayer, grace before meals, the reading of Scripture and the practice of the presence of the living Christ.

It is argued that times have changed; and, without doubt, they have. But surely it cannot be doubted that certain bed-rock realities are timeless and do not change with changing years? God is still the Head of Christ; Christ is still the Head of the church; the husband is still the head of the wife; the parents are still the head of the family; and the father is still the moral and spiritual head of the house. It is unthinkable, therefore, that the children of Christian parents should be allowed the exercise of unrestricted freedom in matters of religion, worship and spirituality. If the times have moved away from God who will dare move with the times?

Infant baptism is an expression of the covenant teaching that the children of believing parents are 'heirs of the covenant of grace' and that, in baptism, God brings the little ones of the fold 'under the influence of that special grace which is found only within the family and household of faith'. The children of converted parents are not to be regarded, or brought up, as other children who are foreigners and strangers to grace. They are special children, to be cherished for the Saviour and to be monitored, schooled, disciplined and finally engraced into Himself.

Being weak and foolish, of course, we often use erroneous language. We speak of 'claiming the children for covenant grace' or of 'handing over the little ones to covenant grace'. Neither of these expressions is found in the Bible, and neither could be found since they seem to assume that man makes the prior move i.e. we hand the bairns over to God. But infant baptism is witness to the truth that the action of God comes first. Grace is prior to faith, and the most important agent in a baptismal ceremony is neither the father nor the mother but Christ. It is simply required of the parents that they have a true and saving faith in Him, that they themselves be inside the covenant and that they promise to give the child a godly Christian upbringing. I recall shuddering with horror when I once heard a Christian father say that he regarded his sons as 'the rotten miserable sinners we all are, in need of conviction of sin, of repentance and of conversion'. He had no sense whatever that they might conceivably belong to the world of grace. Alas he got the children he deserved.

Am I saying that the children of believing parents are automatically saved? No, not really. But who can say when the Holy Spirit does His work of regeneration? Faith is necessary for salvation, we often assert, and faith can come only with years of discretion and understanding. Yes, indeed. But faith is not the *ground* of the New Birth. Faith is *evidence* of the New Birth. Faith is the visible fruit of which being born again is the hidden root. 'Except a man be born again,' said Jesus, '*he cannot see*.' And lack of seeing bespeaks blindness.

Young folk can wander and break our hearts. That goes almost without saying. Many come to Christ the hard way after years of rebellion and waywardness. Parents often die in faith without having seen the promises come true, committing, almost with their last breath, their bairns to the holy care of a saving God. And young folk, especially in their teens when they want to assert their independence and strike out to 'try life' for themselves, can be infuriating to older Christians who have tried the broken cisterns and found them to fail. Yet the covenanted young must come to Christ. The Word of God and its certain promises are sure and steadfast even when, and perhaps especially when, they are contradicted by the evidence before our eyes.

It is shocking and grievous, almost beyond what words can express, to see some professing evangelical parents allow their families so much latitude and leeway in spiritual matters, as if children were to be the masters of their spiritual futures and destinies. 'As for me *and my house*,' said Joshua, 'we will serve the Lord.' I do not believe that in this area of life there are any 'mysteries'. God honours faithfulness. God answers prayer. He has covenanted and sworn to be not only a God and Father to us but also the God and Father of our children. I rejoice to say that a growing number of husbands and wives in our fellowship have proved, in this very issue, that children grow into Christ and into a manhood and womanhood that is pleasing to God. What greater crown could they desire for their love for one another? And from their consecration I do not exclude the power of intensive prayer.

Yours sincerely,
THOMAS SWANSTON

PS: John Macpherson has been telling me that the disobedient and wayward children of Christian parents must be reckoned as covenant-breakers. Do you not think this an interesting thought?

43
BAPTISM OF NON-MEMBERS*

Dear Friends,
It is right that a minister, from time to time, should share with his people some of the things that trouble him in his work. Here is a matter that I want you to think through with me: it has disturbed me for several years and given me some rare twitches of conscience. It concerns the baptism of children whose parents are not members of the church.

This may seem rather remote and unimportant, but it rose to the surface at a recent meeting of the Kirk Session when we discussed the church's failure to hold both her adult membership and her young people. One of our elders, Mr. Eric McIntyre, said that the church in our time would have more spiritual authority, and make a more telling impact on our generation, if she kept to Christian principles and exercised proper discipline over her members. Another elder, Mr. Herb Macdonald, added that the failures of the church could be traced to 'lack of both leadership and discipline'. We cannot expect the world to be impressed by our message when we are so casual about setting our own house in order.

Here in the Highlands we have rather a special set-up. In common with every other congregation of the Church of Scotland we have a Members' Roll. This is made up of all those who have made a reasonable confession of Christ before a congregation of His people. They have told the world that God is their Father, that Jesus is their Saviour and Lord, and that the Holy Spirit is their indwelling Comforter. We all know, of course, that some of these confessions are hypocriti-

*October 1973

cal since the confessors give little evidence of repentance, of the second birth of the Spirit, of conversion, of newness of life. Paul puts it like this: 'They are not all Israel who are of Israel... Those who are the children of the flesh, these are not the children of God' (Rom 9: 6,8).

It is not our calling, however, to sit in judgment and say who are and who are not Christians. 'The Lord knoweth them that are His.' We simply have to take folk at the face value of their confession. At the very least they have 'taken a stand' for Christ. They have hoisted, as it were, the family flag. A 'member' may later on, by false teaching and indifferent life, turn out to be an unbeliever. In that case he is an insincere professor. But until he shows himself to be so, then we must accept him as a child of God.

In the Highlands also we have Adherents' Rolls. These are made up of people who do not fully profess Christ, but who wish to identify themselves with the work and worship of a congregation. Adherents give many reasons for not committing themselves to membership. Some say that they are 'not ready'; others that they are 'not worthy' to come to the Table; and a few honestly admit that they do not come to the Supper because they have not had 'the change' (i.e. the change of the New Birth). No-one doubts that there are true believers among adherents, some of whom are excellent and devout saints, full of faith, of the Holy Ghost, and of good works. Their unwillingness to 'come forward' is due to shyness, or to an over-strict upbringing, or to a false fear of holy things. It also needs to be said, gently but plainly, that a few hold back for less worthy reasons. We all have a certain amount of native guile in our natures, and I'm afraid that some do not want their lives to be interfered with. They will not commit themselves to Christ lest they get 'too involved'.

As Presbyterians we believe that the children of believing

parents are heirs of the New Testament of God's grace. So we hold that they should be baptized, and marked with the outward sign and seal of the covenant - in this case water, just as Jewish babies were covenanted to God in circumcision. (The Westminster Confession of Faith makes it clear that water baptism and circumcision are not in essence saying different things. They are two rites, but they stand for the same reality, namely the committal of the child to the covenant grace of God, and his separation from the world to belong to the Lord. This was as true for a Jewish child as it is for a Christian.) But here is the rub: when parents bring a child to church for baptism, the vows we ask them to take are the *vows of church membership.* They are the vows which answer the questions we put at the Service of Admission of New Communicants. But *how can we* ask adherents to take these vows when they have never confessed Christ?

Take the idea of 'vicarious faith', i.e. faith exercised on behalf of another who is too weak to trust. The best example of this in the New Testament is the story of the man who was taken to Jesus and lowered down through a hole in the roof. The Bible says that it was 'when Jesus saw *their* faith' that He healed the man. *Their* faith - the faith of the men who brought the man. He was too poorly and sick to do anything for himself. In fact, in the story he does not say anything at all. In the same way a baby cannot trust Christ. He is too young and lacks understanding. So we baptize him on the strength of the parents' faith. But how can we baptize the babies of adherents on the strength of the parents' faith, if the parents have no faith?

It can well be argued that perhaps adherents have a true and living trust, and confess Christ in their hearts. Fair enough. But if a man confesses Christ in his heart, why does he not confess Him with his lips? Why do *believing* adherents not take the final step, hoist their colours for Christ, and take a stand with the Lord's people in service? If adherents are prepared to stand before a congregation and take vows, surely they must know that this obliges them to come to the Supper, since it is vowing the vows that makes us members?

Some critics of our denomination tell us that we are now a church without discipline. Certainly among the churches we are now almost a byword for laxity. It is *almost* true to say that a man may believe what he likes, and live as he pleases, and still be reckoned a good 'church member' unrebuked and unchastised. But in the Highlands we can hardly complain at these criticisms, for in practice we have put the Sacraments of the Gospel on two levels. The Lord's Supper is somehow seen as a first-class sacrament, for the far-ben, top-grade, consecrated Christians; while Infant Baptism is all right for the more ordinary folk, whether they live Christian lives or not. That is why *more* parents come to the Font than to the Table. But must we go on having this system of first and second class Sacraments?

I know that churches can be too stern and too strict, and by their legalism can, and do, drive men away from Christ, alienating and estranging them. I would be the last to turn a frosty, unwelcoming face to any who genuinely seek Christ and His blessing on their homes. Experience, however, suggests that not many of the adherents who have sought baptism for their children are in any way interested in the affairs of the Gospel. Very few attend church regularly. Most come to worship neither before nor after the child is baptized. Only a handful could begin to tell the difference between 'christening' and 'baptism'.

Do you see my dilemma? Church law is church law, and sinners are sinners and apt to stray and be foolish. No doubt. But are we to go on being a church without standards, without discipline? Meanwhile we go on asking questions of adherents in church, and expect for answers *vows of membership.* But am I thus asking men and women to sin their souls? They have never ever professed such vows. Do you see my problem, and appreciate how unhappy my conscience is?

Yours, with growing affection,
THOMAS SWANSTON

44
PERSONAL EVANGELISM*

Dear Friends,

The subject of personal evangelism is one that has concerned me for some time, and I want to think with you about this now. By 'personal evangelism' I mean the man to man, one to one, heart to heart, eyes to eyes communication of Christ; and the burden of my message is that either Christians have lost this rare art or else, having not quite lost it entirely, fail to practise it in any measure.

Our difficulty is that we tend to fall into two kinds of error. In the first place, we try to excuse our silence in the presence of unbelievers by muttering vaguely of personal modesty, failure of self-expression, wordlessness, lack of aggression, the fear of appearing too 'pushy' in the manner of sectarians. Some have even held that such characteristics, in the world of religion, are national and that dour Scots do not find it particularly easy to speak of their faith since 'religion is a private affair'.

In the second place, Christians have often assumed that public worship is the only, or the main, occasion for evangelism. For us the 'preaching of the Word' is the great thing and the pulpit cannot be anywhere other than central. If only, therefore, we can get men under the sound of the Word, there is some hope of their being saved. It is unfortunate that because of this there has grown up in many reformed circles, especially here in the north, the idea that the minister or the professional evangelist is the primary agent in the conversion of souls, and that he is the proper person to lead seekers to

*October 1980

Christ and salvation. In practice this has meant that when Christians have wanted to see their neighbours influenced for the Saviour they have taken them along to worship, and have often used this as an excuse for not engaging in man to man, one to one, heart to heart, eyes to eyes personal evangelism.

With regard to these two points above, it is always interesting to see how eloquently and volubly men can talk of the concerns and subjects nearest their hearts (e.g. golf, fishing, football, music, art, church activities, culture, politics). I recall one professor in divinity college who could 'stand and deliver' for any length of time, to the point of weariness, on all sorts of socio-political matters, but who had little to say of Christ. What Jesus said of Peter was aptly and tragically true of that man, 'Thy speech betrayeth thee!'

And whether we dour Scots are quite as taciturn, as sullen and as wordless as is sometimes believed, is a debatable point. Celtic oratory is proverbial (is it not?) even if the Welsh Celts seem to have a greater measure than we Irish Celts. And we should beware of using 'Scottish dourness' as a grand excuse for saying nothing at all. Man is a creature of easy options when and where he can find them, and we all are given to liking cheap short-cuts. To my mind it is obvious that personal evangelism is more costly than simply asking a friend to attend worship. 'What think ye of Christ?' is not quite in the same category of question as, 'Would you like to come and hear the minister?'

The urgency of all this is seen in the indisputable fact that in the past thirty years attitudes to, and the language of, evangelism have changed. After my own conversion to Christ during the Tell Scotland Crusade, when Billy Graham came to the Kelvin Hall, it was somehow assumed that committed and surrendered believers should become soul winners. 'Firebrands' was one of the current terms used of those who were aflame for God and for souls, hungry for trophies for the King. Somehow one hears less and less of this language, and one would be hard put to it to draw up a short list of Christians who could be called 'soul-winners'. Matters reached a new and disheartening 'low' for me when I heard a young man saying that he did not think he had ever influenced a soul for Christ. What was more he added that he would not know how to lead anyone to the feet of the Saviour. And he was held to be a bright Christian! 'One of the two who heard John speak, and followed him, was Andrew, Simon Peter's brother. He first found his brother...' (John 1:40,41). Times have changed!

You realise, of course, that I don't want to idealise, or glorify, or romanticise the past, otherwise how far back would we have to go for methods? To Sankey and Moody? To the Bonars and McCheyne? To the Wesleys and Whitefield? To the English and Scottish Puritans? Or to the Reformers themselves? We are all under an obligation to make Jesus Christ contemporary to every generation, and to cause Him to live to the understandings of our fellows as vitally as we may. And yet times *do* appear to have changed! 'We can hardly wait for the next campaign to start,' said an enthusiast. 'We are hoping to see many saved.' But do we not expect men to be saved every week when the Word is preached in the power of the Spirit? Have we ceased to believe in the Holy Ghost as an experimental reality? Do we not count on God to be at work as we, His fellow-workers, work with Him? Campaigns and special efforts may be useful in themselves, but they can never take the place of the private, personal encounter. Man to man, one to one, heart to heart, eyes to eyes. This is the evangelism of the future, and may soon be the only evangelism allowed if western Christendom is engulfed by totalitarian regimes.

Consider the phrase that was once in common use - 'hand-picked fruit'. Nowadays we have machines for harvesting crops and lifting potatoes. We even have machines for picking raspberries. But farmers will tell you that machines damage the crop. Fruit lovingly picked by hand is less likely to be harmed. Which thing is a parable. We have lost the art of picking fruit by hand, of culling and choosing men and women personally for Christ. In the end of the day, this must be done with words. Just as cartoons of the Gospel are not enough, so portrayals of Jesus in life and deed are not enough. Sooner or later He must be spoken - His Name, His claims, His promises, His warnings, His overtures, His invitations to men.

And yet the deepest word has yet to be spoken. Personal evangelism presupposes a vital message, and one cannot have such a message without a vision of the Crucified. If that has dimmed, or been sullied and spoiled by coldness of heart or by secret backsliding (our fellowship is riddled with men and women who have drawn the line with Jesus), then the call is not for personal evangelism but for a sore repentance - a change of mind, leading to a change of heart, leading to change of life. Many who have been to the Cross need to come back there again. The born-again need to be born-again again, if that does not strain the point too far.

It was said of Jesus that He 'spake as never man spake'. Let's learn all over again how to speak to men of Him who spake as never man spake. Man to man, one to one, heart to heart, eyes to eyes. My fear is, you see, that so many will one day stand before Him and have to show no more than the barren fig tree - nothing but leaves. 'We speak what we do know, and witness to the things that we have seen,' and 'That which we have seen and heard we proclaim' (John 3:11;1 John 1:3).

Yours warmly, with growing affections in the work,
THOMAS SWANSTON

45
PAROCHIALISM*

My Dear Friends,
We Scots are a people of paradoxes; some might even say of contradictions. We are inveterate wanderers, adventurers, explorers of continents and challengers of the unknown. Highland clearances and evictions, together with the vicissitudes of history, have made us so. Thus we have scoured the world to found banks and new cities, chart strange seas, and pepper mountains and maps with clan names.

But you cannot deny that we are also guilty of appalling parochialism. As students we used to joke about Scottish narrow-mindedness by telling the apocryphal story of how, on the morning the Titanic went down, a local north-east rag carried the headline: 'Aberdeen man drowned at sea'. It is well to joke about that sort of limited vision: but it is no joke at all to think of the failure of congregations to lift up their eyes to wider missionary horizons. Do you know any living missionaries? Can you name half a dozen? Do you correspond with any? Do you know the name of our own congregation's official prayer partner? The only expression I can find to describe narrow, parish-bound religion is 'kailyard Christianity'. It is a gross hindrance to the work of Christ in our day, and will survive among us only over my dead body. Brothers and sisters, I am against kailyard Christianity. And if you are for it, then I cannot be other than against you.

Actually, the Church of Scotland had a poorish start, historically speaking, to missionary enterprise. The traditional date for the Scottish Reformation is 1560, but the first

*March 1975

missionaries did not begin to go out in any numbers until the early 1800s. Why the 240 years of starved vision? It has been argued that the reformed church was still finding her feet, and had too many internal problems with which to cope: problems of relationship with the State, of church order and government, and the ever-growing difficulties created by schismatic, breakaway bodies. And there is, to be fair, an element of truth in all this. But the early church too had her problems. There were heresies, divisions and hypocrisies from a very early stage, and there was the might of the Roman Empire to contend with. Yet the early Christians turned that world upside down, problems and all! It is a question of having that vision of the Crucified without which 'the people cast off restraint'.

The General Assembly of 1796 was a high watermark of blindness in this respect, and yet a turning-point too. Proposals were made that the church should carry the Gospel to the heathen abroad, but this was bitterly opposed. One minister rose and, in a fluent and able speech, argued that we had heathen enough to convert on our own doorsteps and, besides, we would need to wait until the heathen saw the light of civilisation first before we brought them the light of Christ. When he finished a clumsy, white-haired man, Dr. John Erskine of Greyfriars Church, rose and called across the Assembly: 'Moderator! Rax me that Bible!' He read the first ten verses of Acts 28. 'Think you,' he said, after he had closed the Book, 'that when Paul wrought his miracles at Malta he did not also preach Christ to the Barbarians and explain whose Name it was through which such power was given to men?' He went on to plead the missionary cause of the Saviour, and said that it was our duty to bring redemption to people of other lands, and not merely to use them for trade. His plea - and this is almost unbelievable in our emancipated age - was actually refused by the Assembly!

Consider, therefore, the expansion of the churches' missionary borders in last century, coupled as it was with the spread of worldly empire and the growth of capital; and compare that expansion with the contraction of the churches' missionary borders in the past 50 years. It is a sobering prospect, and it can be argued that the speed of recent contraction far exceeds that of the previous expansion. Some 70 years ago one third of the world atlas was coloured pink, and belonged to the British Empire. Now the Empire is no more; we scarcely have a Commonwealth; and two thirds of the world surface is now dark red, and closed to outside missionary interests into the bargain. But the question arises as to who closed the borders? There was a day when Russia and China were wide open to the Evangel of Christ. Western Christians, tragically, failed to enter. Surely it was God, the Lord of history, who closed the gates as judgment on the church's unbelief and infidelity to her great commission?

But where does your religion end? For many it ends with their own skin, reaching no further. These are the folk that say that their religion is a 'private affair'. It certainly is, and noticeably and painfully so in many cases, for their religion is private almost to the point of non-existence. For others their religion ends with the walls of the kirk: they cannot see further than the church's activities and organisational life. For them 'a good-going congregation' is the be-all and end-all of religion, and is what Christ died for. For others religion ends with the boundaries of the town, or with the fringe of the Highlands, or with the coasts of Scotland. But where does yours end? Surely you cannot believe that when our Treasurer sends off our contribution to the Mission and Service Fund we have fulfilled all righteousness?

There is a parable for us in the tension between Jerusalem

and Antioch as centres of evangelical outreach in the early church. Jerusalem tended to be rather Jewish, whereas Antioch was the gateway to the wider Gentile world. Jerusalem became the home of the rather narrow, exclusive, legalistic, parochial, provincial party, inward-looking and slow to move out and claim the Gentiles for Christ. History shows that this community eventually became a backwater where very little happened. God marched on, through outward-looking Antioch, into the world. Those who did not march with Him were left behind.

All of this is illustrated in a story told by Prof. J .S. Stewart in one of his sermons. The story goes that a lady once came to her Bishop protesting that she did not believe in missionaries. 'Madam,' said the Bishop, 'you have no right to believe in missionaries. You do not believe in Christ.' The Bishop's point is well made and I hope it reaches us all loud and clear. If you do not believe in missionaries the sombre probability is that you do not believe in Christ. Fellowships that have ceased to believe in, and care for, missionary outreach at home and abroad are not dying; they are already dead. They may well survive, but they do not live.

Your servant in the glad bonds of Christ,

THOMAS SWANSTON

46
LACK OF VISION*

Dear Friends,
Perhaps you have heard the story of the Aberdeenshire farmer who is alleged to have prayed thus: 'Lord, bless me; and dinna forget my Brussels sprouts'. We smile at the man's naivety; but is a smile the proper reaction? The Bible proclaims the Lord's eagerness to bless farmers, especially farmers who pray. Scripture also teaches us that this same Lord who is willing and zealous to bless His creatures (more willing and zealous to bless than they are to be blessed by Him) even has an interest in vegetation. The Old Testament in particular has much to say on the Lord's care for trees, for crops and harvests and for the soil itself - as witness the fallow years commanded by Him so that the very earth could, with men, enjoy God's sabbaths. We ought not to smile at the farmer's naivety (the Lord of creation being anxious to do good both to him and to his Brussels sprouts), but we ought rather to grieve at his parochialism and narrow-mindedness. The world is a big place, much larger than the largest of our cabbage patches. Yet how many Christians today live in spiritual vegetable plots and have adopted Brussels sprouts mentalities?

I cannot but think of poor Sam Weller in Dicken's *Pickwick Papers.* Sam lamented the fact that he could not see much, or far, or well. 'Yes, I have a pair of eyes,' replied Sam, 'and that's just it. If they wos a pair o' patent double million magnifying' gas microscopes of hextra power, p'haps I might be able to see through a flight o' stairs and deal (soft-

*March 1989

wood) door; but bein' only eyes, you see my wision's limited.' Sam's difficulty was his limited vision. His weakness is epidemic among the saints. Only a choice few, it appears, have faith sufficient to lift up their eyes to see beyond the palisades guarding their kail-yards to the broad horizons, the evangelical possibilities and fields white unto harvest. Where there is no vision of this sort of magnitude, the people surely perish (Prov 29:18).

I wonder if we in Scotland are peculiarly susceptible to lack of vision? Joy Hendry, writing in *The Scotsman* of 7th January of this year, complains about the poorish quality of the offerings on Radio Scotland over the Christmas and New Year periods. She says: 'The turn of the year fairly brings out the kailyard Scots from the woodwork, and we get on radio a near unadulterated diet of Scottish country dance music, pipe music and the old chestnuts of Scottish song... New Year proves annually that kailyardism is alive and well in Scotland...' Kailyardism is indeed alive and well, but it is not new in the churches. The date of the Scottish Reformation is traditionally taken as 1560. But, in fact, 200 years passed before the Church of Scotland started to think about sending missionaries into the world to convert the heathen. Ideas suggesting that General Assemblies should bestir themselves to consider the cause of world evangelism were barely tolerated. There's lack of vision for you and a Brussels sprouts mentality!

It could be, and often is, argued that we in Scotland were taken up in those years with internal problems, with creeds and statements of faith, with the organisation of parishes and schools and kirks, with doctrinal matters and the dangers of schism and fracture in the Body of Christ. Fair enough: there is some truth in this. But the early Christians had major problems: yet they had the vision, the faith and the courage to turn the Empire upside down! Do you not find it interesting that the disciples of Jesus were first called 'Christians' not in Jerusalem, as one might expect, since the Lord had died and risen again there, but in Antioch? Antioch was the place with a vision of the needy world beyond the cabbage patch of Palestine. From Antioch the first ambassadors of the Cross set sail; in Antioch the worldlings sat up and started to take notice of the Gospel. But Jerusalem, with its barren petty-mindedness and visionless-ness, became a backwater and the blessing bypassed it and moved on.

Is there an answer to lack of vision? The question leads to another: 'Where should our religion end?' Ought it to be a purely private affair, ending with the points of our religious noses? Does it stretch beyond the walls of the kirk to compass Inverness? Does it extend to what the Lord is doing in Scotland today? Do you *know* what God is doing in Scotland today - in the schools, in the colleges and universities, in the caring ministries of our own denomination? Do you have a vision of Europe, or of Africa, or of the Far East, or of China, or of South America? A casual visit to the free section of the Christian Literature Bookstall might open blinded eyes and prove a revelation. Or are we forever to be thirled to parochialism?

Parochialism. Aye, there's the rub! The word, incidentally, comes from two Greek words: *para* - alongside, and *oikos* - a house or dwelling. The parochial mind is taken up with events and happenings in the immediate vicinity - alongside the dwelling! While that is well and good for some of the time, the parochial spirit, anxious only that the Lord should attend to our Brussels sprouts, has ever been a hindrance to the spread of the Gospel and can prove an enemy of the onward march of Christ in the world. Such a spirit has been, and still is, something of a plague in Highland Christianity. I met an elderly Christian lately who had never heard of Hudson Taylor and the work of the China Inland Mission. One could be forgiven for reeling aghast in the manner of a Sophoclean chorus!

I jalouse that what we lack nowadays is a sense of adventure and of the heroic in Christian living. Abraham went forth in the obedience of faith 'not knowing whither he went'. There were elements of risk, of danger and of daring in such a step. Can we not rise to the likes of this today? Kailyards are all very well; and Brussels sprouts are good for you. But Jesus said: 'I must go on to the next villages to preach for that is why I have been sent.' *I must go on!* To that end it would be helpful if we were all to lay on the altar of sacrifice our fondness for self-preservation. At the end of the day those who hold on to their lives lose them. One cannot have one's life and be saved. Jesus said so. And to become a Christian at all, far less a Christian delivered from a cabbage patch mentality, will need more than a casual visit to the free section of the bookstall: it will require nothing less than a new sight of the Crucified. When, and if, that happens we will, in the words of Thomas Hardy, be ready to be up and doing, 'scorning parochial ways'.

Yours sincerely,
THOMAS SWANSTON

47
EIRE*

Dear Friends,
In July it was my happy privilege to be one of the speakers, in Southern Ireland, at the Greystones Convention for the Deepening of Spiritual Life, and I should like to place here some public record of that exciting expedition and venture. I shared the platform with Rev. Maurice Marshall, himself Irish by birth and nurture. He is a minister in the Church of England and a man of thoroughly Reformed outlook and sympathies. Sharing Calvinism we shared so much else!

Two impressions of Eire indelibly abide: a famine of the Word of God, and a hunger for it. Undoubtedly the two go together. If we never miss the water till the well runs dry it seems to follow, by analogy, that we are most aware of pangs of hunger when the cupboard is bare. And the cupboard is very bare in many places in Eire, both in Rome and in Protestantism. Let me enlarge on these two, on the famine and on the hunger.

Without wishing to be needlessly polemical and controversial it is true, I think, to say that the vast majority of Roman Catholics live in an ignorance of the Gospel that is almost total. Religion for them is a question of masses, confessionals, prayers to Mary, telling rosaries, engaging in good works, and faithfully obeying the priest. Not only do the majority not know the Gospel and the Word, but they also scarcely understand the teachings of their own church. In a sense they are not expected to, since it is not the place of ordinary believers to usurp the privileges and the powers of

*October 1979

the clergy. It is simply required that worshippers come to mass and confession, put in offerings and be obedient.

It is only fair to say here that much of this is little different from a great deal of contemporary Protestantism. It could cogently be argued that, with a few changes in terms, not much separates the estate and condition of most Catholics from the estate and condition of most Protestants. What, after all, is the difference between two corpses? One may die richer or poorer than the other, or better informed, or better dressed. But each is dead. A Catholic who is not born again of the Spirit is in precisely the same position as a Protestant who is not born again. Each is dead, and neither is a Christian. One is a Catholic unbeliever, and the other is a Protestant unbeliever.

In Eire the population is 96% nominally Roman Catholic and 4% nominally Protestant. The historic Irish problem is largely of English origin, caused by the oppressions of absentee landlords who lived on their country estates in England, or in their town houses in London, and collected rates and taxes from Irish peasants whom they had scarcely ever seen. Cromwell is still called the 'Scourge of Ireland'. From that imperial and rapacious past we reap today the bitter harvests.

Mr. Marshall recalled some of his younger days when Protestant lads tried to evangelise the Irish villages. Simple folk would eagerly rush to receive tracts, only to tear them up and scatter the pieces to the winds. Bibles too were gladly received and immediately burned. And any evangelising group could be sure that at the end of the village street, when the Gospel visitation was over, there would be a band of bully-boys ready to give the heretics a good punch-up.

But there has been a famine among Protestants too, and they with Bibles in their hands - God's full larder! In this matter of neglecting the truth, how much more culpable are professing Protestants! The tradition, both in northern and southern Ireland, has been one of evangelisticism. The term 'evangelistic' refers to certain methods and emphases - to appeals and altar calls, to enquiry rooms and to a rather limited understanding of what constitutes the 'simple Gospel'. There has been a preoccupation with fundamentals and elementary Gospel truth - the need to repent and be saved, the need for primary forgiveness, the need to be born again, the necessity of conversion, the coming judgment, the realities of heaven and hell. But Hebrews says, 'Let us leave the elementary doctrines of Christ and go on to maturity, not laying again a foundation... and this we will do, if God permit' (Heb 6:1-3).

I am bound to say that I was mildly pressurised by some to turn every meeting into an evangelistic occasion, more or less, and press for 'decisions'. These pressures I gently but firmly resisted and rejected. The convention at Greystones was founded for the 'deepening of spiritual life' i.e. for the advancement of Christians, for growth in holiness, in sanctification, and in service. Why should it be allowed to degenerate (I chose the word advisedly) into yet another Grand Gospel Campaign? Conveniently, such efforts often leave unscathed the consciences of juvenile and worldly Christians. Surely it is well known that judgment begins with the house of God, and that the greater part of the New Testament was written for people who were already committed to the Saviour? Christians in Eire have been starved of the deeper things of the Word, and expository ministries - the week by week systematic opening-up of the treasures of the truth - are almost unknown. 'The hungry sheep look up and are not fed.' Herein is fulfilled that word spoken in Amos, 'Behold, the days are coming... when I will send a famine on the land; not a famine of bread... but of hearing the words of the Lord' (Amos 8:11-12).

But how all of this has changed and is changing! There is a new hunger for Christ and the Word, especially among younger Protestants and Catholics alike. I had already seen something of this in the States, having worked on the streets of Los Angeles with Catholics influenced by the charismatic movement (the movement that seeks to recover the full range of the gifts of the Spirit for all Christians). Some Christian bookshops tell of a sell-out of Bibles and literature to Catholics, including nuns and monks eager to learn the Gospel as they have never known it before. It was Pope John who actually opened up the way for this in what he called 'aggiurnamento' - bringing the church up to date, opening the windows and letting in the sunshine, allowing the Spirit to re-enter and blow away all the cobwebs of needless tradition. At that time I did suspect that Rome was about to bring upon herself her own ruin, for any Roman Catholic turning to the Word immediately becomes aware of the vast discrepancies between what the Bible says and what Rome teaches and practises.

It would be unjust here to omit the part played by the neo-pentecostal movement in this quickening and awakening. Nevertheless, once seekers have acquired a taste for the Word, as distinct from having had a desire for the gifts of the Spirit, these hungry Catholics would put many Protestants to shame. Never could I have imagined myself leading a Bible Study and Prayer Fellowship in a Roman Catholic school, with the Heart of Jesus in one corner, and the Bleeding Heart of Mary in another, and a crucifix above! Yet such was the case as, along with a nun, sister Germaine, I led the gathering. On another occasion I was asked to do Bible Study with some Catholic wives recently influenced for Christ. So many turned up for the meeting at a farmhouse deep in the Irish countryside, that we had to organise a creche in the garden for all the children. We studied the 'tests' of being a Christian, in First John. Several nuns, a monk, a lay brother and a Jesuit came to the Convention. 'More of Jesus; more of Scriptures!' - that was the cry. Some Christians from Cork wondered if I could go south to give Bible readings there. Seemingly, at one recent meeting, nearly 400 Catholics and Protestants came together to study and pray. And a similar group from Limerick asked me to come over to the west to preach.

Quite apart from all of this, there is real evidence of a new work of God among young people dissatisfied with traditional Gospel services, and longing for something richer and deeper. It was a little disheartening to see this hunger was not being satisfied by local churches and preachers who were merely nibbling at the fullness of the Word. My counsel to these young folk was that they should meet together to pray that the Lord would raise up in Ireland a whole new generation of men not afraid to declare the whole counsel of God, as distinct from parts abstracted from the whole and erroneously labelled '*the* Gospel'. And it may well be that the young should themselves be prepared to be just such men. How should a sovereign God not do such a thing? How should a sovereign God not decree that the next spiritual awakening should come through Rome? Why not, indeed, when one considers what 'Protestants', the heirs of Biblical tradition, have done (or, rather, have not done) with their heritage.

Inevitably, in such a situation of flux, there are immense problems. A wary and watchful eye needs to be kept on the excesses of the charismatic movement. Men and women cannot live on 'experiences'. And experience-centred religion, rather than a Christ-centred or a Word-centred one, is doomed to despair, for one is impelled more and more to seek newer thrills and more exciting 'highs'.

Almost inevitably, too, as Catholics turn to Christ and the Word, there is bound to be an increasing awareness of contradictions. If the Bible is the last word, the final court of appeal, the ultimate authority, many of the teachings of Rome are at variance with it - the doctrine of the Mass (Christ dying again and again on Roman altars), the Immaculate Conception (the belief that Mary herself was conceived without sin), the ascension of Mary into heaven, the prayers of Mary on behalf of sinners, the prevailing power of the prayers of departed saints, Requiem Masses, salvation by good works rather than by grace alone, and the entire structure of the Papacy. And there are tales to sadden as well as to cheer. I heard of one dear Christian lady, a nun in a Carmelite convent for over forty years, who was converted to Christ and in whose heart the Spirit did a real work. Superiors were summoned, including the archbishop, and she was dismissed - sent out, cut off without a penny and with scarcely a decent garment to clothe her. She lives alone in a small flat, rejected by her own flesh and blood.

There is also the problem of labels. When Catholics do come out of error, what name do they adopt? Are they now 'Protestants'? Or born-again Catholics? They cannot call themselves 'ex-Catholics', since Catholics will listen to Protestants and even to born-again Catholics, but not to 'ex-Catholics'. And one must be careful with terms. Rome, of course, believes in 'baptismal regeneration' i.e. that children are born-again in baptism. Some Catholics tend to describe their new experience of Christ as a coming to fruition of what had already happened to them in Baptism, a realising of what took place then. But, on the contrary, since we are not made Christians by Baptism, the New Birth within takes place when the Spirit comes from without. It is not the germination of a hidden inner seed, but a brand new life from the outside.

The last problem is also a serious one: the new movement has, so far, generally taken place outside the churches. It has not reached the heart of the establishment and has not received an unqualified blessing. The vast majority of the clergy view with grave misgivings and displeasure the turning away of the faithful to the Bible and to first hand spiritual experience. Indeed, in many areas, priests keep careful scrutiny of what goes on, and deviations from the norm are frowned upon or strictly forbidden.

The challenge is to pray for our good friends in Eire. There was little hint or awareness of the violence in the North. All good Christians deplored the godlessness and anarchy of terrorism. My last impressions were of a charming Celtic people, filled with laughter and good taste, given to hospitality and, from a Christian standpoint, full of promise. The kindnesses showered on me by John and Joan Cardoo in Carrig Eden (the old Christian Endeavour conference centre) were overwhelming, and the fellowship enjoyed there was a rare thrill. Pray that God will bring to perfection the good work that He has surely begun. After all, aren't the Scots, the Irish?

Yours affectionately,
THOMAS SWANSTON

48
HUNGARY*

My Dear Friends,

I want to put down some permanent record of my recent visit to Hungary; and my first words must surely be of profound gratitude for all the prayers which upheld me on a tightly-scheduled mission. It is one of earth's most humbling and thrilling experiences to be thus sustained by prayer, and so enabled to declare God's honour, and sing His song, in a strange land. I am bidden by various Christian groups to convey their thanks for all the gifts which you sent to them, and which have been such a blessing to their bodies and souls.

It was good to renew fellowship with Rev Janos Dobos, minister of the Scots Mission in Budapest, who is maintained by the Overseas Council of our own denomination. The Scots Mission has a long and honoured history, having its roots in last century when the English engineer and sculptor, Clark, was commissioned to build the first chain bridge across the Danube at Budapest, so linking the old and new parts of the city. Since those early days the Mission has sustained a living ministry, especially to Jewish communities, but the ravages of war, with its traumatic movements of population, have rather put an end to this. Our property has been confiscated by the Communist regime, but we do have an agreement with the government by which we are allowed the use of a hall in which to conduct worship. The rest of the building is now a school, and there are moves afoot to remove even the hall. A gymnastics teacher, pleading the need for a new gymnasium, has drawn up a petition, signed by 600 parents, asking

*January 1975

the government to commandeer the hall. This they have, as yet, been unwilling to do.

It was a great personal joy to meet again our dear brother in the faith, Miklos Szarka, who is the assistant minister in a large Budapest church. He carries on a vital work inside the more routine work of his congregation. It was also useful to contact beleaguered Christians suffering because of heavy floods. This has been the wettest summer and autumn within living memory and the river Danube fairly sizzled along in spate. There were disastrous floods, especially on the eastern side of the country, and the grape harvest was so ruined that students and school pupils were bundled into lorries and taken to rescue what they could of the vintage. It was a great pleasure also to be able to send, by the hand of a Czech brother visiting Budapest, material assistance to our friends in Czechoslovakia who are having difficult times.

It is not possible to understand the Christian situation in Hungary without knowing something of the country's history. When one thinks of Hungary one imagines a monument of human suffering, a pillar built of strata of persecution and repression. Interestingly enough the fundamental culture is Celtic, for the Celtic tribes appear to have begun their migrations westward from the Danube basin. Indeed, there was in Budapest an exhibition of Celtic culture from the area, and it was a strange experience to see patterns, designs and motifs which we normally associate with Highland culture. This Celtic civilisation, however, was soon overrun by wild, warlike tribes who came from the east, perhaps from around the Urals in Russia. These were the Magyars, the foundation of the Hungarian people. They had a culture and a language all their own, and these have survived centuries of change. In fact, the language is quite unique, having no relatives. The nearest to it is Finnish since the Finns appear to have been

Magyars who broke away early from the parent tribe.

Then came the Tartars, wild pagan horsemen armed with sabres, who scythed their way westward in a campaign of rape and pillage. In due turn they were defeated, to be replaced by the Turks as the greater part of Hungary was incorporated into the Ottoman Empire. Those were bitter, cruel days when the saints were tyrannised by Moslems. It was the era of the Turkish bey, the landlord who ruled by slave labour and the whip. So overjoyed was western civilisation at the final defeat of the Turks that the Pope commanded that all the bells in Hungary be rung at noon forever to commemorate the triumph over the infidels, and to this day you may still hear bells heralding that victory.

In due course Turkish terror was replaced by that of the Hapsburgs, most famous among whom was the Empress Maria Theresa. Hungary had for long been known as 'Mary's country', because of an early legend that St Stephen, the first Christian King, received his kingdom directly from the Virgin Mary. It was therefore small wonder that the Jesuits should make the land the headquarters of the counter-reformation, and all Protestants suffered in those sad and weary years. Strict laws were enjoined against them: no Protestant Church could be built within the walls of a town, and no church could have a main door leading on to a main street. But the Hapsburgs too, were brought to divine judgment, and the next stratum of suffering was World War I, at the end of which significant territorial changes were made. The greater part of Slovakia (now in Czechoslovakia) used to belong to Hungary and many Slovaks, in fact, speak Hungarian as their native language. On the eastern and western borders also, great slices of land were taken away, and now two-thirds of Hungarian-speaking people live outside Hungary! To crown these trials came World War II, with the horrors of Jewish persecution under the master-hand of Eichmann. The tragedy was that, in the early years, Hungary foolishly threw in her lot with the Nazis, and this meant that at the end of the war she was terribly and fearfully punished, particularly by Russia. It was almost inevitable that Communism, in the form of strict Stalinism, should take over. Those were the days of sudden arrests, of the secret police, of torture and the quiet, un-noticed disappearance of personalities. Such was the resentment in the land that an uprising against the Russians was staged in 1956, and in those brief, tragic days of horror, 78,000 Hungarians died. The walls of the buildings in Budapest are still pockmarked by the shells. But the uprising accomplished this much, that it put an end to the whole Stalinist regime and opened the way for more liberal government.

The sadness of Hungary's long struggle is perhaps exemplified in the dictum of a famous Cardinal who, in a previous century, said that only three things should be done with 'these Hungarians'. Firstly, they must be made beggars: and he almost succeeded in this, for the popular image of a Hungarian is that of a gipsy fiddler in pretty peasant costume, scraping catgut for coppers to stay alive. Secondly, said the Cardinal, we must make them good Catholics. In this, too, he almost succeeded, for 85% of the population is still nominally Roman Catholic. Thirdly, he said, we must make them Germans: and in this he almost succeeded, for German was the language of the Hapsburg Empire.

The suffering is also symbolised on church steeples where we find not a Cross, but a cockerel crowing in the new day. It is easy to see this as a symbol of Resurrection. But above the cockerel there is a gold spiked ball. The first impression is of a sunrise, crowed in by the bird. But, no. It is nothing less than a cruel mace, one of the weapons used by knights in ancient wars, and it is raised as a testimony to the blood that was shed for Christ and the Gospel's sake. Since the turn of this century there have been two revivals in Hungary, one after the First World War and a second, and more significant one, after World War II. The interesting thing is that the second of these reawakenings sent an army of young men into the ministry. The Lord laid His hand on plain fellows, joiners, plumbers, electricians and carpenters, converted them to Christ, and ordained them to the ministry of the Word and these are now the backbone of a growing evangelical nucleus in the Reformed Church.

When, therefore, one is asked what the Church is like in that land, one must ask a question by way of reply: 'Which church do you mean?' For there are two churches. The old Latin tag holds true: Ecclesiola in ecclesia, a church inside the church, and I saw both. The ecclesia is a fairly large body, governed by bishops, who are ordained for life, and by moderators who are appointed for twelve years. It is the ecclesia that one is actually encouraged to see by the Communists. One is permitted to see churches that are open, and where there is not a suggestion of persecution or psychological pressurisation. There is no doubt that many of the leaders of this church are smooth men who have compromised with the regime. This is a Laodicean body, which is neither hot nor cold, but lukewarm, and is thus an abomination to the living God. In this church one is entertained and feasted with fine foods and wines. One sees splendid manses, magnificently furnished; and the cause is not hard to find, for many of the salaries are subsidised by the state. The reason is that this is 'repayment' for property that has been taken away from the church by the Communist government. But who is fooled by such specious arguments? These are the men who are paid to say the right things, who live in comparative affluence, luxury and ease and, which is no surprise to find, who have absolutely no Biblical position whatever. They have, in fact, departed from the historic Gospel of Jesus Christ.

But within this Church there is another Church. It is always so. They are not all Israelites who are of Israel. They are not all true Christians who are in the church, for it is possible to be inside the church but outside Christ. There is a little true church inside a larger corrupt one, and this ecclesiola is made up of some 500 men dedicated and consecrated to the Person and service of the Lord Christ. But, because they have a real message, they are regarded as 'dangerous men'. They preach eternity. They preach the Apostolic Gospel, and for this very cause are banished by the regime, under the hands of the bishops, to the backwoods, the remote villages, the mountain fastnesses and comparative obscurity. For them life is hard; salaries are poor, travel conditions are almost impossible and congregations are scattered. Yet these are the very men who are making an impact for Christ upon the land. I went to one service supervised by a compromising worldly minister. There were six people there. That very evening an evangelical was preaching and there were over 400 in the congregation, mostly young people hungry to learn of Christ.

It is foolish to ask Christians whether they are pro-Communism or pro-Capitalism. This is not really a live issue for them. Hungarian Christians are good patriots, as one might expect them to be. It is improper to expect a Hungarian to be a good American, or a good Scot, or even necessarily a good Capitalist. The issue is *not*: 'Are you for or against the regime?' but: 'Do you confess the revival?' *That* is the leading question, and by it is meant: Do you confess the things for which the revival stands? These are no less than the fundamentals of vital gospel religion: 'Do you confess repentance, faith in the Lord Jesus Christ, the new birth, the need for holiness and a sanctified walk before God?' *These* are the issues at stake. So the question which I ask you now is: 'To which Church do *you* belong?' There is an Israel of God inside natural Israel, and there is a church of Christ inside the church. The smaller church is the one that stands for Jesus, for revival, for the Word of God, for prayer, for conversion. The other church does not really stand for much at all. To which do *you* belong? Do you confess the revival? But, of course, that is a question which would prove a terrible embarrassment to many in our own denomination.

Yours with growing affections,
THOMAS SWANSTON

49
CZECHOSLOVAKIA AND HUNGARY*

My dear friends,
Surely it is right that this month I should bless God publicly for His goodness to us on our mission to Czechoslovakia and Hungary. His loving-kindness did not exclude moments of adventure, and even of fear. Our poor car took a terrible punishment on some appalling roads and the silencer and exhaust system came home (like Caesar's 'All Gaul...') divided into three parts, albeit primitively welded. And there were two encounters with the police. We were stopped in Prague and had our visas examined by an officer who appeared to be in radio contact with the occupants of a car which had followed us through the streets. More ominously, our car was emptied and searched, and we were detained for two and a half hours by border guards who suspected us of trying to smuggle literature. Thus we arrived at our destination for that night - weary, crestfallen and discouraged. But the Lord looked down and rescued us.

Extol the Lord with me,
Let us exalt His name together.
I sought the Lord, He heard and did
Me from all fears deliver.

They looked to Him, and lightened were,
Not shamed were their faces.
This poor man cried, God heard
and saved him from all his distresses.

*October 1975

The angel of the Lord encamps
And round encompasseth
All those about that do Him fear,
And them delivereth. (Ps 34:3-7).

May this self-same God honour and reward all whose generosity was a rebuke to my unbelief, and whose open-heartedness was an occasion of wonder in these days of economic straits. I am bidden, by those who have received your gifts, to convey their warmest gratitude and Christian love for your care. I mention especially the syringes delivered to a pastor suffering from diabetes; the spare parts for an ancient car desperately needed by a brother who has an itinerant ministry in sixteen preaching stations; the money given to a pastor who urgently needs a new vehicle for service in fourteen churches; the gifts delivered to some saints busy building a new church extension for which, miraculously, they have been given a building permit by the authorities; the tape recorder to be used in pastoral work, and monies handed to a pastor formerly imprisoned for his faith.

Special thanks are commanded by our brother Miklos Szarka and his wife, Gyopar, who have moved into a country parish outside Budapest. The folks there are mostly of peasant stock, and it was a joy to serve with Miklos at the Lord's Supper, to preach at the Evening Service of Thanksgiving and to address a promising Youth Fellowship of some thirty teenagers eager to hear the Word. Worship in his place is a solemn affair and the folks are traditional and conservative. From all God's servants, therefore, helped and blessed by your offerings of coffee, tea, soap and tinned foods, Christian greetings and gratitude.

But what are we to make of the church under Communist regimes today? May I make four rather negative points?

Firstly, it is wrong of so many Christians to suppose that Eastern Europe is one country - as if communism presented a monolithic, united front to the world. Language, culture and history divide the nations of the socialist block. Rumania (the Dacia of the Roman Empire, the prison house to which convicts were sent) is a different proposition from Poland; Czechoslovakia is quite unlike Hungary; and Albania is a world apart, having closer relations with China than with the nearer Soviet Union. Even within countries there are major differences. Slovakia (which is part of communist Czechoslovakia) has a language, and indeed a Socialist Government all of its own. Within Yugoslavia, Serbs and Croats are separate peoples. Thus Eastern Europe is not one but many.

Secondly, it is irresponsible and unwise (as well as untrue to the facts), to speak of an 'underground' church in every country. There is no need to speak of 'underground' churches in Czechoslovakia or Hungary, for there are none. Whatever may be the case in other atheistic regimes, the churches in these two lands are over-ground. It is true that Christians are victimised, and subjected to many kinds of psychological and social pressures but, if you want to worship, the church is there, often on the main street.

Thirdly, it is too heroic and theatrical to speak of the need to 'smuggle' Bibles into every socialist country. In fact, there is no need to do this in the two lands which we visited. There are plenty of Bibles in Czechoslovakia and Hungary, and it is an established fact that earlier this year Government permission was obtained for the import of 25,000 Bibles in Slovak. While much is heard in the West of the 'smuggling' of Bibles, we should not forget the patient faith and perseverance of the world's Bible Societies, whose labours have not reached the headlines but which have, nevertheless, enabled the lawful introduction of Bibles into some communist lands.

Fourthly, it is erroneous to suppose that the perfect church exists under communism. No perfect church exists in this world. The perfect church, with its perfect minister and perfect ministry, exists only in Heaven. Therefore, it is natural to discover that amongst Christians 'over there' the problems are almost exactly the same as they are in this country. Only the environment is different. Perhaps this is why we heard that the real enemy of the church is not communist government but the growing secularisation of society. Communist regimes do not ask that populations turn into rabid Marxists. All they ask is that common folk lead worldly, materialistic lives, listen duteously to dogma, and keep quiet.

The conditions under which Christians have to live vary from district to district, and are controlled by many factors - the attitude of the local police, the sympathy of Party officials, and relations with the State in general. Matters appear to be hardest near the West, and in two provinces we found that saints have to live in a world of privations, of petty rules and prohibitions, and of denials of freedom which we take for granted. In an eastern province on the other hand, there were signs of hope. In one place, incredibly, one pastor still may enter the local school and teach Scripture. At least one fellowship has been given permission to reconstruct and extend its premises for worship; and a pastor told us that in the past year over twenty people had come to Christ in his fellowship and had been admitted to full membership, 'including many intellectuals'. Everywhere we found an attention to the Word, zeal for truth, and joy in coming together for Christian fellowship. We are especially impressed by the numbers and the quality of those attending youth groups, and it is thrilling to see how unashamed they are to confess Christ publicly in an alien and untoward society.

But the darkness, which cannot put the light out, is inescapable. In the school where the minister may teach Scripture, only those children both of whose parents sign a special form may attend his classes. This at first sight may appear promising. But is it? If parents are not well grounded in the faith, or if the children come of a mixed marriage (of a believer with an unbeliever, or of a Protestant with a Roman Catholic) they may not wish to jeopardise or prejudice the child's future education by allowing him to attend such classes. All teachers are atheists and are committed, in one way or another, to the spread of godless, totalitarian communism.

We heard of children who attend Sunday School being asked to stand up in class in order to be derided and mocked by their teachers and their fellow pupils. We heard of schools where questionnaires were issued with these queries: Who is the real head of your house, your father or your mother? Is grace said before meals? Do your parents pray and read the Bible? Do you go to church? What do you like in church - the singing, the friendship of the people or the preaching? Do you believe all that the minister says?

The Scripture commands us to 'rejoice with those who rejoice and weep with those who weep', therefore, I cannot over-emphasise the fact that Eastern Europe is one of the greatest mission fields in the world today. I stress the importance of Christian visitors going there as 'tourists'. This can be a time of relaxation and of encouragement for believers. I wonder if the time has not come for married couples, who are not burdened by small children, to start thinking of such a possibility? Christians in Czechoslovakia must think that Scotland, to date, is composed almost entirely of celibate clergymen!

The risks, of course, are there. If I may lay down guidelines, simple and few, to help any who feel led to engage in such work:

1. Recognise that your name and passport number will almost certainly be noted and fed into some computer for future reference.
2. Recognise that if you are so bold as to try to introduce Christian literature in Slavic languages you put yourself at immense risk, and you also compromise seriously the position of any whose names may be found on your person.
3. It is extremely inadvisable to carry names and addresses, either on slips of paper or in notebooks. If discovered, these will certainly be confiscated by the guards.
4. The day may soon come when it will not be wise even to carry an English Bible for private devotional use. It gives a clue to the customs authorities as to the nature of the tourist.
5. The ideal number for travelling (unless, the party sleeps in a minibus or dormobile) is one or two. Christians tend to have restricted accommodation and can offer only limited hospitality to visitors.
6. Be assured that the police know full well the names of all pastors, elders and office-bearers, all who attend church, preaching brothers, and all who correspond with Westerners.
7. The purpose of a visit is not to take an interest in cultural differences, but to bring spiritual edification to Christ's suffering children. That must be the criterion of every venture.

The Prophet Jeremiah speaks of God's heritage, the

church, as 'speckled bird of prey'. Any bird of rare plumage which escapes from a cage soon becomes a victim. Why? Because she is the odd one out; she is a rarity, and stands out from the rest. She does not fit in. Therefore she must die. This is what the true church is like. The church is God's budgerigar, God's oddity. Therefore, living Christians suffer because they do not fit in with this world; they do not belong here.

For the first 300 years of her history, the Christian church was a persecuted minority in the Roman Empire. Only when the Emperor Constantine professed conversion did Jesus suddenly become fashionable, and there grew up that marriage of State and Church which has so bedevilled Christ's work to this day. What has happened in Eastern Europe is that the church has moved back to the pre-Constantine position. And, as history is moving now, I wonder when our turn will come to take that same step?

Again we give God the glory for the faith, the devotion, and the sacrifice that made our mission possible. We did not lead - we were led; we did not carry - we were carried; we did not bear - we were borne. Yet it is infinitely good to be home again!

Yours with growing affections in Christ,
THOMAS SWANSTON

50
EASTERN EUROPE*

Dear Friends,
It is said that Mr. Gorbachev's mother is a Christian. Be that the case or not, she certainly is a devout member of the Russian Orthodox Church and goes to worship each Lord's Day escorted by security guards! She named her son Mikhail, and there is something of dark, divine irony in that, for Mikhail means: 'Who is like unto God?'

Who, indeed, is like unto God, who casts down the mighty from their seats and exalts them of low degree; who, seated securely on His everlasting throne, laughs to scorn the puny tyrants of the earth who rise to challenge His authority and sway? And do you not think it curious that such a man, with such a name, should have been instrumental in the fulfilling of heaven's decrees for the liberation of the captives and the oppressed? But what are we to make of these recent tumults in Eastern Europe? Is there a Christian perspective?

Events have moved, as we know, with bewildering speed. Barriers and obstructions long held to be impregnable, and declared to be so, have crumbled before men's wondering eyes. The Brandenburg Gate in East Berlin, closed for 28 years, was reopened on December 23rd 1989, and the Berlin Wall that hated symbol of division, is gradually being knocked down. It is reputed that an American millionaire has offered to buy it in its entirety for 60 million dollars! The Czechs have started to dismantle the Iron Curtain between their homeland and Austria. Our elder Archie Roberts once said, on another auspicious occasion: 'The peacocks of today

*July 1990

are the feather dusters of tomorrow!; And surely the Marxist birds of yesteryear have had their proud scarlet plumage set in sad disarray. To return to reality and change the metaphors: the judges now find themselves in the dock; erstwhile guards are behind bars; persecutors are themselves up for arraignment, and secret informers are publicly exposed for the Judases they were. All of this is highly interesting; but I ask you again: 'Is there a Christian perspective?'

In the 1990 April/May edition of the *Themelios* magazine (a UCCF publication for those involved in theological and religious studies) Christopher Wright writes under the editorial heading: 'Responding to the God of History'. He suggests that the winter of 1989-90 will rank with other dates and revolutions such as England in 1689-90, America in 1776, France in 1789 and even Russia in 1917.

The point is well made that the God of the Bible is not merely the God of the Bible; nor is He merely the God of Abraham, Isaac and Jacob and, therefore, the God of Israel; nor yet is He simply the God and Father of the Lord Jesus Christ. He is the God of history before whom the nations are as nothing and who takes up the islands as a small thing. History may be for us a thing of anguish and torment, of blood and loss and heartbreak, of war and guilt and tragedy; but the assurance of Scripture is that in all the tumults and seeming disarray the sovereign Lord of history, of time and of space is working out His purposes according to His infallible and inerrant laws of righteousness, justice and truth. In this very matter none can stay His hand or say Him nay! And surely Isaiah has a prophetic and apposite word for times such as these:

> 'Surely the nations are like a drop in a bucket;
> they are regarded as dust on the scales;

He weighs the islands as though they were fine dust.
Before him the nations are as nothing;
they are regarded by him as worthless
and less than nothing.
He brings princes to naught
and reduces the rulers of this world to nothing
No sooner are they planted,
no sooner are they sown,
no sooner do they take root in the ground,
than he blows on them and they wither...'
(Isa 40:15,17,23-24 NIV)

Thus far a spiritual insight into the times. But there is more. What has happened in Eastern Europe is a direct answer from God to the persistent, urgent, believing prayers of the saints for over seventy years. For that length of time, and for much longer, praying remnants in what is left of Christendom have come to grips with the Lord in intercession and have cried to Him to show mercy on His elect in their bondage and humiliation, and to bring the wicked to judgment. One thinks of the cry of God's servant in Psalm 18. There the man calls to the God who hears and answers prayer. 'In my distress I called upon the Lord; to my God I cried for help' (v6). And God, who is ever true to His nature, heard and answered thus: by sending an earthquake (v7), darkness and major disturbances in the heavens (v9), hailstones and coals of fire (v12), thunder (v13), lightning storms (v14) and cataclysmic events in the seas (v15). And in all these traumatic and fearful happenings the Lord's hand was reaching down to draw his chosen 'out of many waters' (v16).

Do you believe in prayer? Do you believe in the living God, the God of history, who alone hears and answers and saves? Do you believe that prayer shakes kingdoms and, under the throne, governs, rules and transforms human affairs? Are you ready for earthquakes, for the shaking of the heavens, for storms and upheavals as the answer to your prayers?

Thus far a second insight. But there is more: and here you will forgive me for exercising holy caution. I spoke recently on the phone to our good brother Miklos Szarka in Biatorbagy, on the outskirts of Budapest. He surely knew privations under the old regime and tasted bitterness and frustration under worldly and carnal 'bishops' of Christ's kirk; and he has a realistic and sober attitude to the changes. We both agreed that there is abroad a new spirit of hope. But we also agreed that where there is hope there is also danger. In Eden, the Paradise of God, there was found a serpent (Hebrew: shining one); in the royal house of David there was a vile Manasseh; among the twelve there was a Judas; at the heart of the revival in the early church we find Ananias and Sapphira, a husband and wife team, dissembling before the Lord and telling monumental lies; and in the Apocalypse the Harlot wife of Satan apes the chaste Bride of Christ. I say again; where there is hope there is danger; where you have the Christ you also have the antichrist; and all the best-made plans of politicians, however well-intentioned, must reckon (although few do) with the reality of Satan, enemy of God and man. Do we not believe that he is as interested in the upheavals as we are? Any assessment of the situation must therefore face three realities:

In the first place, no conclusive reckoning can be made now since all the revolutions have been different. The 'velvet revolution' in Czechoslovakia, with an almost complete absence of desire for vengeance and retribution, is not paralleled by the awesome and bloody events in Romania. In Poland the Roman Catholic church played a large and strategic part in the happenings. Many of the revolutionary gatherings were held in churches and presided over by priests. But we cannot wonder at this: it is almost an unwritten law that to be Polish is to be Roman Catholic. The Virgin Mary is still hailed as 'Queen of Poland' and it is more than significant that very few Protestants have been active in the movements for change. Indeed many Protestants aver that they enjoyed more freedom and religious liberty under Communism than they did in the days when Jesuits and hard-line, authoritarian priests held sway! There was a day in Poland when to become an evangelical believer was to risk social estrangement, loss of one's job and, in earlier times, loss of life itself. In the Soviet Union the Orthodox Church, extensively compromised with the powers that be, virtually ever since the Bolshevik Revolution of October 1917, does not appear to have concerned itself much, in any active way, with the changes. Orthodoxy is a strange entity, and can accommodate itself to whatever regime is in fashion and whatever philosophy is held, however anti-God.

In the second place, revolutions do tend to change with the passage of time. When a baby is born, interested and curious relatives crowd around, often looking for 'signs' that they can recognise in the little one's features. Is that dimple on his chin not inherited from his grandfather? And the red hair must come from his mother's side! And that retrousse nose... was its like not seen on his father's face when he was brought into the world? But, unfortunately for us all, babies' features change with passing years. The dimple may vanish; the red hair may change colour; and the retrousse nose may straighten itself out. We simply are unable, looking down into the cradle, to make final pronouncements on what the infant will become in later maturity. In much the same way we have several infants in sundry cradles in Eastern Europe, not a few showing signs of political and economic promise. But the features we discern in these early, pristine stages will almost certainly change over the years. And, apart from all this, we need to face the chastening fact that political freedom is not necessarily the same as spiritual revival. We in the west have enjoyed rich political freedoms a-plenty for years, many of them dearly won in costly conflicts between Church and State. But where are we today? Can we say that our western liberties have fostered godliness?

In the third place, every social upheaval and tumult must make allowance for the essential nature of man's heart without Christ. 'The heart of man,' said Jeremiah, 'is deceitful above all things and desperately wicked. Who can know it?' There is scarcely a movement in history, however virtuous, however high-minded, however exalted in its principles, that has not been corrupted and ruined by the sinfulness of the human heart. Already it is being said that many Securitate men are well placed in the new government in Bucharest. Across the open borders to the East have rolled vans bearing pornographic literature and foul videos. Jehovah Witnesses, Mormons and eastern cults are all highly active now where once they were banned. There is a strong interest in seances and in the occult. Hare Krishna devotees have been seen dancing through streets in Czechoslovakia.

In a recent edition of *The Independent* newspaper, Edward Lucas has a worthwhile article on the sudden rise of crime in Czech cities. Under the title 'Starsky and Hutch in downtown Prague' he tells of sleazy, unsavoury nightclubs; of gypsies actively and openly engaged in prostitution; of pimps and pickpockets, and of the fear in the hearts of many that the leaders of organised crime will soon emerge to open up markets in drugs, arms and other sordid forms of racketeering. Already the figures for robbery with violence and rape have risen alarmingly.

Once upon a time, not so long ago, there was a British politician called Asquith. On the occasion of the reintroduction of Budget material to Parliament he was asked what the changes would be. 'Wait and see!' was his famous and quotable reply. And although that advice may not be romantic enough for some fiery tastes, it is at least realistic. As Christians we simply have to find grace from the Lord to be patient, not in a woebegone spirit of Islamic resignation but prayerfully, expecting God to complete every good work which He has begun. As Isaiah said: 'He that believeth shall not make haste'; and this is recapitulated by Paul: 'Judge not before the time'. Wait and see, in earnest intercession! And if it took seventy years of prayer to bring down the ramparts of godless Marxism, how long will it take to shake the walls of the more sinister foe gradually insinuating itself into western lands - militant Islam? The call is for prayer warriors. You are either prepared, in these days of boundless opportunity, to become one or you are not. The choice is as simple as that.

Yours, looking to the future.

THOMAS SWANSTON

51
CONCERNING CONVERSION TO CHRIST*

Dear Friends,
I want you to read this letter patiently and carefully. It contains some urgent challenges which need to be issued in these days.

Somewhere at the back of my mind there is a theory - unproven and perhaps unprovable - that, in the business of conversion to Christ, God tempers His methods to our personalities. To put it crudely and primitively: gentle people tend to come gently, while more violent people tend to come more violently. No-one can doubt that there are many kinds of conversion experience, but it almost seems as if some of us need a sturdy shaking down before we admit our sinnerhood and surrender to the absolute claims of the holy Son of God. Does the experience relate to the kind of people we are? Do dramatic and frantic psyches, filled with dramatic needs, summon forth a dramatic encounter with Christ?

In my salad days, when I was green in judgment and much given to brash and somewhat chauvinistic evangelism, I tended to measure all conversions against my own. Some of you may know that it took a car accident to bring me finally to my moral senses, to warn me of eternity and constrain me to bow the knee to the lordship and sovereignty of Christ. I foolishly and erroneously took that monumental encounter to be the norm, the standard. But all conversions are not like that.

I have been persuaded over these years of ministry that many worthy churchgoers come to a saving knowledge of

*January 1991

Christ as they sit quietly and unobtrusively through worship, the Word and the Spirit of God working silently and effectively in their hearts and souls. I have been deeply touched and moved to hear such speak of their personal knowledge of the Lord Jesus, of His sacrifice for them and of their love for Him. Such modest and unpretentious professions have humbled my arrogance and rebuked my pride. God is truly here on earth what His heaven will be hereafter - filled with surprises! He has His bairns (which means 'born-ones') in the strangest places, and He knows His own from the foundation of the universe. Some of you who read this are in this blessed category. It matters not when you came to Christ, or where or how. The great reality is that you have come and that you shall be in heaven at the last, saved, safe, secure and satisfied for ever.

And yet...and yet...it is undoubtedly the case that many of you are not in this blessed category. If you take a long, slow, cool look at your spiritual estate you are bound to confess that you are not converted at all. You do not claim to be. You never, in fact, mention conversion to Christ. And I wonder what this awesome silence can mean. For my own part I never label anyone as 'converted' unless there is some evidence to support what the label says. It is fundamentally dishonest and unworthy, and does violence to another's integrity, to persuade him, or anyone else, that he is converted when, in fact, he is not. You do not tell a committed member of the Boy Scout movement that he is really a member of the Boys' Brigade travelling in disguise.

In such matters there is a disarming simplicity in God. Either you are converted or you are not. You may be converted and unaware of the fact. You may be unconverted and living under the illusion that you are a true believer. I suspect that some who profess to be Christians are, in reality, fantasising about their condition and living in a world of self-deception, notwithstanding the 'decision for Christ' which they may or may not have made earlier in life. But, in the end of the day, God and His simplicity come to the fore: at the last there will be only the final separation of heaven and hell, of light and darkness, of gain and loss; and the ground of the separation will be the difference between conversion to Christ or the absence of it.

I am aware that many regular churchgoing folk can be offended by such language and find it distasteful. We should all strive, however, not to allow the language to keep us from the truth, and the question of 'taste' is irrelevant. I did not invent the language, nor did I make up the rules of the Gospel! Those who object to the language and the rules should complain not to the preacher but to the Great Original. Somehow 'conversion' among religious people, is seen as something that is necessary for drunkards, liars and for people who have led notoriously wicked lives. 'Conversion' is the sort of thing that goes on at Salvation Army meetings, or at Gospel rallies, or in Mission Halls or during revivals of religion. It is scarcely the sort of experience required of decent, upright and respectable folk.

Unfortunately for us all, when Jesus spoke about the necessity for conversion He was addressing some of the most decent, upright and respectable people of His day. Religious folk need to be converted for the plain and painful reason that being religious is not quite the same as being Christian. One may be a fine, dedicated and helpful churchman or church-woman and yet be a lost soul. Churchianity is not Christian-ity, and religion, of itself, never saved one soul nor ever brought one sinner home to glory.

To press the matter: what difference spiritually can there possibly be between an unconverted bishop and an unconverted drunkard? The bishop may sit in his palace, robe himself in the finest lawn and carry about with him the odour of sanctity. The drunk may lie in the gutter on a Saturday evening. You would be unlikely to find the bishop lying in the gutter and, in much the same way, you would not find the drunkard swathed in episcopal clouts. But, in the sight of a holy God, each is a benighted, lost soul standing in need of conversion, and, unless each turns in 'repentance towards God and faith in the Lord Jesus Christ', each will go to hell. There is enough in Scripture to suggest that the bishop's hell will be all the worse for his having played the fool on the very steps of the altar. To *be not far from the kingdom* is to be yet on the outside, and the nearer to God the greater the danger.

You need to be converted to Christ. It is an affair of necessity, and there are no exceptions. But conversion does not stand alone. It is the fruit, the sacramental, outward evidence of another experience. Below it, beneath it and before it stands the New Birth of the Spirit of God. Strictly speaking the word 'conversion' means 'a turning'. The Old Testament word for it carries the idea of coming home to God. To submit to converting faith in Christ is to turn from your wanderings, to renounce your sinful past and to trust in the shadow of the Saviour and of His finished work. Conversion, the transformation of a life, is a visible sign that a man has been born of God, born from above, born twice and born of the Word. And until a man has had that living, saving, evangelical encounter with Christ he is not a Christian at all. He cannot be. It is not possible. Not to be born again is to be without God, without Christ and without hope in the world. Religion, piety and spiritual traditions are all fine and good; but they do not, and can not, save. God never intended them to do so.

There is, therefore, a primacy, a firstness, in the New

Birth. Until a man is born again he is dead, dead in trespasses and sins, dead in his unbelief, dead towards the living God, dead to the Lord Christ, dead to the Word, dead to service and dead to prayer. And the tragedy of every dead man is this - he can do nothing to help himself. Corpses do not pray; they do not serve God; they do not even know that they are dead. They take no vital interest in the Lord's work. Missionaries are of no concern to them. How could they be? Can the dead evangelise the dead? Can the dead speak, or hear, or see, or move? The first experience that a dead man needs is not reformation (how do you reform a corpse?) nor yet a revival (how can you bring to life again someone who never was alive in the first place?), but regeneration, a new nature. 'If any man be in Christ, he is a new creation: old things are passed away: all things are become new.' But until the Holy Spirit comes to a man in regenerating grace and power in that way, the man remains dead.

It has disturbed and wounded me to watch some of you dear, precious folk, in my years among you, fighting against your conversion to Christ. You have tried to hide this, unsuccessfully, from me; but you cannot seriously suppose that I am so easily deceived. Some of you have known the Gospel from earliest childhood's years; you have come from godly homes. You know all too well that you need to admit your sinnerhood; you know perfectly well that you need to repent of your sins and turn to Christ; you know that you stand in need of a Saviour to love, comfort and deliver you; you know in your heart (oh yes, you do!) that you need to be born again. But the years have passed, Gospel opportunities have slipped away and you postpone indefinitely the great decision. Sometimes you have tried to conceal the truth behind a veil of religious words, as if such a facade of spurious piety could shield you from the searching gaze of an all-seeing

God! And I well believe that, in your better moments, you fully intend to come to Jesus... tomorrow, or next Sabbath, or next month... or even next year. But the fatal flaw in your procrastination is this - that you do not intend to come to Jesus NOW.

Alas for us all, whether we are Christians or not, NOW is the only time given to us by God. All the clocks in His eternity stand inexorably at the eleventh hour. They proclaim that this immediate instant is God's accepted time. If you are going to be saved, you must be saved now; if you intend to become a prayer warrior for Christ, you must become a prayer warrior now; if ever you are to learn to become a soul-winner, the time to learn is now; if you purpose to live a holy, separated, sanctified life for God, the time to do it is now. Tomorrow you may call in vain. And it is precisely thus that some of you have frittered away your lives, putting off the day of surrender and capitulation.

'The harvest is past, the summer is ended, and we are not saved,' says Jeremiah (8:20 AV). If you know Mendelssohn's 'Elijah' you will recognise this verse as the basis for the opening chorus. A loose paraphrase could run thus: 'Sowing time has gone; the reaping time itself is behind you; the winter is coming and your larder stands empty'. The day will come for us all when earthly sowing times have gone and all our earthly harvests are ingathered. Then comes the winter. But a winter faced with an empty spiritual larder is a bleak and forbidding prospect. I beseech you, therefore, to come to Christ and be reconciled to God before it is too late. Do not play games with God; do not fool around with Christ; do not trifle with the things that belong to your peace. Let the words of these Victorian verses crystallise the Gospel invitation:

'The Saviour now calls you in grace to receive Him;
O let all your sins go, and make Him your Friend!
Now yield Him your heart, and make haste to adore Him;
Your harvest is passing; your summer will end.'

'O escape to yonder mountain,
Refuge find in Him today!
Christ invites you to the fountain;
Come and wash your sins away.
Do not tarry;
Come to Jesus while you may!'

Yours, as earnestly and affectionately as ever I wrote,
THOMAS SWANSTON

52
BETTER THAN SONS AND DAUGHTERS*

Dear Friends,
Early on in my Christian life I discovered some lovely verses in Isaiah. Their beauty has never left me, and their rich truths have deepened with passing years of ministry. Here is the passage:

'Let not the foreigner who has joined himself to the Lord say;
"The Lord will surely separate me from his people."
and let not the eunuch say:
"Behold, I am a dry tree."
For thus says the Lord:
"To the eunuchs who keep my sabbaths,
who choose the things that please me
and hold fast my covenant,
I will give in my house and within my walls
a monument and a name
better than sons and daughters;
I will give them an everlasting name
which shall not be cut off.
And the foreigners who join themselves to the Lord,
to minister to him, to love the name of the Lord,
and to be his servants...
these will I bring to my holy mountain,
and make them joyful in my house of prayer." '
(Isa 56:3-7)

*March 1991

Lest you are tempted to think that God is prejudiced towards the male in question, you will find his female counterpart in an earlier chapter:

'Sing, O barren one who did not bear;
break forth into singing and cry aloud,
you who have not been in travail!
For the children of the desolate one will be more
than the children of her that is married,
says the Lord.' (Isa 54:1)

What are we to make of these extraordinary words and glowing promises? It is possible, of course, to understand 'eunuch' and 'barren one' literally, in natural terms. But it is wiser, and certainly more profitable, to take them spiritually. Jesus did speak about certain choice folk who were 'eunuchs for the sake of the kingdom of Heaven' (Matt 19:10-12). The gentleman and lady to the forefront here cannot be other than separated saints, reserved for the exclusive and peculiar use of the Lord in a life of fruitbearing. These passages have little to do with the call to either celibacy or to marriage. Both single and married Christians may be set apart in this way for destinies of signal, special and costly service. The issue here is not one's vocation under the good providence of God; the issue is that of practical holiness.

And yet all is not well in this garden of consecration. The bare winds of alienation and estrangement ('foreigner... separate...from his people...') blow upon the eunuch, and he suspects himself to be something of a withered soul ('a dry tree'), denied the pleasure and privilege of natural offspring ('sons and daughters'). The lady, too, senses that her life is empty and unfulfilled ('barren one...not in travail'). But what is the essence of these experiences of aridity?

I think, almost automatically, of two kinds of loneliness. The first is the sort to which all men, Christians alike, are exposed and which is one of the scourges of our century. If I may interject a personal word here: I do not know the meaning of this sort of loneliness. It is a feeling, a state, a condition to which I am a stranger. This may be partly due to the fact that from our mother's side I inherited an almost pathological independence. But there is another reason. In later teenage years I sought to cultivate the rare art of detachment, the ability to rise above circumstance. In the Christian life, of course, absolute independence and absolute detachment are neither possible nor desirable. They can breed the most appalling heartlessness and callousness. One has wearied, throughout thirty years of ministry, of the wintry smile, the chilly stare, and the icy insularity of some! Nor can it really be doubted that the loneliness of which some complain is a form of self-centredness and self-indulgence, a pampering of the ego as well as a cry for help.

I shall never marry. That much has been certain for many years, and the prospect of that kind of domesticity is no longer of any interest to me. Some fine, well-meaning friends have thought otherwise, planning other ways for me. It has been a major operation disabusing them of their fantasies, not to mention their preoccupations! Both marriage and celibacy are vocations under God. Some serve most fruitfully in the one and some in the other. Each is a holy state capable of being sustained with honour, although our benighted generation has opted for a low view of both. Once a Christian has bowed in grace and sweet surrender to absolute divine sovereignty, God's choice in the matter presents problems only to those who either are unaware of his will - 'good, perfect and acceptable' as it is (Rom 12:2) - or who, having discovered what his will is for their lives, or for the lives of others, are somehow displeased or dissatisfied with his decrees. Obedience never stands far from personal sanctification in the Christian pilgrimage. It is wrong to disobey God!

But there is a second kind of loneliness. It is the spiritual loneliness found in the zealous Christian who has outstripped his fellows in the race for spiritual perfection. I call this 'the loneliness of the long-distance runner' after a film which appeared in the 1950s. To press on with Jesus in the path of full surrender means, almost inevitably, that the competitors thin out as the race proceeds. Many are left far behind. There is no loneliness in the world quite like this. It is unique and stands on its own. But the rewards are breathtaking. It was said of Mallory and Irvine who lost their lives on the high peaks that, when last seen, they were heading for the summit. That's the spirit!

Is it this that lies at the heart of the desolating experience of God's servants in the garden of consecration - not natural loneliness, and not the separation between chaste celibacy and faithful marriage, but the forlornness, the spent-ness, experienced when a life is laid on the altar without reserve?

A number of years ago a book appeared entitled *Spiritual Dryness.* It spoke of the real possibility of the most dedicated Christians passing through deserts in which the very springs of grace appear to have turned to broken cisterns, mocking the thirst of the child of God. Have you ever passed through such areas of dust and ashes - the long, grey ravines, the sense of withering and of desiccation, the suspicion that you are a spent force? John Donne captures something of this in one of his 'Holy Sonnets'. In his 'Hymn to God the Father' he voices his dread that, at the last, after he has worked and prayed and served, he will be judged a castaway, a reject, an also-ran:

'I have a sin of fear that when I have spun
my last thread, I shall perish on the shore.'

Is this the dark night of your soul? Be of good cheer, sweet friend! To the eunuch and the desolate one in the garden come the radiant promises of God. The man is assured of 'a monument and a name better than of sons and of daughters'. His memorial, his work and character, will never be forgotten, long after sons and daughters have passed away. The barren, desolate lady will become a mother in Israel, a Deborah, the spiritual progenetrix of generations yet unborn. A missionary nurse, serving in the Edinburgh Medical Missionary Society Hospital in Nazareth, recently hailed me as her spiritual grandfather; and a teenage lad saluted me of late as his grandfather in the faith. The Lord's sense of humour is surpassing wonderful. But is that not how the kingdom grows?

Be of good cheer, sweet friend, in your garden! Your heart shall yet blossom as the rose, and the wilderness and the solitary place shall be glad because of you.

With my deep and abiding affection in Christ,

Yours lovingly in God,

THOMAS SWANSTON